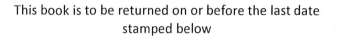
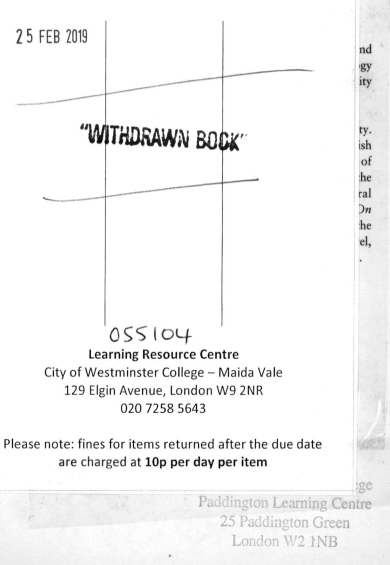

By the same author

Non-fiction
Talk: An Analysis of Speech and Non-Verbal Behaviour in Conversation
The Psychology of Language and Communication (with Andrew Ellis)
Survivors of Steel City
Making It: The Reality of Today's Entrepreneurs
All Talk
England After Dark
We Are the People: Journeys Through the Heart of Protestant Ulster
On the Ropes: Boxing as a Way of Life
Hard Lines: Voices from Deep Within a Recession

Fiction
The Corner Boys

HEAD
TO
HEAD

Uncovering the Psychology of Sporting Success

GEOFFREY BEATTIE

VICTOR GOLLANCZ
LONDON

First published in Great Britain 1998
by Victor Gollancz

An imprint of the Cassell Group
Wellington House, 125 Strand, London WC2R 0BB

A Gollancz Paperback Original

© Geoffrey Beattie 1998

The right of Geoffrey Beattie to be identified as author of
this work has been asserted by him in accordance with
the Copyright, Designs and Patents Act, 1988.

A catalogue record for this book is
available from the British Library.

ISBN 0 575 06358 0

Typeset by Production Line, Minster Lovell
Printed and bound in Great Britain by
Guernsey Press Co. Ltd, Guernsey, Channel Isles

98 99 5 4 3 2 1

DEDICATION

This book is dedicated to my brother, Bill, who used to climb around our yard wall back in Legmore Street and demonstrated to me what a love of sport is all about. He died climbing Nanda Devi in the Himalayas.

CONTENTS

Acknowledgements   9
Introduction   11

Ellery Hanley   25
Alex Ferguson   34
Naseem Hamed   53
Liz McColgan   78
Chris Boardman   99
Vinnie Jones   121
Brian Moore   141
Devon Malcolm   162
Kelly Holmes   180
Herol Graham   203
Gary McAllister   226
Va'aiga Tuigamala   244
Jonathan Edwards   269

ACKNOWLEDGEMENTS

My main debt of gratitude must go to Tony Phillips, who was the BBC producer for the Radio 5 Live series from which this book derives. Tony is both extremely insightful and very funny, and it was a great pleasure to work with him. We spent many hours together in various parts of Britain, but the time never dragged. I would also like to thank Mike Averis, sports editor of the *Guardian*, who first asked me to come out of the closet as a professor of psychology in an interview for that paper.

I would also like to express my gratitude to Mike Petty at Gollancz, who saw some merit in trying to move from a radio series to a book and whose enthusiasm for the project never waned. A number of people gave me a great deal of necessary assistance in this process of translating my efforts from radio to book form. Foremost among these was Heather Shovelton, who provided invaluable assistance by spending many hours transcribing tapes and checking the finished manuscript. I would also like to thank Zoe Beattie, Pippa Vlietstra and Carol Beattie, who all made a number of important editorial suggestions along the way. Finally, I would like to thank all the sportsmen and women who agreed to be interviewed. I, at least, learned a great deal.

'Serious sport has nothing to do with fair play. It is bound up with hatred, jealousy, boastfulness, disregard of all rules and sadistic pleasure in witnessing violence: in other words it is war minus the shooting.'

George Orwell,
'Shooting an Elephant' (1950)

INTRODUCTION

Prince Naseem Hamed, boxer, on fear: 'To tell you the truth, I don't think I've *ever* been frightened in boxing, but I hardly ever get frightened as in "frightened" outside boxing either. I can say that fear really never gets to me. I'm not one of those fighters like Nigel Benn who says "I thrive on fear." As I myself say, "I walk through fear." If somebody else wants to be frightened, let him be frightened. Me, I just want to laugh all the way to the point that I get into that ring and I walk around. I hear my music and then I start buzzing. I start hearing my music and I start getting going. All the way to the ring I'm thinking about what I'm going to do to my opponent, big style.'

Liz McColgan, runner, on her own body image: 'I think I look fat compared with other athletes because I've been more or less told that. If you look at any report from London last year, it was all, "Liz has got a weight problem," "Liz is big." It really does bother me because if you're going into a race, you're going into it to perform well, and then somebody turns around and says, "You're fat." I'm not fat, I know I'm not fat. I look at any other person in the street, any Joe Bloggs walking down the street, and I know that I'm not fat. But in terms of the skin-and-bone athlete, the distance runner, I'm not in that mould.'

Chris Boardman, cyclist, on his attitude to his sport: 'To go back for a moment to the Olympics, when you're sitting on the line, you're thinking, "Oh, there's 176 countries watching this live, and the next four and a half minutes can change my life completely, or not, as the case may be." That's probably the most pressure that you can ever get in life. At least, I thought it was, until I moved on further in my career! To be absolutely honest, I actually don't like cycling. Cycling is just the medium that I've chosen. I am a natural competitor, and cycling is just the medium that I've chosen for that. I don't ride a bike because I want to do well – I need to do well just to be normal. I don't think that this is particularly healthy, but I think that to be at the top in a sport, especially this kind of sport, you have to be slightly mentally unbalanced.'

Head to Head is a book of interviews that explore the psychology of sport and sports people. It is said that the difference between winning and losing is all in the mind and that, when it comes down to it, the difference between a winner and a loser – two perhaps similar individuals with all the same natural attributes and the same number of years of dedicated training – is all psychology in the end. But what kind of psychology? What are we talking about? Is it just mental preparation, or is it the complex cognitions and attributions they make for success or failure. Is it the way that they can control their emotions, or is it a great psychological understanding of others, or is it a great psychological understanding of themselves? Is it great psychological insight at all or is it the great psychological lies that they somehow manage to tell themselves? In this book I start to explore just some of these issues by interviewing a wide variety of successful sportsmen and women from very different sports: solitary sports, like running, cycling and boxing, and team sports, like rugby, football and cricket; explosive sports, like the triple jump, and endurance events, like the marathon. Some of these sportsmen are at the start of their career, some are nearing the end. And there is one football manager.

In each of these interviews there were a great many things that I wanted to learn. How do great sports stars prepare mentally for competition? What do they do before the big fight or the big match? How do they psych out their opponent? How do they think about their opponent? How do they think about themselves? What, in fact, does their corporeal and mental life consist of? What is their attitude to their sport? What kinds of attributions do they make for success and failure? What do they think of their team mates? What is winning a world championship like? What kinds of emotions affect them? What, in other words, are they really like, psychologically speaking?

In each of these thirteen interviews a leading sportsman or sportswoman was prepared to sit down with a psychologist and talk, to describe aspects of their sport and parts of their lives and to explain how some of these things might fit together. We spoke in a variety of locations, in a room in a club-house, in a spare office in the building where the person worked, even in the backroom of a pub in the middle of the morning, on seats reeking of stale cigarette smoke. Sometimes the interviews were conducted in the interviewee's own home, with the artefacts of their daily lives as a backdrop: Vinnie Jones's gun collection, Herol Graham's state-of-the-art hi-fi, bought when he was raking in the money but now virtually obsolete. Apart from Prince Naseem Hamed and Herol Graham, whom I had interviewed previously for my book *On the Ropes*, which was about the lives of boxers in the north of England, I had not met any of the interviewees before. I had in most cases, therefore, a few uncertain minutes to establish some kind of rapport with them, to put them at their ease and to get them talking. This was especially important, because all these interviews, with the exception of that with Ellery Hanley, the rugby league player, were originally conducted for the radio (parts of the interviews were broadcast in two series on Radio 5 Live between 1995 and 1997).

What did my interviewees have in common? Quite simply, I suppose it was that they were all major sporting figures who were psychologically interesting in some obvious way or other. There was Prince Naseem Hamed's supreme self-confidence and his apparent inability to feel fear; there was Vinnie Jones's aggression, revealed through his disciplinary record; there was Alex Ferguson's perennial success. These almost seemed like character traits that were going to be explored in the course of the talk. Some of my other interviewees were selected because of specific things that they had been through, things that may have had a major effect on them psychologically – things that we have trouble imagining. These could be sudden, like

Jonathan Edwards's extraordinary jump into immortality in the triple jump, or Gary McAllister's penalty miss against England in Euro '96, or more drawn out in time, like Kelly Holmes's dismal Olympics. They may even have been things that were drawn out over several years, like Herol Graham's climb to the top of world boxing and the years afterwards, when his friends and his money drifted slowly away.

What was I hoping to achieve in these interviews? The first goal was really quite modest: it was to allow some glimpse into the lives of my interviewees, sometimes into the extraordinary pattern of everyday life that underpins great sporting success. Liz McColgan, for example, told me about the structure of her typical day, a day organized around her training runs:

> I normally get up about five and then I run about six. Anytime between six and seven I go for my first run and then when I come back Peter [my husband] goes for his run. Peter looks after our daughter, Eilish, while I run in the morning. When I come back from my run, and it could be anything between thirty minutes and two hours depending on what I'm doing, I get Eilish ready for school, I take her up to school, and then really it's just a matter of relaxing for the rest of the day until my next training session, because I train again at three. I usually have a nap of an hour in the middle of the day because of the training that I do. It's quite a boring life really. I don't do much at all. I don't do any socializing.

But there was obviously more to all of this than just routine. There was the necessary psychological accompaniments to such a distinctive pattern of daily life that I wanted to explore. Liz McColgan talked eloquently about her compulsion to run:

> If I don't run, the next day I feel about twenty stone heavier. It's just psychological – I feel so unfit if I miss one day running. You've got to remember, I've run every day since I was eleven years old. It's just like taking a step outside the door in the morning. When I was pregnant, I trained right up until the

week I had her, and then my first race was six weeks after having her, and I won it. I actually started running on the eleventh day after the birth.

I wanted to listen to my interviewees and to try to understand them and their lives. I was not interested in offering any sort of label to describe them or any kind of neat categorization of them or their behaviour at the end of the interview. This would have been both unnecessary and futile, a parody of psychology. There were to be no conclusions of this sort. Rather, these interviews were to be explorations or, at least, a start on this exploratory journey. I wanted to listen and probe whenever necessary in order to understand them better. My interviewees were also all different, so there was to be no set pattern to our discussion. I went with the flow of talk, but with a number of specific psychological issues in mind. There were, of course, some recurrent features in the interviews – I did, after all, want to understand my interviewees partly through how they lived their lives – but I was mainly interested in how they talked about their lives, how they talked about their past and their present, how they talked about their success and their failure. I wanted to explore how they understood themselves. I wanted to explore their own psychology of themselves and others, their psychology of competition and their psychology of survival at the top.

The advantage of being called a psychologist, of course, is that people find it more natural than they might with some interviewers to be asked to attempt to recall fragments from their childhood or to attempt to reconstruct what they were thinking the day before yesterday. That was the one major advantage that I had. And occasionally, when my interviewees talked about their past, I thought that it was all quite revealing. Those fragments of their lives that they reconstructed for me often offered some glimpse into their psychological make-up, into the shaping of their character. Jonathan Edwards, the triple jumper, told me about what he was like as a boy:

I think that I'm very different now from how I was as a boy. I think the thing that's developed over the last two or three years in me is the capacity to be independent. Before, I was very worried all the time, I was very tied up with what people thought. What should I do? What would people think if I did this? What would they think if I didn't? And I've become much more able to make a decision based on what I feel I should do, regardless of anyone else. I don't mean to their detriment, but just that I can go down a line that I believe is right and go for something without worrying what everybody else is thinking. There's a verse in the Bible, in Proverbs, which says the fear of man is a snare – if you are so worried about what everybody else is thinking about you, you just end up tying yourself in knots.

I had read other interviews with Jonathan Edwards, but in these he had rarely been given the opportunity to talk about his background quite so freely. Sports interviews are often more interested in the facts of sport – in times and scores, in the mitigating effects of injuries and, of course, in the excuses and justifications for failure and success. The very substance of sport itself. Embedded within all of this there is some, and only some, psychological anecdote, which is usually spelled out for the reader. In my interviews and in this book, I felt less constrained. I felt that I had a brief to let my interviewees go off at a tangent if they wanted. I wanted to hear them explaining in their own words. I wanted to hear the terms they used for mapping out their world. And powerful images sometimes flooded out. Kelly Holmes, the runner, told me about the Olympic 1500-metre final and how it felt: 'There was just numbness, just like having a plate of steak slapping on the ground. That's just how it felt, I just really couldn't feel my foot at all. I obviously didn't feel any pain from it.'

I wanted to understand their psychological experiences of their sport. Their language and their powerful images helped me enormously. A plate of steak slapping on the ground – that's how it felt for Kelly Holmes in that 1500-metre final. Of course, you don't have to be a psychologist to listen to the words people use – any good interviewer, any good listener, does that – so what did I bring to this task as a psychologist? Perhaps it was as much the title as anything else. The title 'psychologist' made my interviewees recognize, before they even sat down with me, that it was their experiences and their understandings and their host of little psychological theories and models that I was most interested in. And perhaps the title suggested to them that they would have the opportunity to tell me about these things in sufficient detail to let me start to understand.

At this point let me add that this perception of such an opportunity may not necessarily have been confirmed by their perception of me as the quintessential patient interviewer. I come to an interview with my own distinctive style. I have a Belfast accent, with a rising intonation, so that it sounds as if I am asking questions even when I am making statements, and a fast speed of taking turns at talk, with a high proportion of brief overlaps thrown in. I include the interview with Ellery Hanley first, not just because it was the first interview in the overall series I did (for *The Guardian,* not for Radio 5 Live), but because it explicitly details aspects of my interview style, not just what I ask. It tells you a little about how I sometimes talk and not just what I say. The reader will have to imagine that same style of interviewing sometimes being used with people as diverse as Naseem Hamed and Liz McColgan, although, of course, my style was moderated to some extent by the demands of radio.

All I can say is that the style seems to work. I may have overlapped with my interviewees, but I listened and I found their language always interesting, always revealing. In the interview with Jonathan Edwards quoted earlier, you can see the kind of language he uses, you can glimpse his self-construction, with all its vivid metaphor and biblical anecdote woven into it. A boy tied in knots through worrying about what others thought of him, a young man walking down a line in life, the snare waiting to entrap the unwary, and self-understanding gained, in his particular case, through reading chapters of the Bible. This glimpse into his background helps us understand how he interprets important features of his new life as a world-famous athlete who has entered all our lives. Take, for example, his decision to compete on a Sunday for the first time. When you hear Jonathan talking about his boyhood, you realize that one way of construing this decision was an important stepping-stone in his own psychological development. As he himself put it: 'My parents were not for the decision and, given the strong influence they have been, it was quite a big thing for me to go ahead and do it regardless. I obviously asked their opinion and they didn't agree, but I said, "Well, I believe it's right, I'm going to go ahead and do it." So yes, I think it was probably very important.'

Devon Malcolm, the cricketer, told me about his first impression of England, after he arrived at Heathrow in the early spring but with a little bit of snow on the ground.

> Once I got to Sheffield, the style of housing was very different to what I was used to. You don't see houses in the Caribbean with chimneys, the houses looked like bakeries. This place was full of bakeries, what's happening here?

This extract may not seem as psychologically rich as the one from Jonathan Edwards, and yet the image of the young Devon Malcolm mistaking all the terraced houses of Sheffield with their smoking chimneys for bakeries gives us some immediate insight into the magnitude of the challenges confronting him in his new environment. Or consider the challenges facing Inga Tuigamala, the rugby player, when his family moved from Western Samoa to New Zealand:

> It was 1974, I was four years old. I come from a small family of fourteen, and Mum and Dad decided that New Zealand was the land of opportunities, and, therefore, we were going to go. But there were twelve of us children at that time, so mum and dad, by law, had to give up the other eight kids for adoption, because the law in New Zealand was that you were only allowed four children to come with you from the Islands.

In these interviews you catch a glimpse of the past, often graphically retold, and how it is reconstructed as relevant to the present. Elsewhere in these interviews we catch glimpses of the lives of famous sports personalities when they are away from the camera, in intensely private moments. There is Inga Tuigamala psychologically preparing himself before the game. He told me that he got inspiration from the Bible, so I asked him if he would bring a Bible with him to the changing rooms before a game:

I do, I usually carry the Bible with me. I don't open it in front of the guys and read it out loud, because I think I've got to respect the ways that they prepare and what they believe in. But I will have my quiet time, and I might take my Bible to the toilet and sit there and read the scriptures from the Book of Psalms or the Book of Proverbs, which gives me the inner strength to say, 'Right, OK, I'm relaxed and I'm focused, and I actually know what I want to achieve.' But I'm not an emotional person, so I don't get hyped up, or what you psychologists call 'over aroused'.

So here was Inga giving us a glimpse into the private moment before the game, the moment in the toilet of the changing room, with him clutching a Bible. You also see him trying to translate the whole process into psychological terminology for the psychologist in front of him. It was as if he wanted me to know that he understood concepts I might use like 'arousal'. It was rare for my interviewees to do this, to try to speak in what they thought was my natural language. More often, they told me about their psychology in their own language, their own theory of how to motivate people, which derived from their years of experience, their theory of how to read tell-tale signs of fear from their opposite number, their practical psychology of achieving success and coping with failure.

Alex Ferguson told me about his psychological ploy for keeping players motivated after they achieved success: 'After we'd won the League for the first time I said, "There are the names of six players in this envelope who I think may let us down this year." I said, "I will review those six players at the end of the season, if we lose the League." So all the players were saying, "It's not me, it must be you, it couldn't possibly be me." So you identify the winners or they want to identify the winners – that's up to themselves.' But there were no players' names in this envelope, just the name of the manager himself. Ferguson is a shrewd psychologist, of course, as his record testifies.

Then there was Naseem Hamed's psychological ploy for assessing the state of mind of Steve Robinson before their WBO world featherweight championship fight in Cardiff in September 1995. I had witnessed the slow build-up to this fight in the gym in Sheffield where the Prince Naseem dream had begun. On the Sunday before the big fight, I was in Brendan Ingle's Wincobank gym. The regulars were all there. Billy the Bag Man, who had been around Brendan for years, was looking for a lift down to Cardiff. He had bad circulation and didn't fancy driving all the way to Wales. Brendan, John Ingle and the man himself were going down on the Wednesday, so Billy couldn't get a lift from them. Billy had 500 quid on Naz to win. 'To make 250. It'll buy the shopping for a few weeks,' he said. Naz may have been getting hundreds of thousands for the fight, but everybody was trying to make something out of what they had learned over all those years, watching what was going on in the gym. Naz wanted to spar with Johnny Nelson. 'Steve Robinson is boasting that on the day of the fight, he's going to be up to nine and a half stone. Johnny is nearly fifteen,' said Naz. 'I'll show you what difference a few extra pounds makes.' Everybody laughed. 'No sparring,' said Brendan, 'twelve rounds on the pads.' Naz was putting on his bandages. He had a T-shirt on with 'All I have to do is turn up' written on the back. Brendan had forgotten his glasses. 'What does that say?' he asked me. I read it to him. 'The cheek of the lad. Some call it arrogance, I call it confidence.' Brendan kept repeating the slogan on the back of the T-shirt. 'All I have to do is turn up.' He was chuckling to himself.

Naz was confident before the fight, but when they got to Cardiff and the weigh-in he started the psychological battle in earnest. John Ingle had told me that just by looking at Steve Robinson he could tell that he had already lost the fight. I asked Naz if he could sense that as well.

Yes, I could sense it. I'd seen the look in his eyes, and I thought to myself that the look in his eyes was not really very positive. I was looking at him and he was looking at me, and we got on to the subject. I pulled him aside and I said to him, 'Steve, you're not really happy with the figures that you're getting for this fight, so I'm going to make you a great offer.' I said to him, 'Look, there's two of us fighting and we both want great purses and you think you're getting the lowest purse. So what we'll do is, if we're both confident that we can beat each other, we should put both purses in one pot and let the winner take all.' So Steve started thinking about it and he was mumbling a little bit, but then he said to me, 'Well, I'll leave it to my promoters and I'll leave it to my managers.' And he was giving it all this rubbish.

Naz nipped in with a little unexpected psychological test that he devised himself. But all sportsmen are looking for tell-tale signs. They are all trying to read their opposite number. They are all using their own psychology. Devon Malcolm told me about what signs of fear he looks for in a batsman.

You see the eyes, but you can also judge when a batter doesn't want to face you. At times, you can also see when a batter is pretending, like there is a quick single and he says, 'Come for two,' when he definitely knows there is not two, he is just trying to psych you out. Well, I know he is scared like hell and that he really doesn't want to get back. He'll probably get a quick single or a long single. He knows that he wants to stay at the non-striker's end, but he is just saying, 'Come for two,' and in actual fact he wants to be at the other end.

Brian Moore, the rugby union player, talked about his techniques for psyching out his opposite number:

It's more a question, I think, of being sharper in reactive terms and being quicker mentally than an opponent. It's not neces-sarily the case that you will intimidate people in that sense, but I think that if you're playing with more vigour, and if you're playing with better and quicker reactions, I think that does intimidate people, because they feel that you are beating them. There is a physical dominance, particularly up front, that you can try to put forward on an opponent. But again, when it comes to a physical act, like being punched or trodden on, anyone who is a coward is not really going to be a true international player. I mean, if it happens to me, I just try and shrug it off and try to make sure that if someone has hurt me, I don't let them know that they have hurt me. That's a very big thing with us, I think, in contrast to soccer. I would never go down after a punch or a kick unless I really had to. I certainly wouldn't make a meal of it, and I would do everything in my power not to let the other person know that I'd been hurt in anyway at all, because I feel that it would give them an edge.

I am fascinated by this lay psychology. It does not really matter what the academic psychological literature tells us about the non-verbal leakage of emotion, about non-verbal cues to fear. Here we have successful sports people who have to live with their theories. In this book we get a glimpse of what some of their psychological theories might contain and of their broad psychological perspectives on life. Vinnie Jones told me about his great hobby, bird-watching, and about his views on people in general and how they compared unfavourably with birds and other animals: 'People are very predictable. Animals aren't. I put the bag of nuts out there for the birds, and it was fascinating to see how many birds came to feed there in the hour and I watch all their little ways.'

On occasion, some of these sports people showed great psychological insight, and yet at times, it was as if they could sense the dangers of being too insightful, of having too deep an understanding of life with all its pitfalls. So sometimes they had their own distinctive explanations for why things were the way they were. Here was the young Naseem Hamed, full of optimism about his chosen sport, boxing, talking about his great idol, Muhammad Ali, who is stricken by Parkinson's disease:

Well, obviously what's happened to him is very sad. I do feel for him, but I can honestly say to myself that I know, for a fact, that it never came from boxing. His Parkinson's disease never came from boxing. I think that he got Parkinson's disease because God gave it to him. I think that what is written for a man is written. I think this only happened to him just to show people that he was human after all, that he was the same as everybody else. So I reckon that it was just written for him, by God.

Then there is the downside of sport – the failure and the insecurity and what it is like to live with this. Chris Boardman explained to me what it was like to ride competitively after an accident in a time trial.

> I'm still getting twinges from it. In one of the road races that I rode in we were doing 55 kilometres an hour in the rain and cross-winds and we were riding in the gutter, very close to other people. Obviously, brakes become fairly ineffective in those conditions, and I hated it, I really detested it, but I made myself do it. But while I was still getting twinges from my ankle, it was like something constantly poking your imagination into thinking, 'Imagine what would happen if you fell off now.' So while those pains are there, it's probably going to be very difficult for me, but I think that I'll be able to force myself to do it. It's most difficult in the rain and the wet because those were conditions where I always had an advantage before the accident.

And throughout all of these interviews, there was this powerful, revealing language, with its metaphors and its constructions, out of which these sportsmen built themselves and their opponents. There was Vinnie Jones, an 'ex-hod carrier', and 'a thug who can play a bit', according to one fanzine. But in this book we glimpse Vinnie Jones's own self-constructions. At one point, he talks about Gary Lineker. He uses the metaphor of the trenches, the images of war. Then he says: 'That was after an article Gary Lineker wrote, saying that he'd rather watch Ceefax than Wimbledon, so my way to sum him up was to say, "Who would people rather have at their side – a hundred percenter like myself or Mr Nice Guy?" This is his language. He sees himself as a hundred percenter, and everything else derives from this. This is the great psychological dimension in his mind that separates the men from the boys – commitment. You are either one hundred per cent committed or you are not. This is one of his core constructs. And elsewhere in the interview I discovered that my image of Vinnie Jones as the ex-hod carrier, which came from the media, was wrong as well. He had worked for a while for his father who was a builder. That was all. Many of these interviews are full of surprises, one way or another. I was constantly having to revise my opinions of the people I was interviewing.

So this is a book in which leading sportsmen and women talk about their sport and themselves. We hear about their lives in their own words, and from this language, with all its nuances and connotations, we may learn a little about sport and the men and women behind it. We may catch a glimpse of the psychology of sport from one hundred percenters like Vinnie Jones and from young optimists like Naseem Hamed, who say that fear never happens to them. We may gain some understanding of athletes who train compulsively every day like Liz McColgan. She says that she thinks she looks fat compared with other athletes, but deep down inside she knows that she isn't really fat – unless she doesn't get a chance to run that particular day. But, then, she never allows that to happen.

ELLERY HANLEY

There were two things I was told that I needed to know about Ellery Hanley before I could approach him. First, that he was the finest rugby player of his generation. Second, that he was a notoriously difficult interviewee. There were some skeletons in the cupboard, it was said, so he did not like to talk to the media. Until recently, he had been silent for six years.

'You will need – er, um – some special skills to get him to talk,' said the voice of the commissioning editor from the *Guardian* down the phone. I couldn't say that I hadn't been warned.

It was now a day later, and I was jostling for position with the seasoned campaigners from the English and the Australian papers at the press conference in the boardroom of the Rugby League headquarters in Leeds. The Great Britain squad for the first John Smith's test against Australia had just been named. It was a media circus: polite questions about the composition and nature of the team from a room full of reporters, and equally polite answers from the players and coach. Most of the questions were directed towards Ellery, who sat serene in the middle of this buzzing confusion. He appeared relaxed with the string of questions about the form of Martin Offiah or of Alan Hunte or of any other members of the squad. And the questions were restricted to matters of form and the intricacies of play. There was a tangible tension lest someone stray from this strict formula. But nobody did. It may have been a circus, but everyone knew who the ringmaster was, and everyone knew the score.

The circus spilled over to the car park, where the newly appointed captain, Shaun Edwards, grabbed the reins of the two dray horses laid on for the occasion by the brewery that was sponsoring the test series and pulled their faces closer to his for a great photo opportunity. My opportunity, such as it was, was to come later. The gentleman from *The Times* and myself were asked to wait behind after the press conference. We had each been promised a one-to-one interview. We had agreed between ourselves that he should go first. Then the Rugby League public relations sprung it on us. Instead of just a ten-minute interview each, why not band together and get twenty minutes' worth. Hanley was led in and eyed us suspiciously.

The man from *The Times* brought greetings from his father, who was apparently from Wigan. 'Really,' said Hanley. I heard it as a question. There was no trace of northern origins in the well-modulated tones of this reporter's speech, which was distinctly received pronunciation. It was time for his opening gambit. 'How are you enjoying your return to that of a high-profile public person?'

I swear I saw Ellery visibly flinch. It wasn't just the content of the question, it was the tone, challenging and condescending in one breath, in one well-modulated tone group. I leaned my chair backwards on its hind legs to increase my distance from the man from *The Times*.

'Can I just do something one second, please?' And on that note, Hanley reached across and turned off the tape recorder of the man from *The Times*. Hanley failed to notice my somewhat larger machine whirring away on the other side of the desk. 'Are you asking me about Rugby League or are you asking me about my life?'

'Are the two separable?' It was the kind of retort that would not have been out of place in an academic tutorial. It was my turn to flinch.

'Yeah, absolutely. Look, I've got loads of work to do, and from my point of view this wasn't intended to be an interview about my life. I thought you were coming to ask me about rugby league and the test series coming up.'

'Well, I thought that ground had rather been covered.'

'One second.' And on that, Ellery was off, in search, he said, of the P.R. man.

'I think that's probably that for the day,' said the man from *The Times*. 'He's famous for this, you know. I wanted to ask him an important question straight out. He accused one interviewer who left his important questions towards the end of soft-soaping him.'

The minutes ticked slowly by, with no Ellery. Maurice Lindsay, the chief executive of the Rugby League, popped in to find out what had gone wrong. This was meant to have been a reformed Ellery Hanley. Surely, he wasn't slipping into his old ways. Maurice assured us that he would try to get Ellery to come back. He told us that Ellery was sensitive. He urged us to tread carefully. The man from *The Times* was rearranging his bush hat.

I suggested to my fellow reporter that, if Ellery did reappear, I should go first this time. The man from *The Times* left the room. I developed my game plan on the hoof. Quick questions with no time for reflection. Ellery was led in. I didn't give him time to sit down. 'I have been reading all this stuff about you. You're the outstanding player of your generation. Why?'

'Well, that's what people say. I don't know if I ...'

'Do you agree with it?' I must say that from his response I am confident that he had never been interrupted before in his entire career in this kind of manner. He looked taken aback for a moment. He was notorious for being the reluctant interviewee, the man who had to be encouraged to talk by laying great slabs of silence for him to tread gently across. Being interrupted as he tried to formulate his views was new to him. He looked, in fact, as if I had just booted him in the bollocks.

I was using the high involvement style of the native New Yorker – fast, high-pitched, machine-gun questions, with a lot of overlaps and no pregnant pauses. No pauses full-stop. I should perhaps point out that I am not a native New Yorker, nor even a non-native New Yorker. So the fact that the short, fast questions were being delivered in a sing-song, Belfast accent rather than a New York twang might have been responsible for the look of shock on his face.

He regained his composure. 'I never think about it. I never take time off to think to myself what exactly I have achieved. I think that I stand out because of the contribution from other players. Individuals play in a team. It's other great players who have helped me make my name. Um ...'

'But that's very modest.' I was at it again, not giving him time to finish, challenging, not with the depth of my questions but with the speed. 'Why don't other team players get picked out then? Why don't others get the kind of adulation that you've received?'

'It just so happens that I've been fortunate and I've played with some fantastic players in Australia, in the Wigan days, and at Leeds. I've played with some magnificent players – Gary Jack from Australia, Wayne Pearce from Australia, Shaun Edwards, Philip Clarke. I've played with players who people don't even mention. We had a player at Wigan called Ian Potter, who was a magnificent player, but he never got recognition because everyone viewed him as a purely defensive player. But he was brilliant. You couldn't win without this sort of player on your side, but people forget about them. I've just been fortunate in that I've played with some magnificent players. We're a team. Individuals shouldn't be singled out.'

I had read somewhere that he could not bear to lose. I wanted to discover how important was the dread of losing in his psychological make-up. How important was this as a contributory factor in making him the outstanding player that he is? I did not waste words. 'Tell me about losing.'

'I have nightmares over losing. If I've lost a game, I can't sleep that same night. I'll be up watching the video and analysing it. The first thing that I do is to analyse my own performance to work out my contribution. Have I contributed enough to the game? Have I put my body on the line? If you don't put your body on the line, how can you expect anybody else to do it? I always analyse myself first. Has my work rate been good enough? Can I improve my play or my defence? The one thing that I've always been is honest with myself. I've missed crucial tackles sometimes, and I know it has been my fault. One on one, and I've missed crucial tackles. I don't hide from the fact. I'm human. I've made an error. But the next time, I'll work even harder to correct it.'

'It must haunt you, though, if you are watching the video after the game, and you see that you've missed a crucial tackle?' I said.

'But what's important is that if you don't analyse the video and be self-critical, you'll never learn. If you can't take self-criticism and criticism from others, you will never, ever learn. If you think that you're a player of some ability and that you're the greatest and you won't listen to anybody, you'll never further yourself. I play at Leeds with an outstanding player called Graham Holroyd. Graham is only a young kid, he's only eighteen, but I've got tremendous respect for him. He's got many assets to his game – his speed, his skill, his great vision. But he's come to me and he's said, "Ellery, I think that was your fault." It doesn't matter who you are. Any player should be able to go up to any other player and say, "You've made a mistake." It's for the benefit of the team. But what is also crucial is the way a player tells you.

'Talking from a coaching point of view, you've got to know your players as well. Man-management is very important. You've got to know how to address the players. Some players react better to a good rollicking and a bollocking. Some players don't like to be embarrassed in front of a crowd of other players. They just can't take it. A quiet word in the ear might be better for that player. I'm the kind of coach who prefers to give a quiet word in the ear, but you have to be prepared to give a good rollicking if that's what's required. Each player is different, and I treat each player on their different merits. We had one player who only came alive when he was rollicked by the coach, Graham Lowe from New Zealand. Each time he got into him, he just rollicked him and really riled him up in front of everybody. His eyes would open, he was on fire. He couldn't wait to get out on to the field. He was that type of player. Others are different.'

Ellery was at a crucial point in his career – his international playing career was at an end – but here was a man who had to put his body on the line, who led by example. Would his coaching style have to change because he was not in a position to do this any longer?

'It will, in that I will need a captain who will be able to lead by example. In a good side, you will always find a quality player who is willing to go that extra bit further, who will work that extra bit harder. That's where you get your captain from. A captain with brains, and a captain who will put his body on the line, and lead

through example. My captain would have to have the same attributes as myself. Shaun Edwards is just like me. He's a winner. He's
very single-minded. He's very competitive, very focused, and he's
used to winning. He doesn't know anything else but winning. And I
think that makes a huge difference. Also, he's got the respect of the
other players. In future, my choice of captain will be crucial in my
coaching.'

I asked him about this word 'focused', a word he used frequently.
Was it the case that players who are focused cannot imagine losing?
And whenever they do lose, they are devastated, because it hasn't
entered their consciousness up to that point. Was Shaun like that?

'Absolutely one hundred per cent. People think that Shaun and
myself are ignorant and arrogant. But it's not arrogance, it's being
focused. In sport, if you want to go that little bit further and be a
winner, you've got to be like that. You've got to be focused
completely and not let anything affect you. People criticize Chris
Eubank. He hasn't lost a fight yet, because when he goes away from
home he still does the same things. He'll still snarl at the crowd,
whether it's his home crowd or not, whether he's abroad or not,
because he's still focused. Surroundings don't matter to him. It's like
a rugby league player, when you're focused it doesn't matter where
you play. It's still a piece of grass, there are still going to be spectators
there, you still have a job to do. Being focused is the secret of
winning. If people perceive you wrongly because of that, that's their
problem.'

I asked him whether he was, as his clippings suggested, extremely
competitive in all walks of life.

'Absolutely. I play squash, and I'm just the same there.' I told him
that I, too, was an extremely competitive squash player. He seemed
genuinely interested.

'Anything I do, I like to win at that sport. I can't bear losing. I play
chess, and I play a high standard of chess, but even when I play chess,
it bugs me when I've lost. I've got a travelling chess set with me at all
times. Of course, sometimes you have to lose. Everyone's human,
you're going to have a poor game sometime or other, but the important thing is how you've lost. I can't bear it if a player hasn't given
anything to that game. Say, for example, a player has just cantered

through a game, and it hasn't mattered to them, that's what upsets me the most. It really upsets me then. Through my life I've always been like that.'

But fear of losing wasn't the only characteristic that marked him out.

'The other crucial thing is that if I do lose I have to be able to identify the cause. It bugs me until I sit down and analyse why it happened. I can't just put it down to bad luck. There's always a reason why you lose in any sport.'

I asked him about his interest in other sports and I got a rather surprising answer.

'I should have probably been a footballer. Don't get me wrong, I'm very happy with what's happened with rugby league, but if I had another life I would like to come back and try to be a footballer. I have the kind of assets that would make me successful in any sport I tried. I go that little bit further. When people stop training, I might go and do that extra bit. We train in the morning. When the afternoon comes, I might go and do a run of 4 or 5 miles. I always believe in having the edge on everybody and doing that extra bit more, which has made all the difference in my life. This attitude would have made me successful at football. Also I had the ability.'

'A Ryan Giggs, eh?' The machine-gun questions were landing all around him, but he was unmoved, unaffected – a natural interviewee, keen to explain. He was telling me about his great dedication to succeed, and how this dedication shaped the pattern of his life.

'I need to train. My body would not allow me not to. When we're abroad, when I get off the plane, I always go for a run immediately. Always. I couldn't just go to bed and think to myself that I'm tired. I just go out and go for a run and adjust to my surroundings.'

The compulsive behaviour necessary to make an outstanding sportsman is just one side of the coin, then there is the flip side. The body in compulsive training and the mind with its great highs and lows.

'It takes me a while to come down after a game. I'm still hyper-active, because I'm still conscious of the game. It's still running through my mind and so forth. As far as the game is concerned, in leading up to the game, I'm always in control. I always know my job.

It doesn't matter to me if we're playing a bottom-of-the-league side or a final at Wembley. I always know that I'm in control, and I never let my emotions run too high. I've seen some players who let their emotions run too high. They're so fired up that they just want to get on to the field and do some damage. That's because they're not in control. It's important to be controlled. In rugby league you have to have aggression, but it has to be controlled aggression. As the Great Britain coach, part of my job is getting my players to control their aggression, to get them focused, to use their aggression rather than being used by it. The Australians are a great side because they are experts at developing these psychological aspects of the game. They are using psychologists to develop their techniques. Psychology is central to rugby league. The Australians have left no stone unturned to improve their players.'

So how would Great Britain do against this great team, which will be using the most up-to-date psychological knowledge to channel and direct the aggression?, I asked.

'I never, ever try to predict the outcome of a game. Every game is different. A game could depend on a refereeing decision, it could depend on one weak player in your team, it could depend on one missed tackle, it could depend on the bounce of a ball. I never try to predict. But afterwards, with every game, won or lost, I could tell you exactly which single factor affected the outcome. I've analysed every game, and I could tell you whether the opposition played with more aggression – more controlled aggression – or whether they were better prepared, or whether they controlled the ball better or whether they had better field position. I could tell you this for any game. For any game ...'

'Okay, let's test it,' I said.

He was game, but the P.R. man had arrived to tell him that they needed to conduct some television interviews within two minutes. He had given me close to an hour in a frantic schedule. He was courtesy personified. He said that he had enjoyed our chat. 'If people are polite and courteous, you don't mind spending time chatting with them.'

But what about my machine-gun questions? What about my precision timed intrusions? I was thinking to myself.

'I've got time for anybody if they're polite.'

The last I saw of him he was standing in the car park with a TV camera stuck in his face. He shouted after me, 'All the best in your squash.'

All the way home I was worried that I had interviewed the wrong man.

October 1994

ALEX FERGUSON

It was a quarter to nine at Manchester United's training ground in Salford. The mildness of the winter seemed to be fading. It was bitter now. Frost covered the car park and the parking spaces reserved for EC and RG. The initials looked out of place in this very ordinary car park. This was a million miles from the glamour of Old Trafford. It was also very quiet. Alex Ferguson likes to get to work early, before the BMWs and the Mercs of the players arrive. A few schoolboy signings wandered about, one sat reading the Sun, *perhaps dreaming of future glories. Ferguson had been there for an hour, with time for them all.*

He had agreed to the interview weeks before, but by the time I got there he had forgotten who I was or who I might be. 'Sports journalist?' he asked. 'No, just a psychologist.' For some strange reason it seemed to reassure him, the most successful domestic manager of the nineties. I wanted to try to understand the man, so I started with his routines, his day-to-day behaviour, and asked him what time he got to work.

I was in this morning at quarter to eight. You know, I leave the house at quarter past seven normally, but this morning I left at five past seven so I was in here earlier.

I have to say that I'm really impressed by that because I'm not that kind of early morning person. Is it because you're an early morning

person or is it because you like to get some stillness in the day before everyone else arrives?

If you live where I live in Cheshire and you leave setting off until after half past seven, the traffic can be horrendous, so I much prefer to get in here early in the morning, get my cup of tea and my bit of toast or bit of cereal and settle down to doing all my stuff before my staff come in at nine o'clock. So I have an hour in which to relax and tidy up things and sort my desk out and prepare the programme for all that I'm going to do in the day. So, it's a convenience.

So were you always an early morning person?

As far as management's concerned, yes. I always feel like getting in early in the morning. It's a vital time, because as you know, when the switchboards start at nine o'clock you don't get an awful lot of time and you get pestered with all sorts of phone calls – various departments phoning you or your secretary phoning – there is an incessant barrage of calls coming in from nine o'clock till ten o'clock.

Is it a time of day when you can get your ideas together as well? Would you do that thinking in the morning?

I do my thinking in the car, everywhere.

Do your thinking in the car? It's all done before you get here?

Yes, you know, 'Oh I forgot to do that', or 'I must remember to do this' and you try to put a mental freeze on it. As soon as I get into this place, I get it down in writing before I forget it altogether.

Keep a notebook in your car! And do you stay here late in the day as well? I mean do you have a long day?

Well, it depends on the day. There are different types of day, of course. I could stay here to maybe after three or I could go over to Old Trafford – O.T. – or sometimes I have a meeting at Old Trafford so I'll leave here at maybe one o'clock. So it just depends on what's happening at O.T., and that's the difficulty of having the training ground 50 minutes away from O.T. You have to sort of combine the two, at times. I eventually end up at O.T. during the day, and I leave there at maybe about quarter to five.

And in a job like yours, managing the first team must be part of a much broader picture of things that you are involved in?

Well, we now have well over 250 full-time employees in the club, so there are all the different departments, and we have staff executive meetings for all the heads of the departments once a month. Then we've got the scouting departments where we have to have regular get-togethers, and they're usually conducted at Old Trafford. So you have quite a cross-section of varied things, plus all the other parts of the public relations side of Manchester United that you have to take care of.

Presumably, you personally have to have a lot of discipline to get through the week, because you are a busy person and you are trying to juggle a lot of commitments at any one point.

Well you certainly need a tremendous discipline, you also need great energy and perseverance. Energy is the most important thing in this job because it does require a lot of work, and the mental part can be quite exhausting, you know. Normally, when I go home at night time, I have half an hour lying on the couch because I feel that helps me.

Do you have any techniques to wind down after a day, because it must be a very stressful job?

Well, I do tend to think that when I get home I'm sort of relaxing right away. I like watching old movies and things like that. I like watching television.

When you say that you like watching old movies, do you have a

catalogue of videos that you watch or do you just watch them when they come on the telly?

I just watch them when they come on the television, UK Gold and that type of thing and Sky movies, I quite enjoy that. Of course, I've got some great old movies from way back.

Do you play any recreational sport or anything?

No. In the summer I sometimes go up to a nearby hotel into the leisure centre and have a swim every day, that type of thing, but once the winter months loom ...

It puts you off. Do you talk about football at home? I mean is it impossible not to or do you think, 'God, I really mustn't do that'?

It depends who's there. At the moment my three sons are away from home so there's just the wife and I, and the wife's not really interested. She's more interested in *Coronation Street*.

But even though she's not interested, would you still use her as a sounding board or something because a lot of people use their wives in that way.

I'm more inclined to work it out in my own mind.

Often people who have got a lot on their mind tend to be quite quiet at home. I know I'm like that. For example, if I've got a lot on my mind, people are always saying to me, 'What's the problem? What's the matter?' And I'm saying 'I'm thinking, just leave me to it, I'm thinking.'

I normally tend to think about things when I'm reading or when I'm watching television. I'm thinking, but it's one of those things where you try to divide your time. You know – my wife, Cathy, she'll want to talk, and you're thinking and you're trying to listen to her and think at the same time.

Is this a skill you have developed?

But it's giving her the time, and it is difficult for wives, married to football managers.

I can imagine. As someone outside football, I have to say that I think that being a football manager must be one of the most difficult jobs in the world, in terms of the kind of psychology you have to bring to bear on the job to do it well. In addition, there's always a clear criterion as to whether you're winning or not. You've got these eleven extremely talented individuals in their own right who you have to manage and somehow shape into a team. How do you read people, how do you motivate them and so on? Can you give me any hints as to the kind of psychology you might use?

The first sort of bedding down of the team is usually formed if you can get really good players. That's fine, but it's really all about developing the character in a person, having the strength of a person's determination that is probably the key to all the best players I've ever had – the self-determination.

You say 'develop a character' rather than 'build a character', so you'd say first of all that people have to have the seeds there within them, which you have to bring on. So it's not as if you have to build a new character – you can't turn a player into a different kind of player, you have to develop what they've got. So does that mean that you can spot those seeds of character pretty quickly within a player? How can you tell?

Well, I think I could give two different examples. When Paul Ince came to the club he was a young man that you just looked at and said, 'He's at war with the world.' You could tell that he'd had a difficult upbringing. I think that his background and his youth have been well documented. He came to us with his energy not channelled the right way. He was argumentative, competitive and belligerent in an argument, but you said, 'Well there's plenty there.' If you could just get him sorted out and take away the, not exactly the chip on his shoulder, but the grudge against a lot of things, then you would have something really special. You wonder whether his being Black has had something to do with it, you never know these things, but also his troubled background. But bit by bit, by working at his confidence and by building up his trust in the people round about him, and showing him that we were on his side and that we wanted him to become the best player in England, you could see, bit by bit, slowly but surely, that his trust was beginning to show in the way that he started to handle everything. And now you see the, I wouldn't say the finished article, but you see a tremendous array of talent now coming together. Or take someone like Bryan Robson. When I first came to the club, he always had injuries, sometimes bad injuries. He had had three broken legs before I came to the club, and just after I arrived he was just recovering from a shoulder injury and had to have a pin put into it, so you said to yourself, 'How long can he go on?' And I must admit my first gut-feeling about Bryan was that if I could just extend his career that would be great. Bryan has such great leadership qualities, and he has demonstrated all these qualities in a game, his desires and his ambition and his fighting quality – everything was mirrored in his game. So my first inclination was to make him a centre back or a sweeper, because I felt that the number of injuries he was getting was down to where he was playing. He was the type of player who couldn't see danger, he was always throwing a foot or a head into places that you would say to yourself, 'I wouldn't go there myself!' I thought that if I take him out of there and put him in the back, I can extend his career. But I did that without really knowing the true person. I only saw a demonstration of him on the football field. He didn't like it. He felt that I was writing him off as a mid-field player of significance, of great influence in the English game. But he didn't complain, he played centre back and we beat Liverpool. I think that in that game, he and Kevin Moran played at the back and both of them did exceptionally well. The next day he got a hamstring injury, and when he came back he came to see me and he said, 'Look, I'm better than any mid-field player in this country, you know.' And I said, 'Yes, but for how long?' But he was still playing eight years later, and he's still playing now, and you know, when you get that kind of character in a person, you could say, 'Well that's the kind of standard that this club has to have.' He was used quite a lot by us, by all the young players, as sort of a marking card for any player coming to this club or for anybody who would stay in this club or who would survive in this club.

He was a great role model, I think that's clear.

He was, and Robbo helped Paul Ince an awful lot in that turbulent period when Paul came to us. There is no question about that, and the good thing about Paul is that he's such a giving person, you know. Sometimes you see him on the football field and he's snarling and he's growling and he's moaning, but that's his competitive edge coming out. Robbo was exactly the same, and off the field, once Incy trusts you, he'd give you his life, he'd give you anything you wanted. You'd say, 'Give me a hundred pounds,' and he'd say, 'Yeah, OK'. He'd never ask why, you know, but the next day he'd want it back!

And was Robson similar to that off the field?

Yes, it's the same with both of them. Once they trust you, they'd do anything for you.

So that's one kind of technique a manager might use, which is to develop a role model to use with other players. Are there any other techniques for developing character in players?

I never give up on the players in the sense of driving them on. I use my own energy to show what is required of people, and I point it out to them when they're not living up to the standard that I've set. This continues and continues until they either die or succeed. But the one thing that does help is success – success brings many things to people, believe me. It brings stature, it brings prominence, it brings renown, it develops ego, which is not a bad thing in football – all these things can be brought about by success. It's amazing how, if you win a trophy, all of a sudden that player sprouts wings – his game comes on, his personality comes on. Success is, without doubt, another way of developing character in players.

Success. But if you're as successful as this team and as you, as manager, have been, is the downside of success not to keep thinking, 'God, I have to keep repeating this.' Does that not generate real anxiety, which is, 'How do we keep to that standard?'

Well that's not the problem. Put it another way, if you don't get that success, if you don't find it or if you don't feel it and you don't experience it, then you're always going to be in the middle of the road. When I first came to Manchester United, the first season was absolutely middle of the road. Manchester United cannot survive in the middle of the road. It's all to do with the traditions and aspirations of the club and the supporters. Most normal people go through life, quite happy to get up at eight o'clock in the morning and go to work, no hassles, and they never really search out what they could really achieve in life. In sport, success is a way of life because, possibly, the one thing that is remembered is who won the FA Cup, but who remembers who was second?

Yes, it's the *raison d'être* of sport.

There are very few winners in the football League each year. There's your League Cup and your FA Cup, and the European Cup is a bonus. So you've got three winners in a year. Now, it's better to experience a win, no matter what the pitfalls are after that – they pale into insignificance compared with not winning. One must experience winning to really know what you're in the game for.

Sure, but having experienced winning, it generates a terrible high, of course. How do people cope with the lows? Say you've had a bad defeat, what is the mood like? In a team that's used to success, is it much worse for them or not?

I think losing is a good experience.

A chastening experience?

Absolutely. That is a great word, chastening, it's a word I used in Barcelona. It reminds you how hard it was to get to where you are. It's all about the work ethic. After we'd won the League for the first time I said, 'There are the names of six players in this envelope who I think may let us down this year.' I said, 'I will review those six players at the end of the season, if we lose the League.' So all the players were saying, 'It's not me, it must be you, it couldn't possibly be me.' So you identify the winners or they want to identify the winners – that's up to themselves.

And are there six names in the envelope?

Ach, no.

This is a mythical envelope? Every year there's an envelope?

The only name in it is mine.

You've mentioned the work ethic there. Do you find your background in Scotland contributes to a work ethic?

Yes, I think so. I think that people who come from a working-class background retain it all through their life, particularly people of my age. I was born at the beginning of the war, and people from that era were brought up in the work ethic. People before then had to have a work ethic to survive, but people born just at the time of the war started to enjoy the changing luxuries after the war. The 1960s changed a lot of people's perspectives, and there was all this freedom that they didn't have before. Things definitely changed – technology came in, cars improved, television came in – but you still have to retain that real reason for wanting to get on in life.

Do you feel very guilty when you're not working, which is the other side of the work ethic?

It's funny you should say that. I went to Rome this year, at the start of the season with international week. It was the first time I'd ever taken a holiday in the season, and I went to Rome with my wife. She wanted to go to Brussels for some reason. So we were going to go there for a few days then I said, 'Why do you want to go there? Why not try Rome, because you've never been to Rome.' So we went there instead. But I'll tell you honestly, I felt so guilty because at that time, the Dublin deal was on the go, and when I left, the Chairman said, 'Would you sell Dion Dublin?' And I said, 'No way. We need him for Europe.' And he said, 'Well, Coventry have been on to us, and they are desperate for him.' I said, 'No way. He's too good, he's too valuable to us.' So he said, 'At any price?' And I said, 'Well, that's different. If they come along and say two million pounds, then you say "Yeah, fine". That's a good deal for the club and it's a good deal for Dion.' So while I was away they offered two million, and I felt really guilty not being involved in the latter stages of the deal. But having agreed to let the deal go through in the first place, I couldn't very well pull out when I came back from Rome. It was too late by that time.

And did you feel that the Rome trip was really a holiday? Did you feel especially guilty because it was like a holiday?

Yeah, that's right, it was four days away. I went to see a game, mind you. I went to see Roma and Foggia play.

Did that assuage your guilt a little bit?

It did, aye.

It was a kind of a working holiday, now?

Aye, I still paid for it though. I never would ask the company to pay for anything like that. I enjoyed going to Roma and Foggia, and I was only in the ground two minutes before the director of Foggia came up and said, 'Alex, what are you doing here?' And he starts talking away to me. He says, 'Who are you here to see?' I say, 'Well you know!' and I just didn't want to give away anything. I just kept him guessing.

You should have given him a lecture on the Protestant work ethic, to see if he understood it. You mentioned the time before the war, and obviously your working-class life has changed a lot over that period of time. I was just wondering if you had any comments on the kind of generation of footballers coming through now. Do you think that they've got the same roots in working-class culture, because I suspect that the kind of Protestant work ethic was inculcated in you through seeing what life was like around you. Do you see what I mean? And in some sense, that has shaped your pattern of life now. But I was just wondering how you thought the pattern of life had changed across one generation in terms of people's traditional values?

I think that what you are faced with now is a different kind of opportunity. When I was leaving school, I could have started in several places. I could have taken examinations for the power engines, Thermotank, related industries in the Govan area, where I was brought up, and settled to be a toolmaker. I could have gone into the shipyard – my brother wanted to do that, but my father didn't want his sons going into that, but one did and one didn't. But I think nowadays that it is different from my days. Young people don't have the opportunities I had, but you cannot underestimate the young people of today. Believe me, they really surprise you. I've some tremendous examples of young people coming into my club who have great fortitude and a great desire to get on in life, probably even more than in my day, because of the lack of opportunity. All they need is a chance. In my old area, Govan, they started, about six years ago, an organization called Govan Initiative, creating small business enterprises for young people, and it is amazing, the response of people. Once they are given that little bit of daylight, once they are given that little glimmer of hope, they say, 'Well, I can do something with my life here.' So, the real difference nowadays is just the opportunities that young people don't have, in the way that we had then. That's the only difference, but believe me, I think that some of the young people today have got probably more desire to get on than we had.

Does that make them more desperate as well?

Only desperate if they don't get the chance, and also if they lose hope and they lose sight of what is going to happen tomorrow. And then all the other problems come into being that we read about every day. It is all very unfortunate.

And do you think that football is something that has consistently, over the years, been something that has given young lads a chance to do something? In some sense there has always been a door there, only for the talented few, but there is a door, there is something that people can aspire to.

Oh yes, I think that is true without a doubt.

I was interested when you were talking about Paul Ince and I liked the way that you focused on things off the field, which told you something about the character of the individual. Do you look for a certain spirit in individuals? You talked about Robson as well, is there a certain spirit there you are looking for?

Well, I think you look for something in a person that causes you to say to yourself, 'Well, they'll handle adversity well, they will be able to respond to losing, they'll also be able to climb the scales because they've got something in them that will make sure they get there.' You know, I used to have a saying that when a player is at his peak, he feels that 'he can climb Everest with his slippers on', and sometimes players have to have that inner drive, so they can say to themselves: 'I don't care if we're playing bloody Real Madrid with ten internationals and they've won three European cups, I'm not interested, I'm going to win this game no matter what.' And I think people like Robson have had that all their life, I think they were born with that, and I think that Ince is developing that. I think he has that same inner self, it just needed to be brought out. There's been a few others – Steve Bruce has got that same tremendous determination. I can also see development in players like Gary Pallister, he's getting better. When he came, he was just a very raw young man, and I think that you can see development in people that way.

And is it something that you just try to nurture as a manager and you let it develop naturally? Is it something that people have got or they haven't got? You can't train someone to have this ability to fight adversity.

I think that once we achieved success after winning the League the challenge put down to them all was, 'The time is right, you either want it all the time or you don't want it at all. You can get out of the club and we'll shake your hand and say, "Great, you've been a great club player, you've won a League for us, on you go, we now have to go on."' Manchester United is like a bus. We can't wait for people who are late, the bus has to go on to the next stop, the club has to progress. We have to go on. You have to force the situation with the players. There is an old saying, 'Put your medals on the table' and all that rubbish, but we don't go into that stuff. I say, 'Do you want it? Do you want another bit of success? Do you want to go through all the pain and the agony again? Do you want the whole bit with everyone trying to beat you? Do you want that again?' And I think then you start to see the development of character, they either swim or they drown. It's as simple as that. At this club, that's the name of the game. You swim or you drown, and the ones who want to stay on will swim. They have to.

That's interesting. In terms of success in the 1994 season are you very disappointed by the European experience so far?

Well, I was shocked by it. Disappointment happens to you almost every day in your life, but I was shocked in Gothenburg. Shocked, not disappointed. I must admit that I couldn't understand it. I couldn't believe it and I've probably analysed it as best as I can now.

Do you go back over a game on video?

Oh yes, yes.

Do you watch it on your own or do you watch it with the players?

On my own.

And you just go through it all and work it out?

I go through the important parts. I go through the goals, and maybe I
go over the goals we lost about half a dozen times. Funnily enough,
I've not watched the Gothenburg game yet. I've been more interested
in the Arsenal game because we got a lot of criticism from the press.
I've watched the video twice now, and I cannot understand why the
press swung that way, but then again you can never understand the
modern press, it's very difficult. But I looked at the video again, and I
was trying to analyse the referee's performance and I just don't
understand all the bookings. I just can't understand them all. But
that is the new way with some of the referees, anyway, to stamp out
dangerous tackles and all that. But that's why it is so confusing
watching that Arsenal game, because I can't understand why Mark
Hughes was booked in the first instance, or young Keith Gillespie, or
why Nicky Butt was booked. I don't understand it at all. But
anyway, we can put a report in and hopefully it can be sorted out
with the people who are in control of all that.

**And is it easy to separate the European experience from what you
have to do in the Premier League for the rest of the season? Can you
keep those things in your professional life apart?**

Well, we really made the rod for our own back by wanting to win
the League, it was no holds barred. For instance, we got an opportunity to sign young Kanchelskis when he was only twenty-one and
we took him for £650,000. We felt that he could develop into a
good player and he has developed into a phenomenal player. We
took Peter Schmeichel because there was no doubt that young Gary
Walsh was having a lot of injuries, and I needed a goalkeeper of
substance. I think I got that with Peter Schmeichel, who is a tremendously strong character. And then Eric Cantona came along, and
we took Eric Cantona and he has brought a vision to the club. He

has a tremendous awareness of playing the game, and this has developed a lot of our players in their tactical and technical awareness. Plus, of course, all English teams have always used the tremendously important Scottish, Irish and Welsh players. Therefore, when you go one-eyed in terms of trying to win a League and the important thing is to get the best possible team, then you don't realize what is round the corner. For instance, once we'd won the League, they all of a sudden brought this new rule in about five foreign players and that took us by surprise and restricted our success in Europe. In 1991 I could play as many foreign players as I wanted, and we won the Cup Winners' Cup in Rotterdam, but now we have this restriction, which does make life difficult, without any doubt.

Can I ask you what it is like managing a team of people with such different nationalities represented in it? Again, it strikes me as being an amazing feat to have a team where English is not people's first language.

Well, I've enjoyed it because I've had to change myself. I had to handle them all differently. For Andrei Kanchelskis, for instance, you had to be sympathetic because when he came across, he was engaged to his girlfriend then he got married immediately. When his wife came across, they didn't know anyone, they couldn't speak English and you can imagine yourself at twenty-two years of age going across to Russia, marrying, settling into a country where it is very difficult to learn the language.

Does anyone in the club speak Russian?

We brought an interpreter in.

Has anyone else tried to pick up a few words?

You can pick up words, but you couldn't possibly speak it. We brought in an interpreter who did very well, and we used the same interpreter for the football part of it for Eric Cantona. But Eric speaks some English and so does Andrei, who has picked it up fantastically well now. So you had to be different for these lads because they are different people, from a different culture. They have a different mentality, and they have different aspirations for life. The British person is built on grit and determination. It has been a sort of standard bearer for life, the grit, the determination, particularly for Scottish people, I always think, and Irish people. When the British go somewhere else, they take that grit and determination with them, and it usually means they succeed. But for people from other countries who come to Britain, they are coming to a world that is full of that, and they have a different culture and nature to us entirely, so you have to consider all these factors when you are dealing with them. That's why I've changed because, like most of the managers in our game, I've been very much a programme person, you know – we start at ten o'clock and do our warm-up and blah, blah – but now I'm far more flexible in my management, not to accommodate people like Cantona or Kanchelskis or Schmeichel but to incorporate their ideas, which have helped us in terms of practice and things like that. It's been interesting.

I can imagine. Cantona's vision – that's probably the best word to describe this gift he has got – where does a vision like that, in football, come from?

Well, I think all the great players have to have it. The great players tend to have a better vision, it's not just Eric C we're talking about, it's all the great players. Glenn Hoddle had marvellous vision as a footballer – great players just have it. I'm trying to think of other English players that spring to mind, like Bobby Charlton, who had marvellous awareness of what was happening round about him, but the great players also need to have an imagination, an imagination about things. For instance, Eric C will produce a pass in the last third of the pitch and I'll say, 'God I never saw that!' If I'm watching a game, I'll usually see the pass, but the player can't see it because his head's down on the ball, whereas Cantona seems to have his head up like a cocker spaniel, if you've ever seen a cocker spaniel running about a pitch chasing the ball! His head's up and back, and he just has that. I think all the great players need that and although they've got that vision they've also got the imagination. The ordinary person, like you and me, just don't see that.

And obviously there's a certain confidence that goes with it.

Well, confidence comes in many ways. Confidence could be lost in a minute and won back in a minute for some footballers. Some people will never lose it, some people never have it, some people have an inner confidence in themselves. I think there are moments when Eric loses confidence. He's not infallible by any means.

Can you tell when you're watching a match if Cantona is losing his confidence? Is there a change in his body language?

I think that he gets frustrated when he's made a few bad passes. He gets annoyed with himself because he has got great pride, but most of the players have got great pride. You know Mark Hughes has got great pride in himself, and he makes mistakes and you can see he is annoyed with himself and he has a kick at the ground and that type of thing, but that's just a way of getting the frustration out of themselves.

Are there any more subtle things you look at when you are watching a match and think, 'Goodness, I can tell when his mood's changed'?

Maybe small ways. I think because of the speed of our game the ball will invariably come back to one or two or three individuals who have made a mistake the minute before, because that's the nature of the game. You make a mistake, but you get the ball back again the next minute, it's such a frenetic game. They have to have an armoury in themselves to say, 'Well forget that mistake, I'll do something different next time.' But sometimes, the players can go through patches of games when they try the more difficult thing rather than the easier thing. We say to players, 'Look, when you are having a bad time just don't be complicated, just keep it straightforward and make sure your easy passes go until your game is back on an even, flat plane again. Just try and be normal to get your game going again.' And I think that players like Eric C will always try to win the game, and that's what makes them so different. He's always on for a pass that wins the game, and that's what I'm saying about imagination, he has a picture in his mind that can win games.

Could I ask what it was like when you first came to Manchester United? Were you intimidated by the club and its reputation?

Well, I was maybe frightened a little bit to begin with because I came down thinking, 'Oh there are great players here, but maybe they've got too old and maybe they've had enough challenges here without winning the League.' So it took me a while to understand what the real needs of the club were. I did certain things that were put in place right away, which helped me in the long term – like the youth policy – but in terms of changing a club round, it wasn't the youth policy that changed it round, it was making decisions at the first team level that eventually got us there. The summer of '89 was an important summer, when I just felt that I had had enough, I just couldn't tolerate it any more. I had to do something controversial. I had to do something that to my mind was positive, and that was to change the whole structure of the first team, and I think I was lucky in some respects. I was unlucky at the beginning, because we started getting injuries that year, terrible injuries, like Robson who was out for most of the season. One of my first signings, Neil Webb, got a terrible injury, and he was never the same after that injury. You end up saying to yourself, 'Am I ever going to get out of this tunnel?'

So was '89 a particularly bad year then?

Yes, I was always saying to myself, 'Am I doing it right or am I doing it wrong?' And I kept saying to myself, 'No, I'm definitely right in what I'm doing.' I knew that I was right, but I was not getting any tangible proof that I was right. But then winning the cup in 1990 was the turning point.

And since then it's just been success really.

Well you see, we never got complacent, we kept our feet on the ground and maintained the high level of desire, right through to winning the cup.

And in terms of long-term ambitions, would you see yourself being at the club for some considerable time yet?

Well, yes. I don't want to be going anywhere now. I've been here for eight years at the beginning of the month, and obviously my contract finishes in two and a half years' time, maybe three and a half years' time, I'm not so sure. I always said that's a point of decision really, how much I want it, how successful the club is and, hopefully, I can be around to formulate the future for the club. We're always talking about the future anyway – it's not about yesterday, it's about tomorrow in this club, and we think that the structure that we've put down will serve us well for a few years yet.

And the Scotland job at some point in the future?

No, it doesn't interest me.

It doesn't interest you?

No.

October 1994

NASEEM HAMED

For a psychologist, the fight game throws up more questions than answers, and the WBO world featherweight champion Naseem Hamed, otherwise known as The Prince, has long since fascinated me. Not only with his obvious ring craft, with all the flamboyance of a latter day Muhammad Ali, but with his mind. Since the age of seven he's been telling anybody who was prepared to listen that he was going to be a boxing legend, and he proved against Steve Robinson in September 1995 that he was well on his way to fulfilling his dream. His record at the time of the interview stood at twenty fights and twenty victories. Hamed seemed to believe that he was invincible. So what, in his psychological background, was it that made him believe that he was so good? As we sat down late at night in a London hotel I wanted to know if he did not feel fear like the rest of us?

I walk through fear. Fear is not one of those things that blocks me, it's not one of those things that happens to me. I'm one of those very confident people who just overcome fear and just flow straight over it and forget about it.

Have you ever been frightened before a fight?

No, I've never been frightened before a fight. You should see me in the changing rooms beforehand. I'm totally the opposite. I get all the guys in, all my entourage from the gym. I pack out the changing rooms and slam some music on, whatever music I'm into, either it's rag or jungle, swing and soul, hip-hop, rap, whatever it is, whatever my mood desires at that time before the fight. We'll be having a great laugh in there, and I mean a great laugh. I'm talking about laughing, giggling, cracking jokes. This is five minutes before the fight. As long as I've got bandaged up and oiled up, I'm happy and I'm ready to go. As soon as they say, 'The television is ready, you're on,' I'm a different person. I'm blind to all the guys around me then and that's it, everything finishes. I'm ready to walk out and I'm ready to do the business. There is nothing else in my mind except to go out, get into that ring in *style*, as you've seen me do, and take an opponent apart and take him apart in style. In style! Especially if I'm fighting for a title.

Let me ask you a very personal question. When was the last time you were frightened of anything then?

To tell you the truth, I don't think I've *ever* been frightened in boxing, but I hardly ever get frightened as in 'frightened' outside boxing either. I can say that fear really never gets to me. I'm not one of those fighters like Nigel Benn who says, 'I thrive on fear.' As I myself say, 'I walk through fear.' If somebody else wants to be frightened, let him be frightened. Me, I just want to laugh all the way to the point that I get into that ring and I walk around. I hear my music and then I start buzzing. I start hearing my music and I start getting going. All the way to the ring I'm thinking about what I'm going to do to my opponent, big style.

The music is obviously very important, then.

The music is very important to me. It's got to give me a buzz. It's got to hit me so that I'm getting a great buzz and I know that it's the right time to fight. I need that energy, that adrenalin flowing, then I'm prepared to do the business. The music has got to hit you. It always does in my fights, along with the tension and all the people there, all the crowd shouting for me or against me. I've heard so many swear words at my fights, people just swearing their heads off and rhymes like 'Hamed, Hamed, who the fuck is Hamed?' And I've thought to myself, 'Wicked, I can't believe this. WICKED! They'll find out who Hamed is.' I've thought to myself, 'Wicked, let them keep shouting.' I can't wait to get out. This is usually the point in the proceedings where you can just see my shadow behind the screen and my music's about to come on.

Just another question about the music. You used the song 'Hot Stepper' for quite a while. Is this the sort of music you listen to when you're not going into the ring or do you like to keep it special for when you make your big entrance?

No, I'll tell you the truth. The first time I heard it was on the telly, but I never thought it was the right tune for me. And then a mate got it, he's called Ryan Rhodes, and he says to me one day, 'I'm going to come out to this music.' So I started listening to it more carefully, and I thought to myself, 'that's a good tune to come out to,' because when you listen to it on tape and plan out what you're going to do, it can sound pretty good. Ryan was fighting on my undercard. I can't remember which fight it was, but I remember the tune and everything, and Ryan says, 'I'm definitely coming out to this tune. It's a wicked tune.' So I said, 'All right Ryan, come out to the tune.' Anyway, Ryan finds out that he's not on, that it's cancelled. Ryan still wants to hear his tune, but obviously he's not going to come out to it, is he? So I said, 'Ryan, I might as well take your tune because it sounds better than mine.' So I took Ryan's tune and came out to it. Everybody took to it and everybody was clapping away to it. Ryan was happy that I'd come out to his tune. There was a great buzz. That's how it all started. Let me tell you something else. I didn't create the front flip into the ring to tell the truth about that as well. Ryan Rhodes was the first person to do the front flip over the top ropes. He was the first one to do it in the gym when he was sixteen or seventeen. I copied that as well.

He was the first one ever to do it?

Ryan was the first one I'd ever seen do that. I'd never tell a lie about where I got something from. If I've got something from him, he should get the credit.

So you copied the tune and the flip over the ropes from Ryan?

That's right, I got them both from Ryan.

What about your boxing style, where did that come from?

Well, I haven't got my boxing style off Ryan because Ryan's basically followed in my footsteps. But I'd seen him do the front flip over the top row and I thought to myself, 'That's a wicked way to get into the ring.'

He must have been very young when he did it.

He wasn't very young. I can't remember now how old I was when I started doing it, but he must have been about seventeen, something like that. He's eighteen now, nearly nineteen, but I'd seen him do it and I'd thought to myself, 'If I can do that and pull it off, with the landing and everything perfect, then you're going to look wicked. You're going to look great, you're going to look spectacular.' But you've also got to know that you can do it. You've got to get in there and produce the goods. You cannot do that front flip over the top rope and be negative in any way, shape or form, or get in there and think to yourself, 'I've got to do this, and then I've got to fight.' It's got to come all in one. You've got to know what you're going to do. You've got to know that you're going to get to the ring, do the front flip over the top rope, dance or whatever you're going to do, and then you've got to take your opponent out. There is no way of backing down after you do that front flip. You can't have any negative thoughts in your mind whatsoever. So when I saw Ryan do it, I thought, 'Ryan, that's wicked.' I think that Ryan should definitely do it when he boxes as well. We practised it together, and we both got it off to a t. I always think to myself that I'll do it every time that I go into the ring, because there's no way that I'm going to lose after going through that.

And do you have any idea, psychologically speaking, what watching that front flip does to your opponents? What's going through their minds when they see you coming in like that?

Well, if somebody did it to me, I'd think, 'Well, that is a confident man. I just hope he can back it up.' I am very confident and I'm like that, so I'm just telling them. I've got plenty of belief in myself and what I am going to do. They can see that because of how I enter the ring. Ryan is confident as well, but he's not really as confident as me just yet, so I don't think that he does it yet when he fights. He might one day. I think that he should, because it does take a little bit of edge off your opponent when they see it because they haven't got the same mental attitude as you.

Now can I ask you about your world title fight in September 1995? Were there ever any doubts in your mind that you might lose to Steve Robinson?

No, there was never any doubt in my mind. From day one, I knew that I was going to be in there with the perfect style. I knew that he was there to be taken, and especially by a flamboyant twenty-one-year-old who was ambitious and strong at punching out. That fight was tailor-made for me, and the night of the fight I showed it. There was quite a bit of animosity in the crowd, but I held my head up high. I just walked in there and took the title off him.

Had you studied videos of Robinson fighting? How did you know this about him?

I actually went to watch him box four or five times before I knew the fight was on the cards. It was about a year before I boxed him, but I'd been watching him and I'd seen his style all the way through. I knew he was perfect. He was made for me. But he obviously thought that he was stronger and had more experience than me. But in my eyes, I knew that I had the perfect style to beat him, which I showed on the night.

Could I ask you how important the psychological battle is before the fight? First of all, when does the battle commence between two fighters? Is it at the press conference? Is it before that? Tell me about the press conference. Is there a psychological battle going on there?

That part of the proceedings is very important because you've got to show that you want it badly. You're there to show your attitude and to show that there's no way that you're stepping down to the champion. So I showed him all the way, from three or four press conferences before, that I was definitely there to take his belt and to take his title. I knew in my mind what I was I going to do. I knew what I was going to do to him. I wanted him to know all this. Then, of course, he had his own view on what he was going to do. He made out that he was the stronger of the two of us, and that he was the strongest featherweight in the world and that he had boxed the likes of Colin McMillan. Everybody had said at the time that he was going to lose on these other occasions, so he said that he wasn't worried that everybody said that he was going to lose to me. But he was wrong. He should have been worried.

Did he offer anything in his psychological armoury to frighten you at all? Was there anything that he could have done to worry or intimidate you?

There was nothing that he ever did to make me think, 'I'm going to struggle here.' I knew that he had a good defence. But all a good fighter has to do is to break that defence up and take him out. You witnessed me break him up and take him out. I knew that his guard was going to be tight, but I got in there. I was in total control. I dictated the pace of the fight. I dominated it. I did what I wanted to him and to the crowd. When I wanted the crowd to shout, I made the crowd shout. I was so happy, I was smiling away. I was talking away. I did everything I wanted to do.

Can I ask you what you were saying to him, because it was obvious you were talking to him during the fight itself?

Obviously I was talking to him. He had turned round to me in past press conferences and said that he was the strongest featherweight in the world. How could he be the strongest featherweight in the world with me there? I was saying to him during the fight, 'You're not the strongest featherweight in the world, Steve. You've told me you're stronger than me. Do you still think that?' And I'm banging him at the same time as I'm saying it, and I'm hitting him so hard that he just couldn't understand where the power was coming from. At this point onwards in the fight he was thinking to himself, 'He really is stronger than me and he's telling me as well.' I could read his mind. So, mentally I was breaking him up. I was destroying him. He was going mentally, and he was going physically at the same time. So he just fell to pieces at the end of it all. I caught him with one clean left hook. That turned out to be the last shot of the fight. This shot was so perfectly timed that his legs just gave way. I picked exactly the right time.

The eighth round was a good round to finish it in, but I'd predicted the fourth. I thought I could definitely do it in four rounds. I thought I'd have broken him up in three – mentally and physically – and taken him out in four. The reason I said to everybody 'in the fourth' is because I definitely thought I could do it in the fourth, plus I wanted to gain a brand new Cartier Panther solid gold watch from my promoter Frank Warren on a bet we had. So I told everybody that I was going to do it in four, because we'd made a bet that if I couldn't do it either before the fifth or in the fifth, then I would lose out on a brand new Cartier watch. But Frank came up to me after the fight and said, 'Listen, you boxed great mate, you boxed brilliant, you can have the watch anyway.' So I was chuffed. I did the business and I got a brand new watch.

John Ingle, who's Brendan Ingle's son, said to me that at the weigh-in, he could tell by looking at Steve Robinson that he had already lost the fight, that he had already lost the psychological battle. At the weigh-in, could you sense that as well?

Yes, I could sense it. I'd seen the look in his eyes, and I thought to myself that the look in his eyes was not really very positive. I was looking at him and he was looking at me, and we got on to the subject. I pulled him aside and I said to him, 'Steve, you're not really happy with the figures that you're getting for this fight, so I'm going to make you a great offer.' I said to him, 'Look, there's two of us fighting and we both want great purses and you think you're getting the lowest purse. So what we'll do is, if we're both confident that we can beat each other, we should put both purses in one pot and let the winner take all.' So Steve started thinking about it and he was mumbling a little bit, but then he said to me, 'Well, I'll leave it to my promoters and I'll leave it to my managers.' And he was giving it all this rubbish.

So from your point of view, psychologically speaking, did that tell you everything you needed to know? You knew that when you made the offer, he wouldn't accept it?

Yes, I knew it straight away. But I knew it all along, to tell you the truth. I didn't really even have to look in his eyes – I knew the look already, even though he was saying he was going to beat me and that he was going to do this and do that to me on the night. I just knew. You can hear loads of fighters say what they're going to do, and they never do it. It's just talk. But everything I've ever said, I've followed up with action, and that's the main thing. That's the only thing in the end. A winner is definitely a winner, so I knew I could beat him from the start. There was no way that I had to look into his eyes and think to myself, 'Can I beat him or can I not?' It was never one of those situations. I had it in my mind from the start that he was going to get beaten, and he was going to be beaten well! One of the best things was to stop him or knock him clean out. Doing it on points is still a good achievement, but it's not as good as stopping a world champion in style. I won every round before I stopped him, so I was really happy with the performance.

It was a terrific performance that night. Can I ask you about your boxing heroes now? Who was the greatest fighter of all time?

The greatest fighter of all time has got to be Muhammad Ali. His style, his charisma, how he got on, how he became a world figure, what he did for the sport in general. Not just for boxing, but for all sport. I think that he's been a credit to sport, not just boxing. I think he has made sport what it is today. At one time in his life, you could definitely turn round and say, the most famous sportsman in the world has got to be Muhammad Ali. You could actually say that about Mike Tyson now, and they're both boxers. So if those two boxers can do it, obviously there are other boxers who can do it, if they set out their stall and know what they are going to do.

Can I ask you how you feel when you see clips of Muhammad Ali today, with Parkinson's disease?

Well, obviously what's happened to him is very sad. I do feel for him, but I can honestly say to myself that I know, for a fact, that it never came from boxing. His Parkinson's disease never came from boxing. I think that he got Parkinson's disease because God gave it to him. I think that what is written for a man is written. I think this only happened to him just to show people that he was human after all, that he was the same as everybody else. So I reckon that it was just written for him, by God.

So do you think that everything that has happened to you so far has been written for you by God?

Yes, definitely. I've got so much belief in God, and I think that God has got so much belief in me. I've had the best upbringing a child could have, and I praise my mum and dad so much for the upbringing I've had. The upbringing has been of a clean-living guy, a genuinely nice, down-to-earth person. What I'm like in the ring and what I'm like the rest of the time are two different things. I do take my hat off to my mum and dad and I thank them dearly for bringing me up the way they did, and I thank God for the position I'm in today. As I say, I am religious but I like to always keep my religion personal and private to myself. I have prayed before a fight, but the prayers will definitely always be between me and God. I've got so much self-belief in what God has given me. I know definitely that I'm blessed with a gift. I've accumulated such an amount of money, but I've always kept my feet on the ground.

I love training, it's part of me. I'm not one of those guys who, when he's made his money and he's thinking that now he's got all the best stuff and he's living the life that he wants to live, just wants to jet out of the game. That's not me. I'm planning to be a legend in this game. I've set my mind on becoming a legend, until the time comes when I have to retire. Until that time, I'm going to keep winning and winning and winning, and I mean winning! I'm talking about winning titles at different weights. Everything that I have desired so far has come true. My dreams are coming true now and it's all a big dream and it's just happening. At the age of twenty-one, it's great for your dreams to come true.

Can I just ask you about your mother? Did she ever have any anxieties about you going into the ring?

No, my mum's very confident in me. As you know, we're all confident in my family That's where I get my confidence from, but my mum feels like any other mother with her son going into fight and with all the dangers there are in boxing. I always talk to her before a fight. I always keep in contact wherever I am in the world. I love my mum, and I can honestly say that at this time in my life, there's only one woman in my life and it's my mum. We sit down before the fight and she'll say, 'Which round do you want to take your opponent out in?' And I've honestly said to her, 'Well, I want to take him out in the second round,' and she will turn round to me and say, 'It's done.' She says to me, 'You just keep training, get your mind on the job – on what you're going to do in the second round, and you will do it.'

Was your mother interested in boxing before you took it up?

She'd always liked boxing, she'd always watch it. My parents like the style and the art and the craft of boxing. I'm talking about good boxing, not just watching two fighters slugging it out in a fight. That looks ridiculous. My parents like the art and craft of two people in a thinking game, hitting and not getting hit, and being good at their craft. Good at their work. So my parents have always liked it.

Can I ask you how you got involved in boxing in the first instance? Now, everybody is familiar with the story that Brendan Ingle, your trainer and manager, saw you fighting three other lads in the school playground when you were six.

Everybody is familiar with it, but I don't even know whether it's true or not!

I was going to ask you whether it's an accurate story or is it just made up?

To tell you the truth, I think it is made up, but at that particular time in my life it was made up for a reason. It did create a lot of interest in me. It did work, and people wanted to hear this story, so obviously it did some good at that time, but when the truth has to come out, the truth has to come out. I can't remember fighting three guys in the school yard. But that's Brendan's story, and Brendan will stick to it. What he saw, he saw, but I can't remember doing it.

Did you get into many fights at primary school?

No. I was thinking about my school days and the truth is that I hardly ever got into any fights at school, at either primary or comprehensive. In the infants school, there was maybe a few little tangles, but that was only as an infant. Obviously at seven or eight, you're going to get into a little bit of trouble now and again.

Do you have any idea what caused the fights at the infants school?

No, at that age fights can be over anything. You can have a little kid looking at you and you're thinking, 'What is he looking at?' And you could walk over or he could come over, and you could bump into each other and obviously you could start a fight over anything, but I definitely remember most of my school days, and I hardly ever got into trouble. No fights or anything. I never got excluded, never got expelled.

Were you good at school work?

Most of my thoughts were on boxing. I had it planned out actually.
Why do people get educated? The only reason that people get
educated is to get a job. The only reason they get a job is to earn
money. Obviously, the only reason they want to earn money is for a
good standard of living, a wicked way to live. So I thought to myself,
'I'm going to cut all these routes. I'm going to be a legend in boxing.'
I trained every day from the age of seven and I thought to myself, 'Be
dedicated, be devoted to your sport, keep your feet on the ground,
keep training. You'll get what you desire.' At twenty-one, I'm world
champion, so I could say my plan worked out pretty well.

**It obviously worked very well. At the age of seven were you very
good at boxing? Were you very good right from the beginning?**

Brendan always said that I'd got it. That's why I thought I was good.
When you find something really easy when you start, you know that
you're some kind of natural. As soon as I walked into the gym, I
knew that the sport was for me.

You just felt it instinctively?

Yes, definitely. It was in my heart, it was there as soon as I walked
into the gym. There were good things coming out of the gym at the
time, like Herol Graham, Johnny Nelson, Brian Anderson.

**I was going to ask you about Herol. Was he an important role model
at the start?**

At one time I used to look up to Herol. He was a good fighter and a
fighter I looked up to, and I said to myself, 'Herol Graham is doing
the business and being a bit of a hero in Sheffield. He's on the television and he's driving the cars that he does and living the life that he
does. I'd love that to be me.' But I knew, full well, that I could
actually be bigger than Herol. But at one time in my career I thought
to myself, 'I'd like to be like him.' And then I got there and I thought,

'I want to be bigger. I want to broaden my horizons and be a lot bigger and drive better cars and be a lot more popular,' which I did do, and I did it at an earlier age. But I did look up to Herol, and he was a great influence at one point in my life. He's one of the best defensive fighters I've ever seen, but there was definitely something lacking in his style. I worked out what was lacking in him, and I trained all the way up to what I had to do with nothing lacking.

Something lacking in his boxing style do you mean?

Yes, there was something definitely lacking there, but I kept it to myself and I kept training and I knew what I had to do. I just accumulated different kinds of styles and put them into one and brought out a winning formula.

Can I ask you about your amateur career? How many times did you lose as an amateur?

I lost about five or six times as an amateur, but I could definitely say to myself that I have never walked out of that ring a loser when I'd lost. I always knew in my heart that I'd really won. I'd just lost for the simple fact that the judges didn't like my style and they'd gone against me. If it was a bit close, I knew I'd still won, but they would say I'd lost on points. Two judges voted for him and one judge voted for me, but in my heart I knew that I'd won. I never *really* lost a fight as an amateur. I beat the guys that I did lose to when I boxed them again.

Were there some that you didn't box for a second time?

There was just the one, but he retired when he was twelve, which is a ridiculous age to retire.

So there is somebody out there who has beaten you, but he retired immediately afterwards?

There is somebody out there who has beaten me. I can't remember his name. I was only about eleven. I was probably on my fourth fight, and he won. As I say, he never won properly, the judges simply went against me. I knew inside that I'd won. You see, they couldn't really find out what I was up to. When they looked at a guy like me, who had lost in the ring but had a big grin on his face, they would look at me all funny. 'Why is he actually smiling when he has lost? Is there any way we can get this guy down?' This is what they were thinking. I'd be looking at them, knowing what they were thinking and I'd be smiling at them. I'd be walking out of the ring smiling because that was the best thing to do, smile.

Do you mean because it would have been a sign of weakness not to?

Exactly. It would have been a sign of weakness. I knew, even at the age of eleven, that I should just smile in the ring. When I got back into the changing rooms I was still smiling and laughing because I knew that I'd won. It didn't really affect me in any way, but unfair judges' decisions did dishearten a lot of kids, and a lot of kids retired because they were getting robbed.

Did you have a fairly flashy entrance into the ring, even then?

Oh yes, I had a wicked gown. I got this gown made for me by a woman in Liverpool when I first got sponsored by a guy in Liverpool. It was a great gown. It was gold, it was flashy, it had shoulder pads – you name it, it had it, and it looked the part, believe me. And when I got in the ring I'd be dancing. I would dance in the ring just like I do now, and I would do the Ali shuffle, and I would shadow box and do what I had to, and that was from the age of eleven and it's just carried on ever since.

In your early days was there ever any racism when you fought in the ring?

There was only one occasion when I fought in London when I was about fourteen or fifteen. I was fighting for a national title that I needed to win. I remember that I broke my hand in the fight in the first round and I carried on to win. It was a unanimous decision over the kid. The kid was so strong and his head was like rock. I'd blasted him with such a great shot that I broke my hand in the first round and I remember that I carried on with one hand. That was the first time in my life that I came across a little bit of racism like 'you black bastard' or whatever. But I knew from then on that you're going to get it, no matter what colour you are. So that was another thing I had to rise over.

Did you ever have any anxieties about becoming a professional boxer? Or is that something that was just written into the script?

That was most definitely written into the script. There was no way that I was going to be an amateur boxer and do so well as an amateur and then not turn professional and gain all the financial rewards as a professional. The apprenticeship that I'd served as an amateur was so long, I thought to myself, 'I can't wait to turn pro.' That was my main goal.

You turned professional at eighteen?

If I could have turned pro earlier I would have done so. If I could have turned pro at fourteen or fifteen, I'd have turned pro and I would have still beaten all the men. I would have still beaten all of them with the style that I had. From the age of fourteen or fifteen, I knew what I was going to do. I knew that I was going to turn pro. It was my goal to turn professional and make loads of money, to become a legend, to win so many titles and make people so proud.

What is the toughest part about being a professional boxer?

The toughest part about being a professional boxer is to sacrifice what you have to sacrifice before a fight. I love training, so it's nothing to do with training. The toughest part is that you've got to get to the right weight at the right time, to peak at the right time to box, to be mentally right. It's hard, but if you do things as pleasure and you enjoy them so much, it becomes easy. If you're doing things day in, day out, you know that it's going to get easier and you start doing things automatically, just like getting up in the morning, having a wash, brushing your teeth. It's so easy, and I've got to a certain point in my life when I find it so easy to get in and train, to peak right, to control the weight, to sacrifice what you have to sacrifice in boxing. Watching your food, watching what you eat, and at what times you eat or whatever, how much you drink, the salts in your body, which you have to put back in – there are quite a few things to pick up. It's hard, but as I say, it does get easy if you know what you're doing.

What do you think are the major pitfalls for a professional boxer?

The major pitfalls? For a lot of fighters the drink really gets to them. They drink so much that they can't lose the weight and it kills their liver, and they don't perform well in the ring. I won't say late nights because it's how you control your late nights. I do have late nights – I like to stay up late. I've stayed up until five or six in the morning and boxed the next day and knocked my opponent out. Before one fight I stopped up all night and all morning.

What were you doing?

I was at my mate's, chilling out, doing what I wanted to do. Basically, I'm one of those guys. In boxing they say, 'You should have early nights. You should get up and run in the morning. You should do this and you should do that.' It's a load of rubbish. If you're not like that, if you don't want that, you don't do it. Me, I'm not the kind of guy who would get up in the morning from my bed at half past four or five o'clock in the morning and start running. That is not me. Running is for runners. That's what I say! I don't run. I train hard, you've seen me train and I train very hard in the gym. When I do get in to train, I train two or three times a day in the gym. I hardly have any time off. I'm one of those guys who will train all through the year. So I do train hard and I might do short sprints. But getting out of bed in the morning to run? Not me. Sleeping at early hours in the night, at nine or ten o'clock? Not me. To bring it back to the pitfalls in boxing, another pitfall is mixing with people you shouldn't really mix with who are going to be a bad influence, and lead you the wrong way. You've got to know who your friends are.

Can you avoid these pitfalls?

Oh yes, most definitely. One of the biggest things, when you do get successful, is girls. I've seen loads of fighters who have picked a girlfriend and it's gone totally wrong for them because they can't control it.

Psychologically that must be really tricky. Because you meet girls and you think, 'Are they going for my personality? My looks? My fame? My money?' What are they going for? How on earth do you work it out?

Basically, you've got to spend time with the girl, you've got to talk to her. If she's the greatest of actors and she carries on acting her part that she likes you because of who you are, your looks or because you've got a nice personality, you can believe her or not. As they say in the paper, 'There's plenty of devious girls about.'

Does it make you anxious? How do you feel when you meet a girl for the first time?

There are some girls I meet and I think to myself, 'I've got to keep her at arm's length because she might be a bit tricky.' You meet girls nowadays and they've met you and you can say 'hello' in a public place, and they can go away and no matter who you are they can make up some kind of stupid story and sell it to the papers or whatever. You look in the paper and you think, 'What is this? Why has it happened to me?'

Presumably, when you read the paper you don't even recognize some of these girls?

Oh yes, you think, 'Where did I meet her?' So you do get some girls who are tricky. You can get set up in life, and when you get set up you realize what's happened to you. I've seen not just boxers but so many sportsmen go down for women.

Tricky women?

Tricky women.

If you go to a night-club and you don't drink alcohol, what do you drink?

I've just been introduced to a brand new beautiful drink by my friend Tim. Coke mixed with blackcurrant.

Would you have a few of those?

Coke and blackcurrant, and I break it up with pineapple, lemonade and orange juice. I drink all sorts.

Are you never tempted to look at the rows of alcohol and say, 'I'll have one of those?'

No, that's something I've never said in my life. As I say in boxing, what I wanted to do and what I'm going to do is something that I've planned from day one. My parents have never tasted alcohol and I've always had it in my mind that I'll never ever taste alcohol. And I've never tasted alcohol, and at the age of twenty-one I can honestly say that alcohol has never gone past my lips and I never will drink it. Were you asking if I get that urge to say to myself, 'I'd love to see what it tastes like?' Well no, because basically what you haven't had, you'll never miss.

That sounds very sensible. You've been with Brendan Ingle for fourteen years. When you were young and you wanted advice, did you go to him about some things and your father about other things?

I've learned a lot from Brendan. Life and social skills, you name it, he explained everything to me. He's been one of the greatest influences in my life. I have to give full credit to Brendan. He hasn't just been like a trainer. He's been there for me all through my life and he's one of the guys in my life, along with my parents, who have led me the right way and had me thinking what I'm thinking today. So I must give so much credit to Brendan. He's been great for me, and at this moment in time he's my trainer and he's my manager and he's been that ever since I was a professional. I knew from day one that he would be great.

In terms of your relationship with Brendan, did he ever feel like a substitute father? Or an additional father?

Yes, he has been a bit like a second father. Because I can honestly always sit down and speak to Brendan about anything. I can definitely look up to him, like my dad. I can sit down with him or ring him up at any time, to go anywhere, to speak to him about anything. It's great when you've got somebody like that. I really appreciate him for that.

In terms of your identity, do you think of yourself as a Yorkshireman first and foremost?

Born and bred.

Yorkshireman and a Yemeni?

I wouldn't say a Yorkshireman, I would say that I was born and bred in Sheffield. I like Sheffield. I'm proud to be born in Sheffield. The Sheffield people are down to earth and it's great in Sheffield. I think I'll always have that as my base. I'd have flats in other places, like London or whatever, and maybe in other parts of the world when I get richer, but I like Sheffield. I would class myself as a Yorkshireman as you say, but I'm proud, I'm so proud to be Arab and I'm so proud to be British. As you know, I've got two bites of the apple and it works for me in the best ways because I'm so big in the Arab world now. It's great to go to any country in the Arab world and know that you're going to be loved and know that you're going to fit in, in the right way and know that people are going to see you and be proud of you. It's great that way, but I always come back to my British roots. I was born here, I love England, and I know that I'd never leave England to live anywhere else. No matter what they say about tax or whatever and tax exiles, I would never leave England, I love the place.

If you weren't a boxer, what would you like to be instead?

If I wasn't a boxer, I'd definitely be involved in sport because all that pen-pushing rubbish wouldn't give me the kind of things that I wanted. If I wasn't a boxing champion I would be involved in some other sport that I'd picked up and devoted my life to, becoming great at it. That is basically me, but I can't really imagine doing any other sport than boxing.

Are you very competitive in all aspects of your life, not just in boxing?

Yes, most definitely, I'm positive in everything that I do. If I'm going to do something, I like to do it right. If I'm going to get something, I like to get the best.

In everything you do, you like to be the best? Does that mean there are certain things that you won't attempt?

No, I'm a trier. I like a good challenge, but I'm not one of those guys who thinks, 'Oh, I won't be able to reach that level, I won't go for it.' I think I'm totally the opposite. I am a good trier and I do mostly achieve, what I want to achieve, and everything that I've wanted so far, I've got. So at the age of twenty-one I think I've done quite well!

Everyone talks about you being a world champion at four or five different weights. Realistically, how many different weights do you think you could be a world champion at?

About four or five different weights definitely. It's all I've ever wanted, so I think I could definitely step up a few more weights.

I look at my body structure at this age, my legs are pretty big, pretty solid. The top of my body is quite big, so I reckon I could definitely fill out more. I'm a featherweight now, but I think I'd like to drop down to super-bantam and maybe win an IBF world title, a different belt to add to the collection. Maybe step up and win a couple more belts, but then you've got the super feather-weight. I think I could definitely go up another three or four weights.

So you see yourself emulating someone like Sugar Ray Leonard who was world champion at a number of different weights?

Yes, it is great to win the world title at one weight, to be the undisputed world champion at one weight and to know that you're the king of the weight. But it's great to win three or four different world titles at different weights, to prove that you haven't just stayed at that weight and beaten people at that weight. When you can go up three or four different weights you're showing people that you're a legend. Nearly all the greatest fighters in the world have got beaten, and I'm definitely planning not to get beaten.

You're planning never to lose?

I'm planning never ever to lose, no matter what. I refuse to lose.

A really interesting psychological question is how would you cope with that first defeat?

How would I cope with it? I would cope very well with it because I remember losing as an amateur. Compared to losing as a professional it would be very different, but I think I'd cope very well with it. All I would do is set my mind to be even stronger. There are guys that lose and flop after that. They can't take it. They can't get back into the limelight. Look what's happened to Chris Eubank, he's a prime example. He's lost to the same opponent twice. He's gone back and tried to do his best to win, and he's failed again. So there's a prime example of his strength mentally, and it can't be very strong. Me, now if I lost, I'd just come back and I'd train so hard and I'd set my sights on winning. I'd let nothing dishearten me. I'd just basically plan what I'd have to do to win. I'd get up to that same point and make sure that when it came to the crunch again that I'd win.

I'm intrigued by this, because as an amateur you may have lost but you felt you were robbed, so psychologically you could leave that ring smiling because you thought, 'Well, they didn't really beat me.' But what would it feel like to really lose? Do you ever lie in bed wondering what it would be like?

I've never ever sat down and said to myself, 'What if you lose? What if you actually lose? What if you do actually get beaten by a better fighter?' I've never sat down and thought that, because my mind is so positive that I can't get beaten. I've gone through every move, every manoeuvre, every style, every way of punching – everything, you name it. I think at the age of twenty-one I've mastered the art of boxing. It's a big statement to make, but at the age of twenty-one I have learned so much and with so many styles that I can put together, fighters can't watch me and say to themselves, 'He's going to box like that against me,' because I will change my style all the time to adapt to beat a different opponent and his different style. I'm not one of those fighters who you can watch and say, 'He'll box in exactly the same way in each fight.'

That's interesting. Is boxing a science? Is it something that can be analysed and broken down into its component parts and taught to someone?

I think watching me has been an eye-opener for some people because I'm totally different to other fighters. Especially in Britain. I think what I do cannot be taught unless someone is in the gym with me day in, day out, month in, month out and watching me train and copying everything that I do. That's probably the only way to do it. It's not just about watching me and doing the same stuff as me, it's also having the same mental attitude as I've got.

And the same biological background? Are you bringing something special to the sport?

Yes, and the background that I've got. It all blends into one. It's a perfect mixture for a world champion. I think the perfect ingredients went into making me.

You've said that you want to be a legend. In some sense you're going the right way about it. There are a lot of kids out there looking up to you. What's the take-home message for those children who idolize you?

I would basically say that my advice to all children who are watching sport in general, not just boxing, is that whatever you want out of life you can go out there and get it, if you set out your mind to it. You've got to devote your whole life to it, if you really want it. It's all in the heart if you want it enough. The advice is, you can get what you want, if you want it enough. You can become a world champion. It's just like a football team from Sheffield – Sheffield Wednesday, Sheffield United – becoming world champions, going to the world cup and winning the world cup.

That's pretty unlikely for Sheffield United really.

But it's what I've done. I've come from a place in Sheffield, not far from Meadowhall, where all the people are so down to earth and I've gone all the way and I've won a world title and I've brought it back to Sheffield. So my advice to the kids is that you can make it. You can do it. You've got to set your mind on what you want to do and you've got to train and be disciplined.

Have you any personal goals that have not been met so far?

No, not yet, I haven't.

Would you say most of your goals were financial in the end, all about having a good life?

No, one of the goals was to secure my family financially, and that has happened. They can always look at me and know that they're financially secure for the rest of their lives. It's a great point to be at when you can turn round and say to yourself, 'I am the man who supports my family.' I have a big family and at the age of twenty-one it's great to look at your parents and know that you can give them whatever they want.

Some people who have moved from amateur sport to professional sport say that once the money starts rolling in, their interest in the sport sometimes, rather surprisingly, dims a little bit. That didn't happen with you?

No, not at all. As you know, I'd planned it all out, and I'd set my sights on becoming a legend in boxing. So it's not that I've said to myself, 'I'm going to earn my money and retire.' I haven't put an age limit for when I'm going to retire. It's not me. Boxing has been great to me and I've been great for boxing, so it has been a perfect mix. I brought a new sparkle to the game. I've brought a different kind of look to the boxing game, and people like it. People watch it on the telly and they get entertained, and people tell me, 'You're a great fighter, you've brought so much sparkle to the game, you're an eye-opener.' All these things can go to your head, but my feet are firmly on the ground.

Do you feel that you know yourself pretty well and you won't let yourself get carried away with all the attention?

I know myself very well. I know what I want out of life. I've set my mind on what I want but I know what can lead me the wrong way and I know right from wrong. So I know what I'm doing.

Do you ever get frightened of the responsibility that being a legend demands?

No, it's just something else that you've got to do. If you're not prepared to take it, then step out. If you can't take the heat, get out of the kitchen.

Is the heat going to be turned up now?

Oh definitely. I'm only twenty-one and I've only had twenty fights. I've had twenty wins, eighteen knock outs. But there's plenty more fights to come and plenty more attention and plenty more occasions when things are going to get hot, but obviously I'm going to be cool. And as you know, I am cool. Very cool.

So what is the one special thing that sets you apart from other boxers in this country?

One of the special things that I've got, which a lot of fighters haven't got, is the right upbringing. As I've mentioned before, I'm grateful and appreciative of the upbringing I've had from my parents. It's a big strong thing in your life, being brought up right. The self-belief that I've got is a real big advantage over other fighters. My religion plays a very big part in my life, in the sense that I know how I feel and what I'm going to do, so God is the strongest thing, in my eyes, that I've got on my side. I know that every time I enter the ring God is on my side. That's one very big advantage.

October 1995

LIZ McCOLGAN

Liz McColgan was brought up on a Dundee council estate, today she lives in an eighteenth-century mansion with her husband and former coach, Peter, and their four-year-old daughter Eilish. At the age of nineteen Liz won an athletics scholarship, which took her away from family and friends to university in the United States. In her golden year, 1991, she proved that she had the mental resolve and the psychological willpower as well as the physical stamina to be a marathon champion. But since then she has been plagued by injuries, illness and disappointment. But Liz is fighting back more single-mindedly and more determinedly than ever. So where does this great psychological desire to run and run really come from? And is long-distance running really as lonely as they say? When we met on a glorious morning in a hotel near her home in Carnoustie, I began by asking her about the loneliness of long-distance running.

It really depends on the individual. I don't find it lonely at all because I quite like being on my own, and when I'm running lots of things go through my head. I thoroughly enjoy my running so I don't find it lonely in the slightest. But I suppose when you think about training, especially for the marathon, which is up to three hours a day on the road, other people would visualize it as being lonely.

What kind of things do you think about?

Well, if you've got any problems whatsoever in your life, I think that the best solution is to get out there and run because it gives you a clear head and you can really think all your problems through. When I'm running I think a lot about how my body is feeling. I could be running along and have a little tightness in my leg or whatever, and I talk to myself to try to release that tension. I think about the pace of my run. I have certain marks on the course that I do because everything is measured out for me. I never just go out and run. I run on certain loops that I know the exact distance of, so I look at the time that I'm running and the pace that I'm running and I just thoroughly enjoy the whole atmosphere that I'm in. I'm lucky that I'm living in a great part of the country. I'm right on the sea front, so it's really invigorating when you're running along and you see the sea on your right-hand side and the woodlands on your left-hand side. It's just a lovely area for running.

You're always making marks on the road. Do you find yourself making calculations all the time?

All the time. All the time I'm running I have my marks set out and I'm looking at my clock, and everything is being calculated in my head because obviously for a marathon it's very important to get pace judgement, and so a lot of the time I'm running along and I'm just calculating what pace I'm going, what eventual time that would give me for a marathon and things like that.

Does that distract you from the beauty of the nature you're running through?

Not at all, because it's all part of it. When you're out running for three hours it's quite a long time to be out just thinking, so obviously a lot of different things come into your head and go out of your head.

The image that I've got of you in terms of races is this picture of you out there front running, and then you look an even lonelier figure.

Well, I haven't front run races for a long time. What happened in the past was that I was running and everyone was saying, 'She's a front runner,' but this was simply because there was no one else in the world at that time who could run with me at that pace. The type of runner that I am means that no matter what race it is I always go out to run the best that I can, and it just so happened that when I was in all those races I would never take it easy on myself. I just went out and I ran as hard as I could and nobody else could run with me. It's a different situation now. There's a lot more competition now, a lot more girls run a lot faster, and so, luckily enough, now I can just sit in and try different tactics.

Does it feel more comfortable to be among a group of people?

I prefer to have room to run. I've got quite a large stride and I'm not the smoothest runner that you've ever seen. I've got quite a rough style, and I think that I can just relax more when I've got a little more room around me, so ideally I do prefer to be out there on my own.

This is obviously a fairly quiet part of the country and presumably you train on your own, so what's it like, if you're used to being on your own, suddenly to be in a stadium with thousands and thousands of other people? Is that distracting in any way?

It's not distracting because it's back to the type of runner that I am. When I'm in a big race I don't see what is happening around me, I haven't a clue where I am or who is watching, or who's cheering. I don't hear anything. I don't see anything. I just concentrate solely on my running. I just go into tunnel vision.

Is the tunnel vision focused on your body and your responses from your body?

It definitely is, yes. It's focused on trying to relax as much as possible, because in distance running, if you're not relaxed you'll not run well. When I'm in a race, especially on the track, because it's twenty-five laps or whatever, physically it is OK, but mentally it is very, very hard to run around and around. So when I'm on the track, if there is someone in front of me, I just focus on the ground, maybe a metre behind them, and I just look at that one spot the whole way round. This then channels all my energies and thoughts into the race and into how my body is feeling.

What about a marathon where you have a much bigger field of people, what does that feel like?

Marathons are slightly different because you've got to be aware of the terrain around you. For example, there was a race that I ran in Tokyo in 1993. I actually won the race but at the 12-mile point there was a hole in the ground, which I actually didn't see until the last minute, and I had to veer around it, and I actually pulled my hamstring muscle in the process. So in a marathon you have got to be very aware of the terrain and the people because you could easily fall or trip or there could be something on the road. Quite a few times people have stepped out from the crowd on to the road during a marathon.

I was going to ask you about spectators, because when you watch a marathon you think, 'Goodness me. Anyone could step out at any moment here.' Are you very wary of this?

Yes, you have to be. You have to be very aware of it because I have been in a situation where people have stepped out and athletes have just fallen. I remember being in a race with Zola Budd, when all the controversy was going on about her getting her passport and things, and I remember a man trying to grab her in a race. You could very easily get injured because you've got to pull up very quickly. So you really do have to be aware of it, especially during road races in foreign countries as they just put the crowd 10 metres either side of you, and they've got flags and things and it's very, very distracting and you've got to really be aware of the situation.

Could I ask how you got into running in the first place, when you were a child in Dundee? What kind of support did you get early on?

The only kind of support I got was from my family. When I started running there really wasn't anyone in the area who was running well. We didn't have Olympic champions in my area. I think there was one girl who went to the Commonwealth Games, but she was never at the very top. She was sort of the star of the club. There wasn't really any encouragement because I don't think anyone could have envisaged that I could have been an Olympian or whatever.

Could I ask you about your very first run?

My very first run was because of our PE teacher, who was a keen marathon runner. In the winter he just used to say, 'Right out you go, run round that field and up that road.' The runs were only about a mile or so. It just so happened that I'd always be either the winner or second. There was another girl who was fairly good and she used to always race me on these class runs. Other people in the class used to go to this place at the school called the Smokies, which was a boiler house, and everyone used to go there and smoke – so half the class would stop there and the other half would be running round.

Did you ever stop there yourself?

Never! Never! I was too busy being competitive with this other girl. This teacher noticed that we were good, so he sent us up to the local Dundee Harriers. There were actually five of us who went up to the Harriers. I instantly liked it, and I was the only one, after three or four weeks, who actually stayed on. Then I made friends there and the Harriers was a social event for me. All my friends were at the Harriers. I didn't really have a lot of friends at the school because they were more into boys and partying and super-lager type things at the weekends. I just wasn't into that. So all of my socializing ended up being at the club.

What kind of people were there? I always think of Harriers as being a lot of older men.

There were a lot of older men and obviously all the little girls had crushes on them. It was a lot of fun. We used to go away on weekend trips and have so much fun. All the older guys were really good with the young ones, that was one thing that was really good about the club. I used to train with them as well, and I ended up socializing and everything with thirty- and forty-year-old people at the club.

How old were you at this time?

I was about fifteen or sixteen. But because you were there since you were eleven years old, you just got really friendly with them. The club was a really good outlet for encouraging the youngsters. It was everyone mixing together. It was an extremely happy time for me because, as I said, all my socializing was at the club and all my best friends were there, and every weekend we'd go away racing and I'd really look forward to it because it was such a big trip out. We'd go on the bus with packed lunches and then coming back we'd stop for chips. It was great.

At that age how often were you training?

Harry Bennett, my first coach, had us training on Tuesdays, Thursdays and Sundays. That was when I was eleven, but when you say training, it wasn't going out and training really hard. I was lucky in the fact that Harry was well ahead of his time. He never pushed us. We used to think it was games. We used to do leaping and bounding and hops and what he called bunny jumps. There were all these little races on the track and it was actually building up our leg muscles without us realizing what we were doing. He used to give us fun things to do. One of my favourite sessions was what he used to call W training. He used to have us zigzagging up these hills. Now that I'm older and wiser and I look back on it, I realize exactly what he was getting at. He was just making our legs strong and building up our muscles because we were still growing. When I was fifteen Harry actually took me to one side and said, 'You're talented and you're at a stage now when you have to decide whether you want to take this one stage further.' At the time he was telling me that the Olympic games were in my grasp and that I would be doing the 10,000 metres. Well, at that time there was no race like that and I just couldn't grasp what he was getting at. I was thinking, 'There's no way that race for women will ever be on the track.' But you know, it did eventually happen.

That's amazing, isn't it?

Yes it is. He had great insight, he really, really did. He said to me at the time that I had to decide whether I wanted to go for that type of athletics or whether I just wanted to enjoy what I was doing and keep on doing the same. At that time I played hockey and volleyball at school and I was quite good at them. He said to me, 'If you're going to go that one stage further, we have to train more and it has to be specific and you have to give up your hockey and volleyball and all your other things.' He said, 'The decision is yours.' He actually said that he thought that I could be an Olympic athlete. It was unbelievable for him to say that to a fifteen-year-old.

Would you go back and tell your parents about what he'd said?

I didn't really. It was like he was a second dad. If my mum and dad told me to do something, I'd just say, 'No, no I'm not doing it.' If Harry said to me, 'Do it,' it was done right away. No questions asked. It was just done. It was a funny relationship that we had. I have a lot of respect for the guy. When he said things to me I never went home and just repeated it. It was just between us.

It was quite private really?

Yes.

Were you afraid that people might laugh at some of these predictions?

It didn't bother me that way because I had a belief in myself anyway. I believed that I was good, and it really didn't bother me what other people thought. I always came up against a brick wall when I was younger, whatever I did in my athletics, because people used to laugh at me. They just didn't understand. 'Are you still doing that running thing?' was what my friends used to say to me. 'Go and get a real job. You'll never make a living out of running.' I got that all the time from my teachers. 'You need to forget about this running thing. You have to study more.' I always came up against that when I was younger.

Were there any alternative jobs you could have got in Dundee?

When I was sixteen I left school without a job, and I was one of Maggie Thatcher's many thousands of unemployed youngsters. So I was put on a YTS [Youth Training Scheme]. They put me in a jute factory. I was stuck in this factory, and for me, a runner it was really unhealthy because it was very, very dirty. I was breathing in all this dust and dirt from all the fabrics. It wasn't the greatest job for me. That was when I got the opportunity to go to America. That was when Harry packed me off to America.

How old were you when you went to America?

I'd just turned nineteen. I got the offer when I was eighteen, but I refused it. Harry then went behind my back and got my parents to bombard me with, 'You're going and that's it.'

So he enlisted the help of your parents?

Yes. I was not going to go, because I'd never travelled before. I'd never been on my own before, I'd never been away from my family, and I didn't like the thought of going back to school – although I liked school, I was glad to leave. I just thought, 'No way am I going. I'm just going to soldier on and do what I'm doing.' When I got a phone call about it, I said no, but they also phoned Harry and he said, 'Yes, she'll be going.' And that same night he phoned my mum and dad, and then he came up to the house and said that, 'Her running can get her to America, and it will get her to see the world, she's got to do it. It's an opportunity she can't miss.' At the time my parents were saying, 'No she's not going', because I was their youngest child. They didn't want me going abroad to somewhere they knew nothing about. But Harry kept on at them. He said, 'You really have to encourage her to go.' The next night he came back up again and said, 'You're going.' The problem at the time was that we didn't have the money. I said, 'We haven't got the money so I can't go anyway.' Harry said, 'Well, I've got the money.' And he personally gave me the money to go. Then an uncle gave me the rest of the money and that was it. I was away. Within a week I was gone.

Whereabouts in the United States did you go to?

I went to Idaho. But I was really sad, because even though he packed me off like that, it was the last time I saw him. He died when I was out there.

So this was like his last act?

It was yes. He died when he was out running.

How old was he?

He was young. He must have been in about his mid-fifties. He had a problem with his arteries.

Did you hear about this when you were out in Idaho?

What happened was that I came home that summer and Harry had arranged for me to do a race at the Cooper Highland Games, and he was to pick me up at ten o clock in the morning and we were going to drive there. But his wife phoned and said that he was dead.

Goodness.

It was unbelievable. I wasn't going to do that race, but my dad said, 'Do it for Harry' and I went and did it. I ran really well.

Did your interest in running wane at all, since it was obviously so tied up with this particular individual?

Because he had been coaching me I thought that that was it. I thought that I wouldn't run again. But then my dad was quite good that way, and he said that I had the talent to do well and that Harry wouldn't have wanted me to just stop running. I was lucky, too, because when Harry had been coaching me he was also educating me at the same time. He was always throwing books at me to read about training and always explaining why we were doing this and that and he'd outline the reasoning behind it all. Even to this day I think that all of my ideas about athletics have come from him. I think that he understood me better than I understood myself. When he died I was able to go on and train because everything had been planned anyway. It was like I was running for him then, for a while.

After Harry did you have a replacement coach?

Not really, people have come and gone, but I have never had the same respect for any of them until now. I am now coached by Greta Weitz. I have the same respect for her, I think, as I did for Harry.

Was your husband Peter your coach for a while?

He never really coached me. It was a joint venture, in that I really did all my own coaching, but Peter oversaw it all. He made sure that I didn't overtrain. But since Harry I really have been self-coached. There have been a few people who have tried to coach me, but I didn't really have enough belief in their training methods. I didn't think that the methods were suitable for me.

I am fascinated imagining your family life, with Peter overlooking your training methods. Doesn't that put strains and stresses in your family?

It's funny because since the two of us are athletes there is a pressure there anyway. We're basically together twenty-four hours a day.

Usually in husband-and-wife relationships one will go out to work and therefore they don't see each other for eight hours or so. Then they come home and talk about their day, so it's great. But Peter and I live together twenty-four hours a day and there are a lot of strains and pressures there. But at the same time, Peter is so laid back it's unbelievable. I can blow my top, and he just sits there and laughs. He is very good that way. There can be a lot of the pressures on my running, but we don't really take them home. We'll sit and we'll discuss something, he'll have his say and I'll have my say, and we'll work out the best solution. And then it is forgotten about. We've got a really, really good relationship, and things really do work out for us.

Could you tell me a little bit about the structure of your day with training and so on? What kind of time do you get up in the morning?

I normally get up about five and then I run about six. Anytime between six and seven I go for my first run and then when I come back Peter goes for his run. Peter looks after our daughter, Eilish, while I run in the morning. When I come back from my run, and it could be anything between thirty minutes and two hours depending on what I'm doing, I get Eilish ready for school, I take her up to school, and then really it's just a matter of relaxing for the rest of the day until my next training session, because I train again at three. I usually have a nap of an hour in the middle of the day because of the training that I do. It's quite a boring life really. I don't do much at all. I don't do any socializing.

What time do you go to bed?

I go to bed at seven-thirty, or eight at the very latest. An exciting life! I have to do that because if I don't go to bed early I'm too tired for training in the morning.

Do you like training so early in the morning because the air is fresher or …?

No, it's just me. It's just the type of person that I am, I'm probably a morning person. I like to get up early. Morning is the best part of the day. It's amazing how many people miss the best part of the day! I run as the sun comes up.

Is that kind of spiritual?

I suppose it is in a way.

What effect did motherhood have on your running?

It didn't really affect my attitude to running. When I had Eilish, she was unplanned and it was quite a shock as I really wasn't planning to have a child that year because my running was very much in my mind. So I trained all through my pregnancy. I was three and a half months pregnant before I knew that I was pregnant and I was training a hundred-odd miles a week. I didn't even know. I was just not feeling right and thinking, 'What's the reason for this?' I was getting fatter and I was thinking, 'Jesus, I'm putting on weight. Why? What's going on?' So I went to the doctor and he said, 'Could you be pregnant?' I said, 'No, no way.' Then he gave me a test, and I found out that I was and I nearly died. I couldn't believe it, but I trained right up until I had her. I think it was about the week before I had her that I was out for a run and I took a really sore stomach, and I said, 'Well, that's nature telling you to stop running,' so I stopped running then.

But how on earth could you do that? I mean, what does it physically feel like?

Well, it wasn't a pretty sight, that's for sure, a pregnant woman jogging along the road. I think that because of the type of person I am, I just love running. I think that if I stopped I just wouldn't know what to do with myself.

Do you feel really guilty if you don't go out for a run all the time?

I do, yes definitely.

Can you sleep?

It just interrupts my whole routine. If I don't run, the next day I feel about twenty stone heavier. It's just psychological – I feel so unfit if I miss one day running. You've got to remember, I've run every day since I was eleven years old. It's just like taking a step outside the door in the morning. When I was pregnant, I trained right up until the week I had her and then my first race was six weeks after having her, and I won it. I actually started running on the eleventh day after the birth. I remember I'd just given birth and this lady came knocking on the door about two days later. She said, 'I'm the physiotherapist and I've been sent round to show you the exercises that you've to do.' I said, 'Exercises?' She said, 'You know, you've got to do all these exercises.' When she came in I was sat there doing all these push-ups and sit-ups on the bed. She said, 'Well, I see I don't have to show you.' I'm just so into my running that it is just second nature to me to do all these things. When Eilish came along, my running was very, very much the main priority in my life. I was travelling all over the world in the first year that we had Eilish. We took her everywhere with us, and I remember coming home to the house and it was as if she was saying, 'Where are we now? What hotel is this?' She was about a year old and she didn't even realize that they were her own toys in our house. That was when it dawned on me that we needed to give her a bit more stability, so we said that we were going to have to start cutting down on all the travelling. So we did that, and obviously she's a bundle of fun now and she has a very stable life. I think that I didn't really appreciate Eilish until I got injured, until I had the operations and I couldn't run a step, I couldn't do any exercises whatsoever. That was when she actually saved me from going insane, because if it wasn't for her I really don't know what I would have done. Everything was taken away from me and I was really depressed and I was told that I would never run again. But I was still her mum and she just got me through the worst time in my life. So even now, when all the running is going well again, it takes second place to her. The running is just not the same to me as it once was. I really appreciate the fact that Eilish is there now, and she is definitely the main thing in my life. I spend time with Eilish and we go to McDonalds or we go to the cinema. I like to do her school work with her and encourage her in whatever she does.

Do you ever see yourself encouraging Eilish to take up running?

I would never push her into running. I don't encourage her now, I don't take her to a track or anything like that. But if you go on genes then she is a thoroughbred! Peter has run all his days and I've run all mine. She's got the genes there, but I would never ever force her into anything. If she wants to start running and she comes to me and says, 'Mum can I go to the club or to a track?' I will take her, in just the same way that at the moment she loves horse riding, so we take her horse riding, and she loves tennis, so I play tennis with her. I'll encourage her in whatever she wants to do. If she wants to sit in front of the TV and become a couch potato, then I'll encourage that! It's whatever she wants to do. There's nothing worse than parents who force their children into doing things, because the children do not enjoy it and they will not succeed at it. They will never succeed if they don't want to do it themselves, and that's what I believe about Eilish. Eilish is funny though – she thinks that everybody's mum and dad runs! Also, I'll come in from a run and she'll say, 'Mum can you run round the field with me?' And I'll say, 'Yeah, OK' and we'll jog round.

Can I ask you about the highs and lows in your career so far? 1991 was obviously your golden year, you won the World Championship in Tokyo, you won the New York Marathon, and you were the Sports Personality of the Year. Were you happy when all that was happening? People often feel an insecurity when things are going that well, they're just waiting for the downside.

I'm a strange kind of person, I think. When everything was going well like that and everyone was saying, 'You'll never eclipse that year,' it was strange because although I had so much success I still never achieved everything that I wanted to. I've still not achieved my goals for my athletics. So when I win world championships or set world records, even though I've won them, I've got a standard that I've set for myself and I've still not achieved it. So even though I won that race or broke that record, the very next day it was head down and away I went because I still hadn't achieved the goal that I had set myself. And that is very much the same now. Although I had a great year it's still not as good as it should have been.

Is your own personal standard ever attainable?

It is a high standard but it is very attainable. I know it is attainable because of my training. I've done it in training, but I've not done it in racing! It's so frustrating. That's what keeps you going, and that is what keeps your feet on the ground and your head down. In training, even to this day, I've run so much better than I have raced all this year, and so that is why I haven't been happy with my year, but I know that my time will come. I know that I've just got to be patient and things will eventually click and I will run that race one day when everything will click and I will do what I have set out to achieve. But it is actually just trying to get everything to be a hundred per cent at that time, and that's what we are working for now. I mean I have had all the injuries that I could possibly have, and I've learned a lot. It's made me grow up a lot, and I think it's just about being patient now and letting my running take hold and to develop itself.

Does the self-belief of yours come from within or do other people have to persuade you of this?

It's me, it's what I want in life and it's the type of person I am. Running is very, very much about the individual. You can have the best psychologists, the best doctors telling you how great you are but it doesn't matter who tells you, you have got to have it within yourself and if you don't have that little spark inside you it will never be instilled in you. Never.

Is that a spark you feel can never be extinguished?

I think it can be extinguished. It definitely can. I think it would be extinguished when you've achieved what you want to do. That is when the light is going to go out.

In terms of your motivations for running, I've read that money is quite important to you. Is this true?

Money is not on my mind whatsoever. I mean it's great that it's there now and I can make a living from athletics, but at the same time, if the money wasn't there I would still be here. I definitely would. I was in it long before money ever came into it, and I'll be in it long after the money has gone. The motivation is definitely the belief that I have that I can attain certain things in athletics. That's what keeps me going.

1992 wasn't as successful a year as 1991. You were fifth in the Olympic 10,000 metres. Could I just ask, is it harder to come fifth than first? Is it more draining when you're still running that distance?

It really depends on your situation. The difficulty with the Olympics was that I had a liver problem, and I didn't find out until things went wrong that there was some problem. Once that was remedied I was a totally different athlete. So the only problem with the Olympics was when I was running I was wondering why I felt so bad. Obviously, since then I have found out why and that there was a reason for the bad performance. Then it all became logical and it didn't really bother me any more because I knew there was a reason. If there wasn't a reason I would have been very, very disappointed.

For the professional athlete obviously the first thing you notice is the bad performance. But since the body is such a complex machine, it must be an extraordinary few months or weeks while you wait to have something diagnosed.

An athlete is very, very finely tuned to his or her body. The slightest thing and you pick up on it right away, especially in running. In order to run, everything needs to be working a hundred per cent, and the slightest problem within the body, whether it be a slight cold or a twinge in a muscle, could be the difference between night and day in a performance. I know that all athletes are very, very health-conscious. You're aware of anything that goes wrong and that is the problem that faced me in Barcelona. I did find the problem and as soon as I got the medical treatment for it, it was a difference of night and day. The performance was way up again.

You have used a lot of words like health-conscious and so on. Can you go overboard on this? Do you think that athletes can become almost hypochondriac about every slight twinge in their body?

Definitely yes. With a lot of athletes, they have the slightest thing and they're limping off. It's not, necessarily, a very good way to be, but I'm quite tough on myself. When I was sixteen I broke a kneecap and I ran a race with a broken kneecap. I've run through a lot of problems that, medically, I probably shouldn't have. I just ignore the problem. I've got quite a high pain tolerance and I can go on and push through a lot of pain, but there are a lot of athletes who when they have a sore thumb or a broken nail, will walk off the race and say, 'I raced badly because I broke my nail.' So it's very much an individual thing as well.

Have you dropped out of any races?

I haven't. Luckily enough, I've never, ever dropped out of a race in my life, and I never will.

Would you see that as a sign of real weakness, if you did?

Yes, definitely.

And presumably that's true when you see other athletes drop out.

Oh yes. I've never ever dropped out. I always finish all my races. Definitely.

Can I ask you about the marathon now? Could you talk me through a day when you're going to race in a marathon?

Well, no matter what time the race starts, I'm always up about six hours before it, because I like to have a good breakfast before I run. In my opinion, a marathon is a mental race – you really have got to prepare yourself for it. So the time before a marathon is spent trying to psych myself up for what I'm about to do. I usually pack my bags and get all my race gear done the night before so I don't need to worry about that. About an hour before the marathon I usually do stretching and get mobile. I warm up a bit. About half an hour before the race, I just sit down and do the mental rehearsal of what I want to do.

And is the mental rehearsal based around you and your body and times, or is it based around competitors or is it a bit of both?

I base it on the actual performance. I don't particularly base it on competitors or on any particular person, but I do visualize myself running with people around me, no faces, just people. I visualize myself and how I feel in the race and how I see the race developing and things like that. I visualize how I finish the race, how I feel after the race and the recovery after it.

Do you feel funny about your body because you know your body is going to have to do this 26 miles? Do you ever feel insecure with your body?

Yes, I think most women athletes all think that they should be lighter or whatever, and I'm exactly the same. Even when I'm at my lightest, I always think, 'Oh, I should be another few pounds lighter.' It's not a great way to be, but I think that it's good for me because it makes me very aware that I've got to be good on my diet and I've got to get the best out of my body. Going into races I always feel that, but especially with marathons. A couple of days before the marathon you've got to eat. You've got to put carbohydrates into your body so that you can perform well. I always put weight on before a marathon because of that and I hate it. I just hate it. The last two days before the marathon are when I'm at my worst. I just hate it.

Do you think that some female athletes who do marathons could have ended up anorexic, if they hadn't been marathon runners, because they are so very conscious of their bodies?

I think there is a major, major eating problem among women athletes – and some male athletes, too. You know, it is not all just women. I'm just amazed at what some people go through. I'm quite big compared with other athletes, but I eat and that is simply because I am healthy. I see so many bad things going on, and it really makes me mad when I see some of the things that girls do. There are so many women athletes who think that they have got to be skin and bone to compete, and it's wrong. I think it is just a media image that they have been sold, and they believe that they have got to be like that.

Do you ever look at yourself running and think, 'God, I look fat today'?

All the time. I think I look fat compared with other athletes because I've been more or less told that. If you look at any report from London last year, it was all, 'Liz has got a weight problem,' 'Liz is big.' It really does bother me because if you're going into a race, you're going into it to perform well, and then somebody turns around and says, 'You're fat.' I'm not fat, I know I'm not fat. I look at any other person in the street, any Joe Bloggs walking down the street, and I know that I'm not fat. But in terms of the skin-and-bone athlete, the distance runner, I'm not in that mould, so that's why I'm a very firm believer that when I talk to youngsters I will say, 'You don't have to be like that. You don't have to be skin and bones to compete.' It's a major problem, it really is.

Because you run so much, is it the case that you can eat almost anything?

No, that's a myth. That really is a myth. Everything has to be in moderation. I've got this firm belief – and you've probably heard this before – that when you've got a sports car you don't put two star petrol in it, you put the best in it, the best petrol, the best oil. You take it in for its MOT and you take care of it. It's the same with an athlete. When you're an athlete you're looking for your body to perform at its very best, which means that you've got to put the best food into it. The food has got to be good quality food and a lot of it. That's the way I've always been. I've got a really sweet tooth, I love chocolate and I love cakes, but I won't eat them because I know they're fattening and they've got wasted calories in them. So I eat a lot of very good quality food and I do eat a lot of it, but it's good food, it's not waste. What I tend to do is, when I have I break I say, 'Have a break, enjoy yourself.'

When you have a break, what kind of stuff would you eat?

When you're training you have got to have one easy day when you recover. So on that day I say to myself, 'That's a treat day'. You can have a bar of chocolate or a chicken curry or a meal out, that is the day that you do it. I think that works really well. You're not depriving yourself of everything, and on that one day you thoroughly enjoy whatever you do. We tend to go out for a meal to our favourite restaurant on that one day of the week.

Do you ever think about what life will be like when your running days are over?

Yes. When my running life is over I will still be able to live to the standard of life that I've got because Peter has invested everything very well, and he takes care of all our investments and things for the future.

What about in terms of how you might spend your day?

It will be very similar to now because I'm very into sport. Obviously, when I give up running competitively I will keep running and doing weights. We've got a gym in the house, so that will always be part of my life. But I think that I will go into other things. I love horse riding, but I can't go horse riding now because of the risk of injury. I love tennis and we've got a tennis court at the house. So I will do other sports as well to keep fit. I'll be like eighty-two and you'll see me on a zimmer frame, zooming down the High Street. I'll always be running!

How will you know when your time has come to stop competitive running?

I'll know. I'm not one of these athletes who could line up, finish twenty-third and be happy with it. I couldn't drop out of race. I've got standards. I will quit when I'm at the top. I'll know when.

December 1995

CHRIS BOARDMAN

At the Barcelona Olympics in 1992 Chris Boardman did something
that no other Briton had managed to accomplish since 1908 – he won
an individual cycling gold medal. Chris won the 4000-metres pursuit
title on his revolutionary new bicycle, a carbon-fibre Windcheetah
bicycle that virtually eliminates drag. The achievement and the bike,
with its high saddle and low handlebars, made a great impression on
the British public. Some, however, said that this revolutionary Lotus
super-bike, with its high-tech image, almost overshadowed one of
the greatest cycling displays in Olympic history.

In 1993 Chris went on to take the prestigious World Hour
Record, riding 52.270 kilometres in the hour. Then he turned
professional. In his first Tour de France, he won the prologue time
trial holding the leader's yellow jersey for three days. But he retired
after eleven days, the victim, it has been said, of inexperience as
much as fatigue and the intense heat. In 1995, he crashed in the
prologue time trial going downhill at around 50 miles per hour in the
wet with poor visibility. When I interviewed him, he had two screws
in his left ankle as a permanent reminder of this accident, but he was
fighting his way back with resolve and determination.

In this interview, I wanted to explore how tough psychologically
you have to be to survive and win in cycling, which is potentially one
of the toughest of all sports. But first I wanted to focus on one of the
high points of his career – the Olympic gold. So that's where we
started, and I asked what it felt like to win an Olympic gold.

A bit disappointing really, which is possibly a surprising answer for a lot of people. I suppose that I was aiming towards this one thing for ten years, and then in a second it was all over. It was like, 'Oh, that's it then, right.' I didn't get the feeling of elation that I had expected would go along with the victory at that precise moment. I'd watched previous Olympic finals on television, and I imagined what it would feel like to be there winning, and I was always thinking about what it would be like. But when it came to it, it was more of a sensation of shock than anything else. It's something that's been enjoyable, retrospectively, over a period of time. It just sort of sinks in slowly, as opposed to being a single moment, when you stand on a podium and feel total elation. So I did feel rather cheated, if you like, because it just didn't turn out to be like how I imagined it would be. Just cheated.

Is it something you play back on the video to remind yourself of how you felt at the time?

No. I ended up bumping into clips of the Olympic games over a long period of time, at various PR events or wherever it was playing, repeat video loops and stuff like that. So I'm rather sick of the sight of it now! Also, I like to move on, I like to think about new things. So it was a great thing to happen, but I like to think about other things now.

A common image of that Olympic triumph was the bike. Is that something that you've grown almost to hate, the fact that everyone thinks of your bike when they think of your gold medal?

Not desperately. But it is true that a lot of the media don't understand cycling, as such. In this particular type of cycling, it was easy to jump on the technology side of the sport. Everyone likes 'space-shuttly' types of technology. With the bike being there, they leapt on that and said, 'Oh yes, that's the super-bike.' It was christened 'The Super-bike', and to be honest, it was a great bike to do this particular job. It certainly looked very different from all the other bikes around, it really looked the part. We probably wouldn't have got a fifth of the publicity without that bike. The bike played its part, but it was a much smaller part than people gave it credit for. But that was OK by me, because in cycling the Olympic Games, oddly enough, aren't the top. In the world of professional cycling, in which I work now, they wouldn't necessarily be able to tell you who had won the Olympic pursuit title, because in my sport it's just not that big a deal. I knew that after the Olympics I would be going on to do other things and that if I was good enough, the common denominator of success would be myself, because I wouldn't always be on the same bike. The next year I went on to break the world hour record, which is the blue ribbon record – the four-minute mile equivalent in cycling. The test here was how far you can cover in a track in one hour. I did this on a completely different bike. So for me it was fine.

The thing that struck me about this world hour record and the 4000-metre event in the Olympics, is the incredible difference in the distance over those two events. Do you think that the public are fully aware of how demanding cycling as a sport actually is?

No! Certainly not! Most people do not realize that the majority of professional cyclists have races on average of over 200 kilometres for a single race, and that a professional cyclist will ride, on average, ninety race days a year. Now, there's no other sport that does anything like that. Take the Tour de France, for instance – up to seven hours a day for three weeks, over seven major mountains in one of those twenty-one days. There's nothing to compare with this, in any sport. I think that it's quite barbaric actually.

I think that you're probably right. If you asked people what was the most demanding sport of all, they'd probably say that it was the marathon. But the Tour de France seems really like running a marathon every day for three weeks. Is it as bad as that?

Well, a marathon goes on for just over two hours and a top marathon runner may run four marathons in a year. One stage of the Tour de France can be seven hours long, and there are twenty-one stages. And that's just one race in an annual calendar of ninety races on average. Some professionals ride a lot more. Personally I ride a lot less, but I have the pressure on me to get results each time. But just think of the distances and the number and all the intense competition. That's how barbaric cycling is.

Do you have any explanation of why the public do not seem ready to recognize how demanding cycling really is? Is it because of the technology? Do they see the bike, the Super-bike or whatever, and they think that somehow the bike must be making it all less physical?

It's very difficult, even for me, to sit back at home and watch the sport and realize what is going on. You cannot imagine the pain, you cannot imagine the discomfort involved. You can see it, but you cannot imagine what it feels like. When somebody is climbing a mountain on a bike and they look good, the whole thing flows and it looks like a very euphoric experience. It doesn't look hard. That's the whole point. It looks as if this athlete is trained to do that. But when you actually feel what it's like, believe me it can be quite a shock to the system. It's difficult for people to relate to. But in pure physical terms I would challenge anybody to name me a sport that's as hard as professional cycling.

So it's hard physically, but what is it like psychologically? How do you keep yourself focused on the job?

Well, because the races are so long, you cannot physically race flat out for that amount of time. It's just not a physical possibility. Therefore, there is a lot of down time within the race. It's never consistent. There is no set routine. It's not that you ride fairly slow for five hours, and then the last two hours is really quick. The bursts of speed can happen anywhere. Somebody lights the touch paper and then sets off the series of attack, and then you have to respond to that until it dies down, or not.

So you have to be psychologically ready throughout the race?

Yes. It really is quite a psychological battle, because you can be riding along just having a conversation with somebody, and then suddenly it flares up and then you've got to react to it. This can happen any time. So I would imagine it's a bit like being in a war zone, where you just don't know what's going to happen, you just don't know when you're going to get attacked. It's a similar sort of thing. So that's a difficult aspect of it.

If it's like a war zone, does that mean that you can have a similar kind of trauma afterwards?

No, the trick is to survive. When I entered the professional world, I thought that I was going to be surrounded by a lot of highly strung nutters, because of what this job is all about. But I turned out to be completely wrong. When I thought about it afterwards, it was obvious that I was going to be wrong, because to deal with this kind of lifestyle, which is so stressful and so intense, you have to be able to switch off and walk away from it. You have to be able to do that very quickly – for example, between the two stages of a race. You have to be able to switch off and even, to a degree, to be able to switch off within the race itself, to be able to say, 'Right, there's no more attacking, now I can switch off and relax.'

Do you have any specific psychological techniques for switching off?

I've worked with a sports psychologist for about ten years. He played quite a significant role in my winning at the Olympics and in dealing with that amount of pressure. To go back for a moment to the Olympics, when you're sitting on the line, you're thinking, 'Oh, there's 176 countries watching this live, and the next four and a half minutes can change my life completely, or not, as the case may be.' That's probably the most pressure that you can ever get in life. At least, I thought it was, until I moved on further in my career! To be absolutely honest, I actually don't like cycling. Cycling is just the medium that I've chosen. I am a natural competitor, and cycling is just the medium that I've chosen for that. I don't ride a bike because I want to do well – I need to do well just to be normal. I don't think that this is particularly healthy, but I think that to be at the top in a sport, especially this kind of sport, you have to be slightly mentally unbalanced.

So have you always been like this? Have you always been a natural competitor?

Sadly, yes.

Even when you were a child?

Sadly yes, even then. Not to a point of extremes, at least I hope not. The people around me, however, would be the best people to ask about that. I am a professional cyclist, because I get a tremendous amount of satisfaction from it. People very often confuse 'enjoyment' with 'satisfaction.' I don't enjoy going out in the rain and training for four hours, but I get a tremendous amount of satisfaction when I get back after training, knowing that I've done that. I enjoy the satisfaction but I don't enjoy the exercise, and it's the same with the sport itself.

Some people would find that quite surprising. So if it hadn't been cycling, were there other sports that you think you could have got involved with?

There are lots of sports that I would still like to try. Middle- to long-distance running quite appeals to me; triathlons appeal to me a lot. I'm actually intending to stop my cycling career at the age of thirty-two, in the year 2000, because that will give me time to try other things, even to an internationally competitive level.

Would it make you feel better psychologically to be a champion in more than one sport, rather than just the one sport?

Oh, it would nice, but this is when you come down to real bottle and self-belief, based on nothing. I mean, to stop something that you are moderately successful at, and then go and do something completely different, which you might not be good at, would be madness, in most people's eyes. Most people stick to what they're good at. They'd say, 'Well I'm making a good living with this, so I'll stick with it.' So I think that this is why you don't see people doing it. But the basic physiological traits should be the same for any endurance athlete from a number of different sports. So from a physiological point of view, there probably isn't any real reason why I couldn't go and do another sport that had the same demands.

I gather that a scientific understanding of what your body goes through is pretty crucial to your preparation for an event?

To me personally, yes. Another person I work with very closely is Peter Keen, a sports scientist and a senior lecturer at Brighton University. I've worked with him for nearly twelve years. I work with Peter because we both have a similar approach. I work with this guy because he can say, 'Do this type of training because ...' and he can give me a good rationale for why this type of training will work. I like to know why things work because it gives me a belief in my training. I prefer to go out and do the hard work knowing why I'm doing it, rather than just doing it because I always have. So I've always been one to believe that knowledge is power, if you like. The more you know, the more you have the possibility to change, to improve. In addition, he can identify which aspects of training might be a complete waste of time, so we'll cut that out and concentrate on something else instead.

I'm intrigued now as to how the physiological bits and the psychological bits might go together, because, say you have a physiologist advising you, telling you, 'You've got a perfect physiological basis for middle-distance running or cycling.' But what happens if you haven't? I mean can a psychologist come in and say that the psychological bits, the belief or whatever, in the end, might be more important?

Our watchword is 'analyse'. You look at everything, either a good performance or a bad performance, and you pull it apart. At the end of the year we have a debrief, we look at everything that's been done. What was good? What was bad? What do we have to do to improve? We analyse everything and build up a plan. I've always been a person who likes to have plans. I don't necessarily say that I have to stick to a plan. I don't mind changing them, but I like to start with a direction, so that I know where I'm going. As far as physical ability goes, there are certain attributes that, when you get to the very, very top, then what you have been given naturally, I mean genetically, is what will separate you from the others. That's when you have got a small group of people who have been whittled down, that have got every attribute they will need to succeed. The last things that are going to separate them are going to be things that you can't change. But I'm a great believer that you can get a very long way, certainly in my sport, on willpower. I believe less and less that genetic inheritance of pure physiological ability is the be-all and end-all in sport. You can get a long way on attitude, on how much you really want success mentally.

How much success is attributable to basic physiology and how much is due to the psychology on top?

It would depend on what level of success you wanted to achieve. To be a good sportsman I would say that it's eighty per cent mental and twenty per cent physical. But to be the very best sportsman, then I think that it's fifty-fifty really. You need *all* the attributes to get to the very top. You need the mental capacity for the tactics; you need the physiological ability, you need the analytical skills – you need everything.

And do you also have to fear losing? I mean how important is that?

I've always been told there are two classes of people: one group succeed because they're scared of losing and the other group succeed because they want to win! You know, one group is negative, one positive.

Which group do you belong to?

Unfortunately, I belong to the negative one. As I said earlier, I have to win just to be normal! I don't do it to get a high, I don't do it to get above the normal state, it's just to reach the normal state.

So if you lose does that mean you are below the normal state?

I get frustrated and I go away and I work hard. I mean the best motivation is defeat. When I've actually set my stall out to achieve a set of goals and then I achieve those goals, it really takes away the drive, because you're trying to be the best and you achieve it, and it just takes away the edge. And you really need that edge. On the other hand, if somebody comes along and beats me fair and square, that really winds me up because I say to myself, 'Oh I might not be the best.' And that really motivates me.

Can I ask you about your early days? How did you get into cycling in the first place?

I was lucky in that I came from a cycling family, my father was a good cyclist. But I did try a number of different sports as a youngster. I did some running and some swimming and I was reasonable at them all, but nothing fantastic. It was easy for me to drift into cycling. If anything, I was actively discouraged from racing in cycling because cycling is a very sociable sport and you don't need to race at all, you can just do your own thing. But all I was interested in was the racing aspect of cycling, so eventually I was allowed to enter a local club's 10-mile time trial, and it just went from there really. I think that I covered the 10-mile course in about twenty-nine minutes, and then the next week it was twenty-eight minutes something. So I could see progression, even though I wasn't actually winning the event. Those times over a set distance were something for me to strive for.

And was this very important because of your analytic attitude towards the sport, because you could see a progression that you could work on?

Yes, I suppose so. I wasn't doing it because I really enjoyed it but because I wanted to be better. I wanted to improve. As I say, I'm probably not a very mentally stable individual in that respect. It's probably not very good for your long-term health, but it just seems to be the way I am, the way that I was made. I stuck with it because I could see the progression even though, at that point, I wasn't winning anything. I was competing against myself then.

You mentioned that your father was a cyclist and also that you have this competitive streak. Was there ever any intense competition with your father in the early days?

No, not at all. Not with my parents. I was very, very lucky with my parents. My father had done it himself. He was actually short-listed for the Tokyo Olympics. He was asked to go and train with the squad for the Olympics, but he decided that he was going to marry my mother and set up home instead. This was quite lucky for me, really! So he didn't need my success. He wasn't trying to live through his son, which you see so much in sport, and it's very sad when you see parents pushing their kids as if it's their hobby. I didn't get any of that. I got a lot of support from my parents, but I got a lot of space as well. I'd be dropped off at a junior squad training session and I'd be left there for a few days, until I wanted to be picked up. So I got plenty of space, which I've always been very grateful for. I was never pushed, I was only encouraged. My mother was actually very good on a bicycle as well, but she didn't like the competitive aspect of it, so she was quite the opposite to me. She got very, very nervous with races, so in the end she just hated it. Not the actual race itself, just the nervousness before it, so she stopped doing it.

I've read somewhere that you were described in your early days of racing as somewhat arrogant.

Yes, I seem to have projected this image, and maybe I am arrogant. I think that a certain amount of arrogance is probably necessary in sport. I think that this impression might stem from the fact that I work with Peter Keen. We sit down and analyse all the information available. We decide which direction we want to go in, and we have sound reasoning to back up our decision. It may not be the correct decision in the end, we've made plenty of mistakes – absolutely tons, in fact – but I like to think that we have learned from them. So when people ask, 'What are you doing?' we say, 'We're doing this because it's going to do this, this and this for us.' The way that we outline this reasoning may come over as very arrogant and over self-confident. And don't forget, I've worked with this person for a very long time. I was quite self-confident at quite a young age as well, so when this kind of talk comes from a youngster of sixteen who's talking to a twenty-five- or thirty-year-old, it doesn't look very good. It probably looks arrogant.

So did you feel like a bit of an outsider in this cycling fraternity?

No, not at all. Virtually all my friends come from cycling. I was actually contemplating it last night when I was in a bar and I saw a guy I hadn't seen since school. You know your teachers always say, 'Your school days are the best days of your life, but you will only realize that when you leave and you look back.' That's what they say, anyway. Well I hated school, I couldn't wait to leave, and I don't regret it at all. I don't retain any friends from school. I mean I might say 'hello' to people who went to school with me, but I wasn't somebody who developed the kinds of friendships in school that have stayed with me. So all my friends have come from the cycling fraternity.

Could I just ask about training now? Would you describe yourself as someone who enjoys training?

No, not at all. As I said, I get a lot of satisfaction from having done the work that I need to do, to achieve what I want to achieve. I think that I'm fundamentally quite lazy. It's as if there's a battle going on inside me – there's one aspect of me that doesn't want to do it, and another aspect that wants to succeed, that wants to win. I have to do all this other stuff in order to win, so it's just a case of which one's stronger really. And the will to win is actually stronger than my laziness! So it forces me to go out and do the training.

But training is something you've been doing since you were a boy?

Precisely, and that makes it a real problem. All the time we're striving for new and different ways to achieve the same goal, simply to make it more mentally stimulating, to make it more acceptable, because to do the same thing for thirteen years is very difficult. When you know beforehand what success is going to take and how difficult it's going to be to get there, it's hard to face. When you know all that's ahead of you, and you know how unpleasant it's all going to be, it can be very difficult. Using pulse monitors to train means that you have a set work load each day, and it's going to be very hard. It doesn't matter if it's a nice day, a horrible day, it doesn't matter if it's windy, wet or sunny, you know that you're going to suffer. And that's all there is to it. That's how I think about training.

How difficult was the decision to turn professional?

It was actually Peter Woodworth, my manager, who made that decision. He presented me with the scenario when we had just broken the world hour record. I hadn't really considered turning professional, I could see what a hard life it was. I didn't want to do that, it didn't appeal to me at all. It looked like a very unpleasant way of doing things, but Peter presented me with a scenario in which he explained that I could either stay where I was and wait to be knocked off the top, or I could try to do something else – to turn professional, to make a good living and to take on some of the bigger challenges in cycling. As I mentioned earlier, the Olympic games is not the top in my sport, so you can try to do even more by turning pro, and if it doesn't work out, you can just go back to where you were before. So it was a case of having no other option, really. There was nothing to lose. The opportunity was there, so I took that opportunity, and for the first couple of months it was very difficult. It was really difficult. It was extremely painful, it was unpleasant and dangerous, or at least I perceived it to be dangerous. I was riding with 200 of the best blokes in the world, and it was very much out of the pond and straight into the sea. I found myself, on occasion, getting left behind on a climb, with a hundred guys riding away from me. There might be a hundred guys still with me, but another hundred guys just rode away from me, and that was very difficult to accept when I had been the big fish in the little pond for a long while.

So it was very hard at the beginning, but I made the breakthrough when I had some success in the second biggest race in France, the Tour de Deuxvilles Libère, which is the next to the Tour de France. Perhaps I should explain a little about cycling. When you ride behind another rider, because you are sitting in their slipstream you are expending about thirty per cent less energy. So it's obviously a lot easier to sit in someone's slipstream, so everyone wants to do that. When the race starts getting very, very fast, everyone starts diving for cover, that is, getting into the slipstream of another cyclist. On television, that's when you see the big, long line. You want to be towards the front of this big, long line to stay out of trouble and to stay in touch with the action. But say somebody has to get into this line to get out of the wind, and they have to push either a world champion or a first-year professional out of the way, which one is it going to be? The first-year professional or the world champion? So this problem occurs right the way back down the line, so that you end up with the first-year pros getting flicked out of the way, and you eventually end up at the back! So there's a catch twenty-two. You have to gain the respect of your peers to make life easier. You can ride at the front, but that is physically very demanding. But if you ride at the front, you eventually get accepted. It was very difficult to cross this barrier but I actually did it. Now I know that I can deal with this job and it's hard, but I don't mind it at all and I get a lot of satisfaction from it now. But for a couple of months there, I was thinking, 'I don't know whether I can deal with this.'

And the fact that you were an Olympic champion counted for nothing?

Not in this new world of professional cycling. It's almost a different sport. The only similarity with the amateur sport is that we both ride bikes. The demands are completely different. In professional cycling, you have to be a cross between a chess player, a commando and a top athlete.

The distances involved in the different races are extraordinary, from 4 kilometres to 200 plus kilometres. What is this like?

The distances are very different, as you say – 4 kilometres up to 260 or 270 kilometres – but the basic physiology is the same. The engine, if you like, is still the same. You train the engine to do something different, you tune it differently, but the fundamental engine is the same.

But that kind of variability is unimaginable in, for example, running.

I think we can all learn from different sports. I think cyclists do far too many races. We tend to use a lot of races for training. That's become the norm, but your body cannot race that amount. In some of the early season races, I'm there literally just to make up numbers and I'm not expected to win because I'm not physically capable of it. I think that we could learn from other sports and do a lot fewer races. On the other hand, there are other sports that could compete a lot more without any massive damage. Runners actually do more physiological damage during a race than cyclists because cycling is completely weight bearing. But they could probably do at least a hundred per cent more races than they actually run. Certainly the higher distance marathon runners. I think we can all learn from each other's sports.

I've also read somewhere that you've said, 'I've got to get used to winning fewer races.' How difficult is that for someone with the competitive streak that you seem to have?

It is very difficult. I used to target races and I would only ride those races when I had the form to do it. I would prepare for that race and then, hopefully, it would come off. I rode as an amateur around 1990 and 1991, and I think of all the races that I finished that year I lost only two. But in the professional environment that I'm now competing in, it's impossible to do that. I'll give you an example – the number one rider in 1994 probably rode about a hundred races and he won sixteen and he was number one in the world, and yet he only won sixteen per cent of his races. So that says it all, really. But, on the other side of the coin, it's probably not a good thing to get used to winning fewer races. Last year, I won a lot of races and I was trying to because I was motivated and I wanted to win. What I deemed to be success as far as the quantity of wins goes seems to be different from everyone else. There will be some professionals out there who would win just one race in a year and would sit back and think, 'That will do me.' But on my calibration, that's not good enough. So it probably isn't such a good thing to get used to winning fewer races. Accept it maybe, but not get used to it.

Could I ask you about the Tour de France? Is that the ultimate competition in your sport?

It is the ultimate in cycling, and I would argue that it's possibly the ultimate competition in any sport. There is nothing like it. It's now the biggest annual sporting event in the world. It's something that has to be seen at first hand to be understood. It's not a bike race any more, it's a spectacle, it's an occasion, it's something unique and special, even in the cycling world. There is the Tour of Spain and the Tour of Italy, which are very, very big races, but the Tour de France just stands alone. And it outstrips, in terms of its importance, the world championships and that's not written down anywhere, it's just accepted as that by the people who are involved in it. It's simply so hard an event that it demands that much respect.

What about your own experiences in it?

My sports psychologist always says to me that you can either treat things as a challenge or you can treat them as a problem. So I like to treat the Tour de France as a very, very big challenge. The Tour opened up new challenges to me – whether I could climb success-fully, whether I was up to it physically, whether I could make my engine efficient enough to climb with the best, I just didn't know. But we're working very hard on it, because if I can't climb, then any aspirations of winning something like the Tour de France are completely finished. You can gain tens of seconds to a minute or two in the time trial if you ride a very, very good time trial, which is a forte of mine. But you can lose tens of minutes in the mountains very, very easily, so obviously that's something that we are concentrating hard on. It is challenging in the extreme. It's refreshing in some ways not to be expected to win every week and to be able to make up numbers, it's refreshing to have some space to learn. Experience plays a very, very large part in a race like that in which you have to use your physical ability over a period of three weeks and use it where it is going to be most effective. It's difficult and I'm now trying to gather that experience as fast as possible.

Does your psychological preparation have to be very different for something that's going to last that length of time? It must be very different to preparing for something that is over in a few minutes, or at least in one day?

It is very different. In pursuit racing, you've got four and a half minutes to do everything that you have to. On the road, however, it is inevitable that a breakaway group will get away at some point when you're not in control, but you have hours to sort that problem out and to try and work out the most economical way, physically, to bring that breakaway group back. In a cycling team in the Tour de France, we have nine-man teams, so if I am team leader for the Tour de France, I've got eight guys there to go and get the leaders back, and I'll decide when it is the best time for them to do that. It then becomes a chess game. There are teams that can only win sprints, so they're very limited, they can only win stages, they're not going for the overall title. But if that breakaway group doesn't come back, then they can't win either. It becomes a war of nerves to discover which team is going to use up their men, if you like, to chase that breakaway pack. If it gets really difficult, you may get some teams getting together and chasing together, so there's a real psychological aspect to the whole thing. There's a lot of bluffing that goes on. That's quite amusing, but it can be very frustrating sometimes.

From the public's point of view, I suppose the most unimaginable thing is with something that goes on for three weeks, something that

is physically and mentally exhausting all day. How do you relax at night in order to wake up the next morning refreshed and ready to do it all over again?

Well, these are all attributes that have to be learned. You have to be able to switch off and walk away from it. And that may mean between races or it may mean within a race between stages. Or it may actually be on the road in a race itself, when it's not going flat out. You have to try to enjoy the moment for its own sake, to enjoy the fact that you're going slow and just soaking up the sunshine, having a chat and waiting until something gets sparked off. Or it might be me who starts the attacking, I don't know. So it's just another attribute that has to be gained, another skill that has to be learned.

Now, let me ask you, how important is personalized rivalry for your motivation to win?

Rivalry is very important to me. It isn't essential, because I strive to be as good as I can be, and I don't have to dislike the person that I'm trying to beat. Miguel Indurain, for example, is probably one of the nicest blokes I've ever met. It makes you sick that he's so good on the bike and he's a really nice bloke as well. A hell of a nice guy. So you don't have to dislike the person that you're competing with, but rivalry certainly drives me on, because if somebody just happens to be effectively holding their hand up and saying, 'Actually I'm better than you as a cyclist,' I want to prove the opposite. Whether I can or not, we work that one out when we add up the scores at the end of the day. But rivalry is very important.

Is there much 'psyching out' that goes on in cycling, like the equivalent of what goes on in boxing? Is there anything like that?

No, not really. I think that it's more subtle than making statements in front of each other and the press. For example, if you're suffering and you're looking at guys, you learn to interpret very subtle cues as to whether this person is on the limit, close to the limit or totally comfortable with the pace. Some people try to hide that information from you, so they may not be grimacing or really showing signs of suffering and pain, but you learn to interpret subtle cues, like skin pallor and perspiration. Most of the time, you can work out who is flat out and who isn't. Riders like Miguel Indurain, however, are the exception. He is the kind of person who always has the same sort of face regardless of what he's going through. I could name some other cyclists like that – you wouldn't know what they were going through. They always have the same face no matter whether they're going well or they're going badly. It's always the same expression with them, so there are quite subtle aspects to all this.

So the ability to control one's body is one attribute of a champion, do you think?

Yes, as I said before, information is power. So on the other side of the fence you want to give away as little information as possible.

Have you ever made any bad mistakes with regards to the misinterpretation of the signals from a competitor's body?

Not as yet, but I'm sure I will. The other side of the fence is when you want to mislead people, to give them disinformation, about the state you're in. That sort of thing only works once with the same set of people. You can trick people by making out that you're suffering, and that's why you're sitting at the back of this group and not doing your share of the work. You're only sitting there because you're really in trouble. Then you go and beat them all in the sprint at the end, or just clip off near the end and ride away. But you only get away with doing that sort of thing once or twice, and on the whole it won't do you any good in career terms, because you don't make friends like that. It's effectively lying to the people around you. I certainly go for concealing how I'm feeling, but I don't try and mislead people. Some do.

Is it very satisfying to mislead people?

Effectively, yes. I've done it once or twice. I remember doing it once in training with a local cyclist called Dave Lloyd. We were going up a climb called the Sunspot. It's a long, long climb, and Dave always had to prove his ability when he was out training. He obviously had to know that he was the best there, and in fact he was the best at the time. Dave was riding up this climb, and in the end there was only the two of us left of the group that had started at the bottom. We were just coming to the top of this climb, where there is a café. That was the finish line for this particular climb, so I just let myself drift off to the back and made one or two noises. When Dave looked round, he obviously thought that he had just dropped me and that I was suffering away. I was about 30 yards back, and then as soon as his head turned back to look forward again, I sprinted as hard as I could and I went straight past him. By that time he didn't have enough time to react and I got the fastest climb. That was it then. He went and rode off up the road and we didn't see him for twenty minutes before he came back. The big group got back together and when we got to the next climb, he buggered off and left us all. So yes, psychology is important, but I try to use it sparingly because once you've used some, if you've played some of your cards if you like, people remember. They won't get taken in twice.

You recently had an accident on a time trial. How are you coping with recovering from that?

Well, in July this year, on the first stage of the Tour de France, I crashed on a wet descent. It was an unusual injury for a cyclist and I fractured my ankle in four or five places, which has now been screwed back together. I broke my wrist. That's a major limb in my sport, there's no getting around it. You can't start training after a couple of weeks, you have to wait until the entire job is finished, which meant three weeks of immobilization and well over two months before I could train. It was great! It was a really good time off and I needed that break, to coin a phrase, and it was very useful in career terms. I've had five full years – I went from pre-Olympics, which people won't have seen in the media, but it was a very intense time for me, when I was trying to make it to the Olympic year in

1992, then the world hour record, which was very, very intense pressure. There is no second place when you go for a record attempt, you either do it or you don't. So that was very intense and right there in the media spotlight. Then I became a first-year professional and then straight away the next year, I became the leader of the team in the Tour de France. It was all going too fast. The whole thing had been very intense for five years, and I think that it's been good in career terms to step back from that and take some time out. There is no way that I would have taken the time off except through physical injury. I spent some time with my family in the middle of the summer, which sounds a bit melodramatic, but it's really good to spend time with the family. I don't see them so much. And physically when I've been with them in the past, mentally I haven't necessarily been with them. I'm too busy thinking about my sport and what I'm going to be doing. But the problem is, my family won't wait to grow up. They won't hang around and wait until dad's finished and then carry on their lives, they'll just carry on independently. Professional cycling and the commitment it requires can be a very big price to pay. Financially, of course, it's very rewarding to be a professional cyclist, but the price isn't just financial, it's very costly in family terms. I started to question that and I'd also started to go through the motions of cycling, I was starting to regard it as just doing my 'job'. I didn't necessarily want to do it any more. I started to think, 'Well, if something forced me to stop now, I've had a pretty good career.' When you start thinking like that, the need inside has started to waver. So the rest has been very good for me. I've enjoyed that time and we've used it in different ways, to look to the future for security after cycling. I think, hopefully, my career will benefit as a result.

Have you made a fairly good recovery in physical terms?

Physically, yes. I've lost twenty per cent of the mobility in my left ankle, which doesn't affect me for cycling but it causes me to limp if I have to run. I lost three and a half centimetres off my left calf and considerably more off my left leg. And there was a lot of muscle wastage, which is actually more prevalent in highly trained athletes. So there are a number of challenges that have now been created for me.

Has the accident caused any permanent anxieties about racing down hill?

Yes, that's difficult at the moment, because I'm still getting twinges from it. In one of the road races that I rode in we were doing 55 kilometres an hour in the rain and cross-winds and we were riding in the gutter, very close to other people. Obviously, brakes become fairly ineffective in those conditions, and I hated it, I really detested it, but I made myself do it. But while I was still getting twinges from my ankle, it was like something constantly poking your imagination into thinking, 'Imagine what would happen if you fell off now.' So while those pains are there, it's probably going to be very difficult for me, but I think that I'll be able to force myself to do it. It's most difficult in the rain and the wet because those were conditions where I always had an advantage before the accident. I didn't like the rain, but I rode my bike well in the rain and I knew where the edges of the pocket were. It just shakes your confidence when you think that you know where it is but you make a mistake and you go down in the rain. So I'll have to re-calibrate myself and get back to that, but it's going to be difficult for a while.

Are you working with your psychologist regarding this?

I think I will. There comes a point, as an individual, where you can either deal with it or you can't. I think that I can deal with it, but he can help. As far as working with teams is concerned, I think that a good sports psychologist is invaluable to get the whole to become greater than the sum of its parts. It's all about communication. What a sports psychologist can do is to structure that communication and to force people to talk to each other and to be honest with each other, which is absolutely crucial, whether people want to hear what's being said or not. This way, they can get the best from a team.

And do you still see yourself as perhaps trying some other sport?

I'd like to. It just seems like such a narrow area of life to concentrate so much energy on riding a bicycle fast. In the past, when I've had to try to justify to myself why I'm spending so much of my life trying to go fast on a bicycle, it seems like such a waste when there's so many other important things going on in the world. There are disasters everywhere, like Bosnia, and I'm almost embarrassed to be expending so much energy in cycling. But I've found ways to justify it in the end and make it acceptable to myself. I sometimes think this is where the psychology really comes in.

December 1995

VINNIE JONES

Vinnie Jones is the hard man of British soccer. He was born in Watford and was, the media tell us, working as a hod carrier before signing from non-League Wealdstone to Wimbledon in 1986. In 1989 he moved to Leeds United, then to Sheffield United, Chelsea and back to Wimbledon. His disciplinary record is apparently one of the worst in the professional game, with ten sendings off and over forty yellow cards to date. Vinnie Jones is the footballer captured for posterity with his hand on Gazza's testicles, the footballer who revealed a few tricks of dirty play in the video Soccer's Hard Men. *But Don Howe has said that Vinnie Jones is a Jekyll and Hyde character. And there are many in the game who simply describe him as 'a diamond geezer'. So is there another side to the chopper, as he's known at Wimbledon? And how do the different facets of his personality hang together, if at all? I drove up a long, winding road in Hertfordshire to meet him in the bungalow that he and his dad had built. I asked him first what he thinks about this hard man image.*

Well I don't know how you define the words 'hard man'. I mean, certainly there are skilful players and there are tough players that give a hundred per cent. I think it's the media that give you the labels, if you like, and my definition is that I'm a tough all-rounder.

Are there some players you could look at in the Football League and think that they're definitely hard, though?

Tougher, tougher, you know. I mean it's very hard now, the game's getting less and less physical, contact-wise, so it's changing all the time.

Do you think that's a good or bad thing?

Well, I think the crowd like to see the fifty-fifty tackles but that, more and more now, the referees see it one way or the other.

Do you think the referees are clamping down perhaps a little bit too much?

Well, there's a lot to be said about it, but then again they're under instructions to have no grey areas so they're under the cosh a little bit. I mean, players are always going to quibble and say that they're overdoing it, but I feel sorry for referees really because their hands are tied. If you mistime a tackle, maybe two years ago the referee would have said 'one more and you'll get a booking', but now it's a booking straight away.

Do you think that kind of toughness in players is a good test of character?

Yes. I like people that give a hundred per cent but then obviously not all positions are like that – you want silky, good, fast wingers and you want players up front who don't generally work particularly hard but then they get their goals, so that is the blend of a good side.

Right. And do you always see it in terms of commitment, because you keep talking about a hundred per cent? Do you think that toughness is really a physical demonstration of your commitment to the game?

Yes. I mean the main part of my game is fitness and getting round the pitch and closing people down and putting your head into what we call knock-downs – you know, getting on to the loose balls. That's your job, especially at Wimbledon, to get it up to the forwards or to the wingers, and there are times when you're going to have to stick out a leg, and you know that you're going to maybe get a bit of a whack from time to time. But there are some players that are not going to put their foot in and get a whack.

But it's something that you've always been prepared to do?

Yes. In my position you have to.

How do you think opposition players feel when they're coming up against Vinnie Jones? Do you like the fact that the name puts a little bit of fear into them?

Well, I don't know. I don't really think about it. I don't know what goes on in other people's minds. I listened to Gerry Francis after the Tottenham game on Saturday and he said, 'You know it's going to be hard at Wimbledon. You know that they're going to be a very fit side. They're going to be stopping you playing and harassing you all the time.' So, I think when people play against myself or Wimbledon, they know that they're going to be shut down quickly.

What kind of homework do you do against your opposite number? Is there any kind of mental preparation you do in terms of thinking about the person?

We watch a video of the other side and then we generally play our own reserves. Say we're playing Blackburn, the reserves would play how Blackburn play and we'd see what problems arise from that. And then say, if the left back is getting out and causing us a lot of problems, we know that that's going to happen when we actually play Blackburn, so we try to rectify that or change our strategy a bit.

Could you tell me about some of the players who you've been particularly concerned with?

Well, there's not many. I had instructions a few years ago to mark Gazza because he was the player who just made Newcastle tick and

Bobby Gould was our manager and he thought that if I went man-to-man on him and stopped him playing, it would stop Newcastle playing, and it did. It worked. And the same in the Cup Final, we did the job with Dennis Wise and stopped him getting the ball, and that helped us win the Cup Final.

Right, can you tell me about Gazza? Was the marking just particularly tight there?

Yes. We didn't want him to get the ball and have time on it and be spraying it about and bringing other people into the game, so every time he got the ball there had to be a challenge on him.

There is, of course, the famous photograph of you with Gazza. Does that photograph make you smile when you look at it?

Yes it does, because there was nothing evil in it and Gazza was having a bit of a crack and I was having a bit of crack and one lucky photographer got the picture.

This might be a very naïve question, but what exactly are you doing in that photograph?

That was just one of the things that one of our old managers used to teach us when we were under-twelves. It was just a bit of a giggle and that's all it was really. It was a bit of banter, that's all. He was giving me some banter. I was giving him some back.

There was no serious intent in it?

No, he was tugging at my shirt and that was my reaction.

And did he say anything when you did it?

He screamed a bit.

Do you mean in pain?

It was more of a crack than anything. It wasn't something where he got hurt.

Right, because I've seen some newspapers that suggest this is the photo that you've got in your trophy cabinet, but I don't see any sign of the photograph.

Well, if you believed everything that the press say, you would believe anything.

I was going to ask you about the press. Are you sensitive to some of the things that the newspapers say about you?

No. I'm sensitive when people make comments about me, people who don't see me play but nevertheless make comments that are unfair about me.

Can I ask you about your disciplinary record? You've had ten sending-offs and forty-two yellow cards. Do you think that's been justified or do you think people are looking out especially for you?

I just think that referees don't give me the same sort of leeway that they do some other players. The minute I do something, it's terrible. If other players do it, it's not so terrible.

And is there anything that you've done on a pitch that you think is terrible? Do you ever do something and think, 'Goodness I wish I hadn't done that'?

There are times like this in every walk of life, when in the cold light of day you think, 'Oh, Christ, I was wrong there.' There are in every business you're in. But then, when I do it, if I'm in the wrong, I put my hands up and I tell the manager. I own up to it. I think that's the main thing, you've got to be honest. But if I'm in the right, I say, 'I'm in the right' and I've always been like that, so people know, if I'm in the wrong, I'm in the wrong. If they've said I'm wrong and I'm in the right, I detest it.

Can I ask what it's like to be sent off? What goes through your mind?

The thing is that most times when you get sent off, it's in the heat of the moment. You just maybe feel lost a bit.

Do you still feel pretty wound up?

Of course you do. Football is a very high-intensity game, and there's a lot of things to be lost – managers' jobs, players' positions, wages. Everything comes into it. And I've always maintained that if you're at the bottom of the League and you're scrapping away and you're a bit desperate, you get involved in things, whereas if you were further up the League and a bit more comfortable, then maybe you wouldn't get involved with those things.

There's a memorable quote I've seen from you which goes along the lines of, 'At the end of the day who would you rather have in the trenches with you, Gary Lineker or Vinnie Jones?' Could you tell me what you meant by that?

That was after an article Gary Lineker wrote saying that he'd rather watch Ceefax than Wimbledon, so my way to sum him up was to say, 'Who would people rather have at their side – a hundred percenter like myself or Mr Nice Guy?'

You seem to use this metaphor of the trenches rather a lot. Is this how you think about football? In terms of trenches, in terms of war? Where does it come from?

Well, that comes from people like Dave Bassett. Managers always refer to things like that. As they say, when the shit hits the fan, you gotta dig in and you got to get points, and managers want players who are going to put their life on the line. I was just asking the question, 'Would you call on somebody like Lineker, if you were at the bottom of the League, struggling? Or would you call on a hundred percenter like myself?'

I suppose that in some senses it's a very natural way to think about football as a war and there are going to be casualties of war on the pitch. Is that the way some managers think?

All managers are trying to do is give you a buzz and to get you in the right frame of mind for the game, to get you hyped up. With Bassett especially, he used to get me over-hyped up.

Do you feel for Dave Bassett, out of a job at the moment?

I phoned Dave Bassett the day he resigned. He said that mine was his third call from former players. He's had hundreds of players under him, but he only had three calls from former players, and he was over the moon that I called and it gave him a bit of a buzz.

What techniques did Bassett use to get you hyped up?

He used to take us down to the army camp and used to concentrate on team work, not necessarily on the pitch. We'd do cross-country runs with a great big log and you'd be in teams of six, and whoever got over the course quickest won so it was a team work thing. Some of the lads would be knackered and they couldn't carry it no more. It was a case of digging in.

And did these two teams of six have their own leader?

Well, the thing is they didn't. But leaders would soon emerge.

Were you the leader of one of the teams?

Yes. I've always been a leader, even in the school playground. I was always the one with the ball, the one who organized the football matches.

What kind of qualities do you think a good leader has?

I think that the main thing is honesty. If you go three or four nil down on the football pitch, you have to keep the others going and keep giving encouragement. If you're having a bad time, it's easy to slag off the other players and jump on them every time they make a mistake. But true leaders just emerge. At Wimbledon, we say to the full-backs, if they get in a certain position, the ball's got to be in a certain place, and if they start trying things and they don't come off, then I would be on top of them, but the minute they do it right I'd be back on to them saying 'well done,' and geeing them up. To be a leader you've got to earn your respect as well.

You lead by example?

You try, but things sometimes go wrong. I think that the manager puts an armband on a captain, but I think the boys really pick their own captain – you just emerge.

I'm interested in this team spirit thing because I did an interview recently with a guy who was a Falklands vet, and he said that all this business of 'King and Country' as the main motivator is a load of nonsense. He said 'In the Falklands I was fighting for my friends, for my mates.' He was in the Paras. Do you think that the same thing applies to football?

Well, that is what I like. I like players who aren't going to let their mates down. If it's not going well, I don't like it when players say, 'Oh, there'll be another day.' To go and play in front of 20–30,000 people has got to be the biggest thrill of your life, so I just can't see how some people cannot fancy it.

And is the thought of not letting your mates down one of the main things that drives you?

Yes. But that comes second. First and foremost you want to do well for yourself.

A few questions again about image. I read that you were once sent off after five seconds against Manchester City.

I was booked after five seconds and then later on I was sent off. Peter Reid had the ball, and he had a bad touch on the ball, and it was wet, and I was roaring in. I just committed myself one hundred per cent. I couldn't stop. I couldn't get out of the way or anything. I missed the ball completely, and just upended him. I just clattered into him. All these things are split second things. It wouldn't have mattered who it was, nobody could have got out of it. Later on, there was another tackle and I just got sent off.

Did you see the second one as a bookable offence?

I didn't take the ball cleanly. But the trouble is now, if you take the ball cleanly and you touch the man, it's still a foul. I see the ball, you know, but some of these players are so skilful that they are good enough just to knock the ball away from you.

Is it ever necessary to intimidate a player on a pitch? If someone is so skilful that you think the only way you're going to work on him is to instil fear in him?

I think that it comes down to respect. If you've got a ball player and every time he gets it, you're beating him to the ball, psychologically you're doing a great job. When I've played with John Fashanu, if Fash was on his game and winning all the headers and roaring about, he would give the rest of us such a big lift. But if he wasn't at it all, the other boys used say to me, 'Vinnie, get your mate going, get him livened up', because we were looking for him to spark it all off for the rest of us.

And did you have techniques for motivating him?

Yes. I used to shout at him! But sometimes Fash just wasn't at it, and a lot of times he knew it. And a lot of times he'd be pulled off. He'd be one of those players who'd have five good games and then one bad game, and sometimes you could tell with Fash before the game that he wasn't going to be at it. The manager didn't really know him, but if you knew him like I knew him and if I was picking the team I would just have said, 'Look, leave it out today.'

Do you think that every footballer has to be a psychologist? Do you have to be able to read people, understand them, analyse them, and predict what they're going to do on the pitch?

If you want to be successful I think you do.

And do you think you just pick up those skills through football?

I think a lot of it has got to do with your background, how you've been brought up, what kind of character you've got. If we go out on a Saturday night, say with twenty of us having a meal and a bit of a disco, I end up starting a few old Irish songs off, enjoying it and then that gets everyone else going. But there are other people who wouldn't dream of that, they would just sit in the corner and that's their evening. But they've still enjoyed themselves. They've had as much out of the evening as I had, but I put a lot more into the evening, I've got everybody going so they've enjoyed themselves more.

You obviously see that as being one of your central characteristics, this business of putting a lot into life.

People say to me that I've never blushed in my life. I don't know where it comes from, but things don't bother me. Last night we went into a bar and it was absolutely packed and people were saying, 'Go on Vinnie, give us a song.' And my mate said, 'I bet you a hundred pounds you wouldn't get up.' And two minutes later I was up there singing!

Are you a good singer?

No, not really, it's just a good crack. We've got our Christmas do coming up and the chairman has got a karaoke thing, and he came up to me after the game and said, 'Look, can you get everybody up and get everybody involved?' And that's off the pitch!

Can I ask you about the video you made about soccer's hard men? What was the thinking behind that?

I didn't make the video. I was asked, to be honest, to say what goes on in football. My agent, at the time, should have vetted it. Since then my new agent and I have copy approval on everything, so there are no slip-ups. Some of the things in the video, in the cold light of day, shouldn't have been said. As the FA said to me, they know it happens but it's not something you can go around talking about. I don't really want to go into it any more, it was ridiculous. I got a fee, the same as Brian Clough got a fee, everybody involved in it got £2000 for their interview, for an hour or so. That was my only involvement, the same as everybody else in it, but everybody says that it was my video. The guy who did it, did it about two years before it even came out and it got sold about five different times, and it just so happened that someone cottoned on to it and said, 'You can't say that.' And then it got publicized so much. It got into the papers and everything, and bang, it was suddenly like a bull in a china shop. It just got all out of hand.

Don Howe has described you as a Jekyll and Hyde character, with this really nice, pleasant side to you. But I get the impression that you don't see yourself as having two sides to your personality but that you just see yourself as having one side to do with commitment and contributing to things. Is that how you view yourself?

Yes. I love company. My wife has the biggest problem if just the two of us are going out for a quiet meal, because it always ends up with about eight of us and she does her nut! I like people all around. My mum does as well, but my sister and my dad could be on their own. My dad is up in the woods all day and all night with his pheasants, knocking about and shooting, all on his own. I'm going out shooting tonight, but I won't be going out on my own. I'll be going with two or three of my mates. The same with fishing, anything, I like to be around people and have the crack and a bit of a giggle.

Could I ask you a little bit about your family background? Where did your interest in football come from?

Well, my grandparents lived 2 miles away from where we lived, and my dad's brothers lived at home because they were all young. They were like big brothers to me and they were all Watford supporters. My dad played for Watford boys, as a school boy. So it was the same as the shooting, you know my dad has been shooting all his life, and I think you can take it or you can leave it. But I was always out shooting and fishing with my dad, up to the divorce, and then it was up to me to make a decision about which way I was going to go. Was I going to go into the same things that I knew everything about, shooting, fishing, football and all the rest of it? I always had lots of mates, so that was the side of my life. Or I could have gone a different way. It's only really since I've become a celebrity, or whatever you like to call it, or well known, that I've had to sort of get away. I couldn't handle living on the estate any more, that's why I live up here in the middle of nowhere. I get all sort of tensed up when I go into a strange pub, or something, because everybody is just turning round whispering, and you just think, 'Have you not got anything better to do? I'm only a human being!'

Do you ever get any aggravation when you're out, because you are who you are?

Well I did. I kept getting into a lot of scrapes because I'm still one of the lads and I've still kept my old mates. When I first started, I went about with Fash and Nigel Benn, but I just thought that this wasn't me. I needed to get back to my roots. I think when things go wrong then I run back to my roots, back to the local pub, where I was brought up and I get involved with them and I can hide away with them.

These are the guys you grew up with, the guys you went to school with?

Yes. I mean a lot of them are still very, very close to me. I stayed away Saturday night, so I rang up one of my mates, who I went to junior school with, and he and his girlfriend stayed here for us. You know, things like that. At Christmas time some of my old friends are struggling for money and they've got little kids and families and nearly every year I have to help some of them out and give them a bit of money, because they can't give their kids what they want. It's hard because I can't say no, because when you're kids you always said, 'If you had money the number one thing would be to look after your mates.' So that's what I try to do, but they always pay back after Christmas.

Do you ever get any stick from your friends because you've become a celebrity?

No, because it pisses me off. I get that everywhere else, I don't need it from them.

Did you have quite a tough upbringing? Was it quite a tough area?

Yes. It was the London overspill, in a big council estate. I think all council house estates are generally fairly tough, and you struggle to get on. We had it a little bit more comfortable because dad was a builder, he didn't bring home normal nine-to-five money, he brought home a bit more. Then he'd get cash jobs. So we had a couple of nice holidays.

Were you in a gang on the estate?

I was in with all the boys. It was a hard part of my life when all the boys started splitting up for girlfriends. Instead of meeting on a Friday night like we did for years and years, all of a sudden Harry wouldn't be there, Joe wouldn't be there and it got whittled down and whittled down and in the end you just went, 'Right do our own thing now.'

The advantage of football is that, in some sense, you stay with a gang.

Yes, it's great for me. The only thing which I think that I regret, which I'd liked to have done, is to have joined the army. I would have liked the camaraderie. Although I like my home life, with my kids and no one treats their kids or their family better than I do, but I do like being with the lads.

Nigel Benn was in the army, did he ever talk about that?

No, because Nigel likes his life now.

The media reported that you started your working life as a hod carrier. Were you working for your dad at the time?

Yes, I was working for my dad. One of my first interviews was after I scored the goal against Man United, and they tried to sensationalize it, saying, 'What were you doing three weeks ago?' I said, 'I was working for my dad, we were building a house, I was doing the hod.' But I wasn't a hod carrier all my life. I was generally just working for my dad as a labourer.

It suddenly looks very different if you describe yourself as working for your dad, as opposed to being a hod carrier.

Exactly. Me and my dad clash very much. He wants things from me that I don't want to do. He likes me going over there all the time pottering about. I like getting on with my own life. My dad hates pubs, and if I spent fifty quid down at the pub he just can't believe I've done that. But he would spend a hundred pounds on a telescopic sight for his rifle.

One other image I have of you is as this country gentleman, but you're saying that just comes naturally from your father, it's something that was always done in your family.

Yes. At the weekends I was playing football, Saturday morning, Saturday afternoon, Sunday morning, Sunday afternoon. And in the evenings I would be out shooting with the old man, or fishing or whatever, and I just got brought into that. It's just something I understand. I was actually fully employed as a gamekeeper, which people don't know.

When was that?

Well what happened was I decided that I wasn't going to do my exams at school. I just thought, 'What do I need them for when I'm going to go and work for my old man?' So instead of doing the last year at school they released me on permanent work experience. So my work experience was on the building with my dad. He was then a shoot captain and he ran this pheasant shoot, and his gamekeeper quit, so I went in there and took over and I loved it.

I've read somewhere that you were expelled from school. Is that not correct?

No, it's crap.

So you were just on work experience then?

Yes, a year's work experience. At school all my reports were sort of Ds, but when it came to sport it was A+. I switch off very quickly from things that I'm not interested in. I couldn't sit in a classroom and take in history, maths and all that stuff. But with things I am interested in, I'm very intelligent in them. I mean at sixteen I was rearing 4000 pheasants from eggs and hatching them and bringing them up and releasing them into the woods. I had to sort out all the temperatures and all the humidity and everything for £10,000 worth of incubators, which I was in charge of. I had Landrovers and the tractor, and if anything went wrong with them you had to get under them yourself and get by like that. So when it comes to that side of things I'm good, but I can't keep my interest going on things like books. I can't read a book. My book collection just contains shooting and fishing books.

The quote about you never having read a book in your life is repeated time and time again. Is this true?

Yes, it is true. I've never read a book in my life. I haven't got the patience to do it. I've got a book called *More Tales of Old Gamekeepers*. That has got different tales and I can read those because they're not sort of 500 pages, they're six and seven pages each. I haven't got the patience to say, 'Right, every time I go to bed I'm going to have an hour with this book.' I'd rather wait until the book comes out on video.

You've got a Jeffrey Archer, though, I see.

Somebody gave me that and said, 'It's a great book.' It was in the other house for five years. I still haven't read it. It's a dust-collector that's all it is.

I've read another quote from you that you only watch the news because of the sport at the end. Is that true?

Yes. Also, I don't know how people can sit and watch soaps. I don't understand how people can just sit there and waste their time watching acting, and it's bad acting and it's crap. It's sheer crap. But I've got a hundred wildlife videos. I can sit and watch them for hours. There was a great programme on Christmas Eve about the red deer in Scotland. I could sit and watch that for ten hours.

What's so fascinating about wildlife?

I don't know. What's so fascinating about your job?

Well some people would say that people are more interesting than animals.

No they're not! Never in a million years. People are very predictable. Animals aren't. I put the bag of nuts out there for the birds, and it was fascinating to see how many birds came to feed there in the hour and I watch all their little ways. The great tit barges the little blue tit off. It's very dominant. The little nuthatch comes down and then the grey squirrel will come along and they're all gone! I sit at that window with a cup of tea in me hand and watch the bag of nuts rather than bloody *Home and Away*.

If you hadn't been a footballer, Vinnie, what would you have liked to have done?

If I hadn't been a footballer I'd have been a gamekeeper without a doubt. My best friend is a gamekeeper, and I'm down there all the time. In fact, I'm going out tonight.

What time would you go out?

Well, at this time of the year I'm very busy, because the foxes are getting into chicken pens and stuff like that. I know that's them and no one minds them taking a chicken for their cubs, or whatever, but the foxes get destructive and they go in and they wipe you out. They just get excited and they go crazy and wipe you out. So they have to be sorted. People phone me all the time round here. There was an old woman of about sixty who rang me today. She's got three geese, and she went out last night and a fox had killed all three of them. That's quite unusual for a fox to kill geese, because geese are quite powerful. This woman was in tears because she'd had these geese for ages.

So you're well known locally as somebody who can sort out this kind of stuff?

Yes.

Are you a fairly good shot then?

Yes. In shooting circles I'm known as a good shot.

What age were you when you had your first gun?

I had my first shot when I was five, with my old man. I've got sixteen guns. That's probably about fifty grand's worth of guns.

Do you ever see yourself as getting involved in football management?

I feel that there is a fork in my life. One fork is staying in football and being a manager, and I think that I've got what it takes to be a good manager. I've always respected Bryan Robson. He's another one hundred percenter. You know when you're losing he's always digging in there, working hard and getting the lads going, and if he's winning he's doing the same. He's made a good manager, so I don't see why I shouldn't make one. I love being with the lads, I love all the crack and all the mickey taking. I love all that. Or the other fork is to start my own game farm, rearing pheasants, duck and partridge full time. I've got enough money to do that. The house will be paid off in the next two or three years. My main goal was to come out of football with no mortgage. I know I'm not too old to be a gamekeeper. I've got a nice big house here, and I've got all my dog kennels, my chickens, pigs, sheep and cows and then in the middle of that I've got a nice swimming pool. It would be hard to leave that to go to a little gamekeeper's cottage. I also like the telly side. I can handle that and it would be nice to have my own show one day. I'd like to be the new Wogan. That would be super if I could do that, as a young bloke. We've had Wogan with all his older people on it, like Joan Collins. I'd like to do it now because all those older people have been done, and there are all these new stars coming up. There could be a tremendous programme with me hosting it, and I would like to do that.

Are there any managers that you have worked with whom you particularly admire? What particular qualities do you think a good manager should have?

I don't know whether the word 'admire' is right. I think when you admire someone it's got to be someone like Mother Teresa. I don't admire people in football because it's their job and they're getting paid for it. I only admire those kind of people who work for charities and things. There have been different ways that managers have motivated me, they've all had different tactics. Some of them have been great with the lads – they get involved with the lads and go out for a beer with them. Others don't do this. Bobby Gould was great. He sorted out the disciplinary side and he gave Wimbledon a new angle. He changed Wimbledon. He said, 'Basically, you can't be Sunday morning footballers any more in the top flight, you've got to become men and you've got to become respectable. It's a good crack going to the games in the minibus and all that, but you can't have that. It's all right living in a bloody flat, but you've got to be better than that.' So he helped me a lot but I've never had a bad word to say about any of my bosses. They've always given me a hundred per cent because they've always wanted a hundred per cent from me. You can't give seventy-five per cent to somebody and expect a hundred per cent back. When I've done well and I've dug in, I like a pat on the back. I like people saying 'well done'. So to answer your question, I would say that all my managers have been superb.

Have you got any particular football idol?

Well, as I said, I don't really admire people in football. But when I was a kid I always used to love Glenn Hoddle. I was a Watford supporter but I used to go to Tottenham, and support Tottenham, because of Glenn Hoddle.

Could I just bring things up to date. You've announced your intention to leave Wimbledon. What was the thinking behind that?

Well, say you work in an office and there are some people who you don't particularly get on with, you have to do it but you feel that the crack is not the same. There's always changes in life and I just feel that I need a new challenge. I mean I have a picture of when I played for Leeds and there were 30,000 people screaming for you. I miss that, I didn't know at the time how much I would miss it. I was lucky, I went to Leeds, then I went to Sheffield United, I went to Chelsea with a brilliant following. I want thousands of people there screaming, it's very hard when you play at bloody Man United, say, and there are a hundred Wimbledon supporters. It's very hard.

Are there any clubs that you'd be particularly interested in joining?

There are, but I want to keep them close to my chest. Obviously there are some big clubs as big as Leeds. There are also some big clubs in the Premiership that I think could do with me. My football career has been like the migrating woodcock really. You never know what's in front of you. You've got all the shooters and the storms in front of you, which are trying to whack you down, but in the end you just want to get to new fields. That's just me. The migrating woodcock. Who knows what new fields I'll make it to in the end.

December 1995

BRIAN MOORE

Brian Moore, one of the fiercest competitors in British sport, is the former English and British Lions' hooker. Known affectionately on the pitch as the pit-bull, off the pitch he was the ring-leader in demands that have taken the game from amateurism to professionalism. He was born in Birmingham and was adopted a few months later by Ralph and Dorothy Moore in Halifax, West Yorkshire. Just before the World Cup in 1995, Moore announced that he was to retire from international rugby, choosing to focus on his career as a London solicitor. I wanted to know what was going through his mind when he announced his retirement.

All sorts of things really, there was a lot of pressure that year. The World Cup brought such a strain on everyone in terms of time, preparation and mental preparation. Harlequins, my club team, nearly got relegated last year and it was a horrendous prospect. I didn't necessarily think that we had been playing particularly badly or even worse than we had been doing this year. We simply didn't take our chances, and I took it very personally because as captain you feel ultimately responsible, even though it is not you that is missing the goal kicks. I felt that very keenly last year, so there was that, along with a lot of work pressures. After the World Cup people were saying that there would be a clear-out of players and anybody who wouldn't make the next World Cup in 1999 was probably going to be axed. I didn't want to get into a situation where I felt that

I was still playing and available and then suffer the indignity of being told, 'I'm sorry, but we want someone else in because they are younger, but not necessarily better.' That would have been very difficult to bear, and I didn't want to leave myself open to it. When Jack Rowell, the coach, made it quite plain during the World Cup, or just before that, that it wouldn't be like that and people would be judged on experience and all sorts of other things, that went a long way to reversing it. I also think that the experience of the World Cup was such that it was so enjoyable, even though we had a harrowing defeat against New Zealand, but the high against Australia was particularly strong. So I just felt that if I could continue to play at that level it was something that I shouldn't deprive myself of voluntarily, without very good reason.

In terms of the World Cup, what was the highlight for you?

Well it has to be the Australian win. To knock the holders out of the competition in circumstances which were so dramatic – it almost defies description. But I think that you can get a picture of it by thinking of all of the most pressurized and exciting moments of your life happening in one particular eighty-minute spell. It was such an overwhelmingly joyous feeling, because we were made underdogs and despite what people say about the Australian team, they were a very good team and we hadn't necessarily been expected to win. To achieve what we did, in those circumstances, was particularly thrilling.

Do you get a high from that kind of experience which you can't get anywhere else in life?

Yes you do. The circumstances are so different from ordinary life you just can't replicate them. I often think about pop performers who are the centre of attention in front of a hundred thousand people – it must be such an incredibly powerful feeling that I can quite understand why they go into drugs to try and re-create some sort of different feeling, because it must be the only area and the only time when they feel ultimately alive. It's very seductive. Actually you have got to try to get yourself to a situation where you can enjoy what it is, but understand that it is a separate and totally divorced part of your life, because if you try and judge the rest of the enjoyment you get in life by the same standards then nothing really compares. Everything else seems mundane and tedious by comparison. The real world is not out there on the field or on the stage, the real world is off stage and it's with your friends and your family and people like that. And if you get those two mixed up, and it's very easy to get them mixed up, I think that leads to a lot of unhappiness. That ultimately leads to suicides and all sorts of other things. If people can't re-adjust then I think they're in trouble.

Did it take you a while to come down afterwards after the Australian game?

It did, but knowing that we were going to be facing the All Blacks in six days' time was a fairly good focusing tool! So yes, it was euphoric for two or three days, but there was a job in hand and then very bitter disappointment after that. Those disappointments live with you so in terms of the roller-coaster of emotions – within seven days there were the highest and lowest points, almost of an entire sporting career.

How did you feel after the New Zealand game?

We just felt devastated and bewildered in a sense, because when we came off the field I felt that we hadn't played too badly. That was because we got thoroughly beaten for fifteen minutes then it didn't matter what we did for the next sixty-five. There was always going to be a lot more points on the board for the All Blacks than there was for us, and that was the way it actually turned out. But when you came off the field you didn't feel as though the balance of the game had gone that way at all. So it was a very odd situation. You were out of the World Cup and it was in circumstances which were just bewildering.

Did you actually talk about what went wrong immediately after the game?

Not immediately, but the next day people had a proper discussion about it, simply because you have got to try to learn from your mistakes. But it was difficult because everyone basically wanted to go home. I think it probably would have been right for the third and fourth place teams to go home anyway after a semi-final defeat.

Was it particularly negative losing to France in the third and fourth place play-offs?

Yes, I'd only played on one team previously that had lost against France and unfortunately after this particular game it went to two defeats. It really is one game that is best forgotten, if that is possible.

So in terms of the possibility of retirement, there is this one aspect of some of the very positive things that you get from rugby. Are there any other anxieties about the possibility of retiring? Do you wonder what's going to structure your life in retirement?

Yes. There is a fear that you might be left with the dominant part of your life completely missing and be unable to fulfil those parts that have been taken up so very fully by an all-consuming sport. I think that I've got a bit better perspective on it now because I do feel that there are other aspects of my life that I want to develop, other parts of leisure time that I just haven't had time to do.

Like what?

Well, I like going to the theatre. Over the summer break I've managed to see a lot of good West End shows. It's something that I lost for a long, long while. I think that I'm actually better adjusted to the prospect of retiring now because I know there are other things that I can actually do to fill the time. I'm quite sure that when I finish, after a suitable break, there will be some sort of role in rugby. I don't know what this role will be exactly, but I hope that it is not so time consuming that I don't have time to develop other things.

Would you like some sort of coaching role?

Maybe, I don't know really. I think I'll assess that as and when it comes.

In terms of the physical aspects of the game, could I ask is there any kind of catharsis on the pitch? Do you feel that you're getting rid of some aggression on the field?

I think that is always the case. That was one of the aspects I used to worry about when I thought about retiring: 'Where is all this excess energy going to go?' I think it's all to do with personal development more than anything else. You have to come to terms with the fact that you don't have that outlet, and I suppose that you must channel it elsewhere, whether it is into work or whether it is into leisure. I mean, I will probably still train very hard in my retirement. But I can't deny that competitive rugby is a form of release that will not be open to me any more.

In terms of your work as a lawyer, do you get rid of some aggression there?

In some senses yes, but it's stylized aggression when you're a lawyer. You can get rid of a certain amount of aggression in litigation when you're arguing, but it comes nowhere near the sense of release you get on a rugby field when you are able to run full tilt into someone and bodily assault them.

Would you buy a punch bag or something like that when you retire? Is there any way of getting rid of it?

I honestly don't know. Hopefully I'll cope with it by working hard and training hard. Just carry on doing something. I can't say for certain whether I will successfully cope with it or not. I hope I will!

Could we now talk about the psychological battle on the rugby pitch? How much of what goes on between the two teams is psychological rather than purely physical? There you are on the

pitch – you're listening to the national anthem, you're looking at your opposite number – what's going through your mind when you're listening to the national anthem and looking at the French hooker?

Well, with the French there are a lot of things going on really. We hadn't lost to the French for so long that it was a question of reasserting dominance, and also we'd had some pretty brutal games against the French, so you know what's coming and it's a question of preparing yourself for that. You play teams other than the French and you know that the battle will be fierce but fierce in a certain way. Up front, there is a totally different psychological battle from those at the back in rugby union. The backs try and stay loose, they are het up but they try and stay relatively jovial to try and keep their attitude positive. The attitudes of forwards is much more bloody-minded and very much more confrontational because it's a very direct physical battle in the way that playing in the backs is not. We have to get ready mentally. There are certainly things you can do – you can warm up properly, you can do a little bit of scrummaging or you can do a bit of work with contact pads to get yourself physically ready. But at the end of the day, it is mainly a mental thing, to get yourself ready to throw yourself around. I think that the only other sports that can be like that are boxing and rugby league, because they have direct physical contact. It's not the case that you can simply approach it in a way where you don't consider what the consequences are. If you do that, then you won't be mentally right.

Do you try to psych out your opposite number?

There is only a certain amount of that you can do now. Quite often the teams don't face each other and staring contests don't really come to pass. Anyway, at that level, if they're any good, people are not intimidated by that sort of thing. It's more a question, I think, of being sharper in reactive terms and being quicker mentally than an opponent. It's not necessarily the case that you will intimidate people in that sense, but I think that if you're playing with more vigour, and if you're playing with better and quicker reactions, I think that does intimidate people, because they feel that you are beating them. There is a physical dominance, particularly up front, that you can try to put forward on an opponent. But again, when it comes to a physical act, like being punched or trodden on, anyone who is a coward is not really going to be a true international player. I mean, if it happens to me, I just try and shrug it off and try to make sure that if someone has hurt me, I don't let them know that they have hurt me. That's a very big thing with us, I think, in contrast to soccer. I would never go down after a punch or a kick unless I really had to. I certainly wouldn't make a meal of it, and I would do everything in my power not to let the other person know that I'd been hurt in any way at all, because I feel that it would give them an edge. I think that if you shrug your shoulders and say, 'big deal', it sends much more of a direct message than an opponent being warned and you having to have treatment and so on, because he has the satisfaction of knowing, 'Oh well, I might have got warned, but I did hurt him.' He'll take that into account next time, but if someone just shrugs their shoulders and smiles, he'll think, 'Well, it's not really worked has it?'

Do you talk to your opposite number in the scrum?

Occasionally. It's so quick now that people are just gasping for breath really! There is a bit of banter that goes on. It's usually short and very much to the point and fairly frank.

What kind of things are said?

Well, I'll leave you to work it out for yourself. It's usually fairly abusive most of the time. One of the difficulties now is that they have microphones so close to the field that most of it can be heard. I don't realize what I say in the game half the time, and when I listen to it afterwards and it's very plain, it is always excruciatingly embarrassing.

From your point of view, is it just a sign of effort and commitment?

I think so, yes.

Do you feel yourself saying things but you can't really stop it because you are so involved?

Almost always, yes.

After a game you need to come down from it. Is this where drinking can help?

I was recently discussing the 'Sally Gunnell approach' to coming down, which is a Mars Bar and a Coke, and rugby players' coming down, which is twenty-seven pints of lager and four bottles of Hooch! This is a question of degree, I think, and I have seen some pretty horrendous degrees of drinking after games. I suppose, at the end of the day, people will just say that with tours and tournaments, like the World Cup, when you have continuing obligations, you just don't do that. You have to take a view on that really.

Has there always been a danger that drinking, in the public imagination, goes with rugby? You can do things and engage in a level of alcohol abuse that if you were doing it individually people would say, 'Goodness me, there is something a bit curious here.' But as you're doing it in a team, it all seems different somehow.

There are fierce drinkers wherever you go, but you're not talking about shy, retiring wallflowers when you are talking about these rugby players. It is as simple as that, people with big body masses tend to drink more and can cope with more, and when you have got a coach that encourages that as well. I don't think that it's necessarily harmful. I don't think that there is necessarily a correlation between that and other anti-social acts. I think that if you compare the level of trouble at an international game with any club soccer game, you can see that rugby and alcohol do not necessarily mix badly!

Now you've been pack leader in the England team. Are you a good leader?

Well, it's not really a question for me to answer is it? I'd like to think that I was, but it's for other people to answer. I think that what I can bring to that particular role is a lot of experience. I have played with a number of different types of players and, hopefully, with younger players that will help. I think there is a need to review how you approach things. I think on occasions possibly I am a bit too critical of people, but that's done in order to try to get them to improve. I think that if I was to look at an aspect of how I approach leadership that's the aspect that I'd have to look at closest. I think the role has limits as well. When we're talking about psychology in sport you can say anything you like to a bunch of players and it will not make the slightest bit of difference, if they are not mentally prepared themselves. You can lead people who want to be led, you can't lead people who are indifferent or not quite mentally attuned, because you can't play for people and that is the difference.

So are you saying that a critical stage of the whole process is getting them tuned in?

Yes.

Are there any particular techniques that you would use here?

I think that you've got to try and vary it in relation to the pack you're facing. I mean, certain teams have certain challenges in certain areas and you must emphasize them. You must make sure that you are prepared and that people are thoroughly happy with the way that they're going to counter those strengths, the way that they feel that their individual contributions can, first of all, beat their opposite number so that they win the personal battle. But also how that contributes to the wider picture in terms of the pack. It is very important to explain to people why one player needs another player to do a certain thing a certain way, and how much benefit that brings. People often don't appreciate just what their contributions do mean to other people. They see their particular games and roles very singularly. I think that they need a reminder of the overall pattern and how they fit into that overall pattern.

And this is part of being a leader, to have a broader view than individual members of the team?

I think so, and if you're a captain the responsibilities encompass all the team not just the pack; this is a wider role and is probably more difficult.

You made a point about being critical. Would you be critical to players on the field? Can that be a dangerous thing?

It can be, but it depends how you do it and it depends whether it is warranted and I suppose it depends who it is as well. Some people respond directly to a verbal challenge; other people are turned off by it; other people require an explanation; other people are motivated by negative challenging assertions; and other people require positive thoughts to be fed into them, for them to be praised and for their positive abilities to be accentuated. So the skill is finding out which player is which and trying not to get them mixed up and trying to give information at the right time. You can't always do it.

A huge amount of skill must go into that. I mean it might seem that someone is thriving on criticism, but in a big game suddenly they're not, it might be just too much criticism or the stakes might be too high.

It's not easy, and I'd be the first to say that I don't get it right all the time. I just hope I get it right more often than not.

Would you like to have been captain of the England side?

Oh yes. It's no secret that I would have liked to have been captain. I don't think anyone could genuinely say that they wouldn't have liked to have been in that position. It simply wasn't to be for me. Will Carling came in at a very young age and was given responsibilities which, the results have shown, he carried very well.

Do you think that you would have made an even better job of it though?

I don't know. I would have made as good a job of it in certain ways. I think that I wouldn't have presented, necessarily, the positive image of the game at the time that Will did. I mean latterly he's had a bit of trouble with the tabloids for various reasons, but by and large, until very recently, his image was as good as they get in sporting terms and rugby benefited hugely from that. They were prepared full-heartedly to accept the public image that he put forward and the fact that he was sort of clean-living, clean-cut, prior to this point. They were quite happy to have that. I'm sure that my image would have been different. I have always tended to respond to questions reasonably directly, and if the answer happens to be one that isn't diplomatic or politically correct, I've never, necessarily, felt the urge or the desire not to say what I have thought. Sometimes it is not the right time to say things and with retrospect you think, 'Well, it might have been better said later or not at all.' But I've never approached it like that, and I don't think that is always appropriate for a captain. Having said that, I don't think the results would have been any worse. I think we could have achieved the same sorts of things because we had some very good players. It might have been more lively and more colourful if I had been in charge. It would have had different repercussions anyway.

Can I ask you how difficult it is to be in the public eye all the time?

It's a very odd situation and it came up on me by stealth really. When I first started playing, even for England, you're very rarely recognized beyond rugby clubs, very, very, rarely indeed. Then, after four years from 1987 to 1991, when the 1991 World Cup came up it suddenly became far more difficult all round. Now it's pro, the publicity is even greater. It's getting more difficult, so people can't avoid it in that sense. It was always difficult for a rugby player to take because you have a job and you are normal in that sense of the word, and you go to work like everybody else. You're not a soccer player where you go to work at half past ten and you train until twelve and then you have the afternoon off and that sort of stuff. You use public transport, which I do every day, which means that you are necessarily exposed to the public in a way that is completely haphazard, and professional sports people usually don't have to face this. So you have to interact on that basis, you also interact in working terms with people in their everyday lives as well. So you're getting one side of fame, but then another side too, which is completely different and you actually weren't getting the rewards. You get all the disadvantages of being recognized and all that sort of thing, but you aren't actually making much money. I mean if you are a soccer player and you earn five million pounds or whatever, it doesn't really matter about the disadvantages because at the end of the day you get a lot of money, so you can justify the energy. It's a bit difficult to take the rough elements without having the smooth cash element there. Also, you want people to write about you in nice glowing terms and you don't want anyone to write anything nasty about you. You certainly don't want anyone to cover areas of your life that you'd rather not have covered. The only thing I would say is that there seems to be an atmosphere, almost a demand from newspapers that, because you've been in the public-eye and you benefit occasionally, when things are bad they have a right to make you comment. I always say, 'I can't stop you writing what you want about me, but I don't have to make things worse if it's bad already. I don't have a duty to participate in my own downfall and if I don't want to give you a comment on something I don't like, then fine. You write what you want but I don't have to assist you!' That's where I stop, but I recognize that it's a very difficult line to tread.

How difficult is it to combine a successful career with a sport?

I think that it's bloody difficult actually, and it's getting harder simply because the time involved in both is growing and therefore the time available to do anything else is shrinking. There is a point coming where in three or four years it will be impossible to do both, and people in sport will have part-time jobs only, and it will be difficult for people in professions to follow them properly. Sports people will have to accept a retardation in their careers. Having said that, if they're actually being rewarded financially for playing then that goes some way towards balancing it out. What you were actually starting to get was a situation where people were losing out and not being compensated. So the game was having it both ways, it was asking people to retain the amateur ethos while asking them to give a professional commitment, but then not allowing them to reap any tangible reward, which was intellectually dishonest really. People will now have to make difficult choices when they're younger, but at least they'll be getting cash for it, so in some ways the decision is not as difficult as it used to be.

Could you give me some idea of the amount of time you would give to rugby in an average week?

Well, I'll give this week as an example. Tonight is training night, tomorrow is England training at Marlow, on Wednesday I'll train on my own anyway, Thursday is a training night, Friday is the day before a game so you're preparing for a game, Saturday is playing the game, Sunday is a remedial session with England. So that's what it consists of. Today, for example, when I leave work I'll go straight to training. I'll get home from training at about quarter to ten, I'll have something to eat, watch *Newsnight* and go to bed. Tomorrow will be the same. Thursday will be the same. Friday will be an early night.

So it's trying to fit in life around all this?

I mean you try to do things. For example, on Wednesdays you try to train before work or at lunch time so that in the evening you can have one night where you could go to the pictures or you could see somebody and go for a meal or a drink. Just basically to remind yourself that there is something out there other than actually playing and training. But that's not to say that you don't train on that day because you still have to. I don't want to make it sound as if there are no benefits, because there are obviously, but you do have to accept a certain type of lifestyle that is not necessarily, in personal terms, particularly developing.

And with this degree of commitment, do personal relationships necessarily suffer?

They certainly get affected in a major way. Not all necessarily suffer to the degree where it becomes fatal, but I think that you only have to speak to a number of wives or girlfriends to understand that the time players spend away is keenly felt, especially when the players have children. This is, of course, in the same way that people who work very, very long hours find that their family relationships and their other relationships do suffer. Again in the past it has been particularly difficult, because spouses have been able to say legitimately, 'Well, you actually only do this for your enjoyment. I don't get anything out of it.' Soccer players are able to say, when they go on a three- or four-week tour, 'Don't complain about this, because this is why we have the nice house and this is why we've got the two cars and why we've got this and that.' But until recently rugby union has been a kind of a hobby and I suppose at least that will change if and when people are professional.

There is a psychological aspect to all this as well, concerning preparation for games, especially big games, when you're necessarily on edge. You also get a degree of disorientation before and after a game because of the nature of the challenge that's facing you. It can't be easy to live with. Very few people who reach international level in any sort of sport are going to be free from some degree of self-obsession and selfishness. It really is a question of how you personally cope with that, and some people cope with it better than others. Some people are so self-obsessed that it becomes almost impossible for them to create relationships and sustain them. For those individuals people often say, 'Well he is just a selfish git really isn't he?' It can be very sad and lonely for people like that. On the one hand, you can achieve so many great things, and we can think of people who are well-known and wealthy and so on, but you get the feeling that they never really have a decent personal relationship because it's almost closed to them. It's closed to them because of the way they're driven. I'm not saying that this is necessarily the case with me, but you have to try constantly to battle against that, because to get to where you are, you've got to have had a lot of drive and self-discipline and you've got to have put yourself first. It's a case of trying to balance pushing yourself forwards with all the normal, and probably more important, long-term goals of having successful relationships, and that's not easy.

It must be very difficult for a spouse or a girlfriend to imagine what you are going through. Is that part of the problem?

It is. I mean they are very understanding but ultimately no one can understand properly because they are not there. People often ask what's it like, so I tell them, 'Well, whatever you've done, exams, driving test, any nerve-racking moment in your life, it's like doing that, but doing it in front of 70,000 people, all watching you to see whether you're doing it properly, and then knowing that there are probably three million or four million watching it on telly, and knowing that when you've done it there will be eight or nine papers all commenting on how you did it, why you did it, whether you did it well, whether or not you should be allowed to do it again, and how this affects you personally.' And I think that if you put it in that sort of perspective it hits home. I mean normally there is just you and the examiner and a quiet room and that's already a lot of pressure. When you know that everyone is watching you, it's much more difficult.

But in the case of rugby it's even worse than that because there is the possibility of injury. I keep thinking that it must be like going into war, like a soldier the night before a battle.

I've never boxed but I can imagine to some extent what boxers go through. I'm sure that soccer players don't feel this, they just want to get out there, they can run around, they can express themselves and it's really positive. Everything is really positive, and it's possible to be keyed up and slightly relaxed as well. I've never felt like that and I'm sure that most forwards have never felt like that. There's a period before a game when you almost think, 'I wish I didn't have to go through this. I know it's going to hurt a lot. It's going to be very painful.' It's not nervousness really, it's a slightly anxious feeling, it's so adrenalin based. It's a combination of a lot of things, including the prospect of success, the thrill of confrontation, the risk of injury, the possibility of coming off worse in a confrontation, the fear of failure, sometimes the fear of success, with teams that don't do well, the possibility and thrill of success itself, it's a very heady mixture of all those things. I don't think you'll get this in many other sports, you'll get it in rugby league and you'll get it in boxing, but the physical contact aspect really does give things a different aspect.

Do you ever have any anxieties about your own mental strength to cope with it?

Well, when you start off you always wonder whether you will be good enough. That's natural. Once you have found out that you can cope at that level, your thought patterns change slightly so you take certain things for granted – you know you can exist with the pace of the game, you can handle the physical nature of the game, you're not going to be out-gunned in those respects. Then you can turn your thoughts to a slightly more positive framework. Instead of saying, 'I just want to be part of the team and hang on,' you can start thinking, 'Well, I actually want to contribute fully, what can I do best for the team? How can I do it?' Not just, 'I'll just do my own job here.' Although your own job is most important and you must do that first. You alter subtly, so the thought processes change slightly.

Right. Can I ask you about your family background now? You were adopted when you were quite young?

Yes, a few months old.

And you had a Methodist upbringing. What did your mother and father think about you getting involved in rugby? Did they have any anxieties?

I don't think so. I don't think that they were really aware of what it was or what it entailed. I've not got any kind of sporting family background. They were aware that I played, but it wasn't until much later, when I was fifteen, sixteen or seventeen, that they thought that it was going to be, more or less, an obsession really. So in that sense they didn't really have a view on it until much later, when it became a bit more high profile, and then they took a keen interest in it. It wasn't that they were disinterested in what I did before then, but it was just not the kind of thing that people in the family did. At that time it was just a school sport that was played, just as cricket was in the summer. It was no different until much later.

Did they ever worry about you in the other side of rugby? You know, the social side?

I don't know. I think that they were amazed the first time that I came home the worse for wear, simply because of their Methodist background. They never drank, so obviously that was a bit of a shock to them. But they were quite tolerant – well, amazingly tolerant in retrospect, which is something I'm very grateful for.

Did they try and give you any advice about it?

Yes and no. They couldn't give me any rugby advice because they knew nothing about it. Regarding the social aspects, they gave me the same advice as any concerned parent. They said, 'Try not to get into trouble.' And apart from that they left it up to me. I think people have to make their own mistakes, and I think a lesson learned yourself is much better in the long run. It would be preferable if you could listen to what your parents said all the time, not that it's always right, but it's never going to be like that.

I've read your autobiography and it says that you went on a quest to find your natural mother. What prompted that?

Well, I always thought about it, but it was never in the forefront of my mind. It's as simple as this really. When you're filling in forms, especially medical forms, it says, 'Have you any family history of X, Y or Z?' and my answer is, 'I don't know. I don't know what my family history is.' If you've never been in a situation like this, you can try to put yourself there and think, 'It would be like this.' But it affects people in different ways. I don't think that people can ultimately ever say what they would feel like. I just felt that there was always a question mark there, and as I got older, it got to be a bit more insistent. When I was young it didn't really register at all, but it became more insistent as time went on, because I began to think that if I left it much longer my natural mother might have died in the meantime. It would have been a tragedy then to have found this out and not to have been able to make contact. Particularly if you found out later, from other people, that she did have a desire to meet you, and the meeting had just not occurred because you hadn't been bothered. So it was that possibility that pushed it more from the back to the front of my mind and that, along with the curiosity, meant that I did what was necessary.

Can I ask about your adoptive parents? Did they encourage you to try to seek out your mother or was it the opposite?

They never stood in the way, but they always had a natural caution. That's because they had seen, in similar circumstances, adopted children take the same route and find themselves suffering a second rejection, which can be quite devastating. It can have some very bad long-term side-effects. They obviously didn't want that for me. But at the end of the day it has not been like that for me, and it's not like that for a lot of people, which is one of the reasons I would not discourage anyone from doing it. Suffice it to say that people have got to understand that it is not a one-way process. So they did have natural caution about it and also, I suppose, there is bound to be some fear of almost replacement really. Which whether justified, or not, is probably always going to be there. I've done my best to try to set that right, because that never was a possibility with me. But it would be unnatural, I think, for them not to have some element of that, at least at the back of their minds.

Was it difficult to trace your mother?

No, in the end it wasn't. It was amazingly easy actually, which made me wonder why I hadn't done it before. But I hadn't done it before because I didn't want to enough. We, as lawyers, use private investigators for all sorts of things, for finding witnesses and so on, and one particular firm found her within two days.

What was it like when you finally met?

The whole thing was odd really. It's very difficult to explain. I had the address and the phone number for a week and I had it in the drawer and I was wondering, 'Shall I ring or shall I not?' Then I thought that you can't really ring someone up out of the blue like that, it would have been a tremendous shock. So ultimately I went to the social services and asked them to do it, and we made contact that way, which is the right way to do it. We talked on the phone and it was an odd conversation really because there is no real precedent for what you say to someone after thirty-three years. You can talk about major topics, and the more banal things that most people fill conversations with seem to be largely irrelevant after that, so it was punctuated with large periods of silence. This is what the first meeting was like as well. A few very major discussions, and then a lot of silence and reflection, simply because you don't know how it was going to work, and as I say there is no precedent so you don't know how to pitch things and it's all trial and error anyway. There are all sorts of emotions wrapped up in it, and I'm still not sure whether I've got to the bottom of most of them. You don't know whether it is positive or negative, or whether you like the person or they like you, and there is no reason why they necessarily should.

Did she know about your rugby career?

No , not at all. It was a complete shock to her. It was a shock to her when she found out as she had no idea. She'd not followed the sport, but my full brother had actually played the same position in school. He was a hooker as well, and he'd watched telly, so he obviously knew who I was. I don't know how you would react if someone came over and said one day, you know, Will Carling is your brother. Again you can't really say how you would react under those circumstances.

What was it like meeting this brother?

Incredibly odd. You don't know what you should feel. In a way you think you should feel close, but in another way you think that's obviously not going to be the case because it's the first time you have met, so you're not going to be close, although you feel you ought to be. Also, because you haven't any shared experiences, the topics ramble without any cohesion from one bit to the next with no proper linkage. It's like meeting a complete stranger. You're left with a feeling of, 'Well, I don't really know how to react to that, because I didn't get as far as I was wanting to and I didn't get as much out of it as I wanted.' I don't know if I felt that there would be a huge bonding, but I don't think it works like that and that is why I tend to think that most things are experience and circumstance driven.

Was there a genetic similarity between you and your brother?

I think so, yes. Unfortunately for him, he looks a bit like me! My sister, who I've also met, has some slight resemblance. It's interesting that as you go through conversations you do find that there are certain traits which are similar.

Psychological traits?

I think so, but also when I spoke to my sister she said that I had mannerisms that are like my brother. There can only be a genetic explanation for that, other than the whole thing is complete coincidence.

What about your aggression? Do you think your brother has that?

No, I don't think he's got that. I think my sister has got more of that and I think my mother has got a bit more. That's one of the questions that remains to be explained. My mum is very competitive so it may have come from there.

What about your natural father? Were you interested in trying to find him?

I've never really got to the bottom of that. That's something I've got to make a decision about. Again, you've got to be very careful in this area. There are lots of sensibilities that you have got to take into account and your desire to know things does not mean that you shouldn't have proper regard for people's feelings. If it's not that important to you, then certain other things are probably more important. I don't know, I continue to keep an open mind about that one. Perhaps one day.

December 1995

DEVON MALCOLM

In 1994 Derbyshire's Jamaican-born pace bowler, Devon Malcolm, was in full flight, demolishing the South African team at the Oval. When England toured South Africa in 1995, President Nelson Mandela greeted him by calling him 'The Destroyer'. But the tour was marred. Not only will the tour be remembered as the first visit to South Africa by an English cricket team since the late 1960s, it will probably be remembered more for the disagreements and arguments between Devon Malcolm and the team management, which all of a sudden became quite public. It all seemed to hinge on Devon's inability, or reluctance, to take coaching advice. But how do you go about advising a leading sportsman to change his natural style of play? What psychology lies behind it, or doesn't? The tour may have put an end to Devon's international career – he was one notable absentee from the England side touring Zimbabwe, when I conducted the interview. When we met in the Derbyshire Cricket Club pavilion, I wanted to talk not only about the low points of his career, but the high points, too.

So far, without a shadow of a doubt, the highest point in my career was in 1994 at the Oval, playing against the South Africans. It was the final test match, where I took nine wickets for fifty-seven runs. I could see all the players were behind me, and it was just amazing, everything clicked. All the balls nicked to the hands off the bat. There were great catches. Any time the batsman played and missed, he was out. Everything just happened – all the players took catches. I bowled probably equally as well in Perth the year before against Australia, but in that game I came out with about two wickets for a hundred-odd and I had about ten catches dropped, everything just went totally wrong. My statistics showed that in the game I had taken two wickets, but I had been creating chances every two overs but nothing happened. Also, I could see the fielders getting frustrated, nice catches coming in and bang they dropped them. They got frustrated and said, 'OK I will catch the next one.' The next one came, and bang they dropped that as well. Everything went terribly for myself and the team.

In 1994 at the Oval, on the other hand, the atmosphere before I went out to bowl was something that I'd never seen before. The changing room at the Oval was kind of split, so you choose which side you are going to use. That morning I got in very early, and I remember just before we assembled for practice, I moved about six times. I just kept moving from changing room to changing room just trying to find a spot that I was comfortable in and I kept moving my case, 'No this is not the spot. No this isn't quite right.' I don't know what was happening there. I was moving all over the place and eventually, after moving about six times, I found a spot and I settled there and that was where I was going to sit. In the final innings, when I took all those wickets, all the boys came across and said, 'This is your day Dev.' And I said, 'Aye,' just like that. Everybody just came up, 'Come on boy, show them, show them Dev.' And I just went out there and knocked them over. You could just feel the atmosphere. It was a whole team thing, everybody was fired up and we knew how to win and we just went out and played some magnificent cricket.

I've seen some descriptions of you where you are described as a 'mood' player. Do you think that is a fair description?

No, not at all. I am a one hundred percent player. I get out there, and all I think about is trying to do my best, trying to do the things to win the game. I am in the team as a strike bowler and I try to strike. At times, other bowlers probably just think, 'OK, I'll bowl a maiden. I'll not go for a few runs.' But I am there to create chances and to take wickets and to let the batsman make mistakes. Other bowlers are there waiting until the batsman gets tired. It's a typical stereotype. I don't see myself as a 'mood' player. It's the same in other sports as well. You look at Gary Lineker. He is a guy there to strike, to get goals, and if he doesn't get goals, then he gets the blame. I'm there as a strike bowler. I'm trying to do my job to strike and to get wickets. Like at the Oval, bang, the catches were held and all that business, great. But in the game in Australia there were all those chances which I wasn't credited with.

I'll refer back again to a game we played in Barbados a few years ago when we toured the West Indies and it was just incredible. I took about seven wickets and I checked, altogether I had about fifteen chances, fifteen catches. Every two balls, easy catches were just being put down and players don't go around and drop those by mistake you see, so that was the thing about it. In those positions, because I am a strike bowler, I create the chances, but because I am constantly attacking the batsman and because of the speed I bowl at, a ball that has been nicked, if it beats a fielder, it's four runs. Deflections have gone for four at the speed I bowl. If a bowler goes for a hook over the wicket keeper, that is another four. The slower bowlers, they probably go for three an over, I'll go for four. The thing about it is at the end of an innings or the end of the day, if I don't take those five or six wickets my figures look bad because you end up with twenty overs, eighty runs, one wicket or whatever, when normally, it is probably twenty overs and five or six for sixty. I've got a good strike rate, so that is where that label came from.

Could you tell me a little bit about the psychology of pace bowling? Could you give some idea of what kind of speed that ball is coming at, first of all?

Top flight, you are looking at between 90 and 100 miles an hour.

It's pretty ferocious then.

It's pretty quick, and if you pitch it with extra bounce and all that, that can be pretty intimidating. But saying that, those guys out there are equipped for it. In the past, my boyhood heroes were guys like Michael Holding and Geoff Thompson. I thought Geoff Thompson was the quickest bowler I have ever seen bowl, and in the early days, batsmen face them wearing just a cap without a helmet. In those times, as well, those guys could bowl as many bumpers as they wanted to, but nowadays, I can only bowl one. The batters these days are a lot more protected in a way. Like I said, these guys are well equipped to deal with pace with a lot of extra padding and the helmet and all that – and rightly so. I've seen batters get struck and doctors saying to them, 'You know, you want to wear your helmet next time.' And they had a helmet on! Imagine if they didn't have a helmet on, you would be talking about deaths on the pitch!

Can you tell if someone is a bit fearful of you?

Indeed you can. But again, most batters coming in to bat early on are nervous and they feel a bit intimidated as well. The thing I said about helmets and all that, when you are running in to bowl, at times you can't really see the batter's face. As a bowler, when you bowl, you make sure you get up into the batsman's face and have a look in his eyes and you get up close where you can see it.

You can see the fear?

You can see it at times. But these guys are still good players.

I can imagine. Is there anything that you particularly look for though? If you were trying to read fear from a batsman's face and you can just see the eyes, what is it that gives them away?

You see the eyes, but you can also judge when a batter doesn't want to face you. At times, you can also see when a batter is pretending, like there is a quick single and he says, 'Come for two,' when he definitely knows there is not two, he is just trying to psych you out. Well, I know he is scared like hell and that he really doesn't want to get back. He'll probably get a quick single or a long single. He knows that he wants to stay at the non-striker's end, but he is just saying, 'Come for two,' and in actual fact he wants to be at the other end. Again, you can see that when there could be an easy two runs and they take a long, easy drive for a single it's because they don't want to get back to the other end. You have got to realize that what I am trying to do, they are trying to do the opposite. I am trying to get them out and they are trying to stay in and trying to make runs.

Who is the bravest batsman you have ever bowled against?

I'll tell you what, nobody likes pace, I don't even like it myself, although I love batting. I love these guys who can handle themselves and don't back away, there are a lot of brave batters out there. I wouldn't want to single one out.

What about you, how do you feel when you have to face a pace bowler?

It is very intimidating facing someone like Courtney Walsh, he could cut a ball back into you or take it away from you. It is very difficult facing someone like that.

Is there any particular personality type that you think makes a particularly good fast bowler?

The thing about fast bowling is that you have got to be very aggressive. Also, you have got to have controlled aggression to be a fast bowler, because at times you go out there and you have a batter and they probably get on top. There are certain batters that dominate, but what you don't want to do is to get silly and try all of a sudden to do the wrong thing, to try to bowl bumpers when you shouldn't. You do try to work a batsman out. I remember my first tour of the West Indies, and in the first test I did all right. In the second test in Trinidad, I did OK as well, I got Viv Richards out a couple of times in Jamaica and he missed the third test, and I took about ten or eleven wickets in that game. Viv Richards came back and I knew I would take wickets, so I had to be hit out of the attack. I've recently seen Lara when he has tried to dominate. Viv Richards always tries to dominate, his job is to get out there and take you on, and he is going to try and dominate the game. I remember a test match in Barbados where he came in and he was going to have a go. As it happens I remember bowling to him – it was a fantastic over, it went for a lot of runs, mind. I reckon in that over there were three chances, four chances, in the end it was very, very expensive, but there were four great chances. A lot of people said, 'That is a rubbish over.' But I tell you what, he could have been out any ball.

Would you describe yourself as an aggressive person?

Yes, but again I am controlled. I'll control it, I've got a controlled aggression. Needless to say, there is no point in getting out there and being silly because if you are silly you make it a lot easier for the batter. All of a sudden the batter realizes that you aren't going to be bowling at his stump and he is going to be making runs. Again, there are a lot of elements that take a lot of aggression out of cricket. For a start, you have got TV, the close-ups, you have got kids watching and you have got the match referee. You have got to be so careful, but if you don't use obscenities, people say, 'He's not aggressive enough,' or whatever, and as soon as you do something that is bad sportsmanship you get called up by the match referee and get reprimanded.

There must be a very thin line, then?

There is a very thin line indeed. A very thin line. You want to control your game and you want your game to be played in the right manner with good sportsmanship. You know that there are kids out there watching, there are people out there who see us as role models, but at the end of the day, some people want you to do the wrong thing. The wrong thing so that you get called up to the disciplinary committee. As I said, it's a very thin line indeed.

Do you psych yourself up before a game? How do you go about doing that?

It's very easy, very easy.

Have you got a mental image of somebody?

You have got to play a game, you have a test match or a county game or a serious one-day game, and it won't just start when you get that ball. You have got a picture of all the guys who are coming up to bat, you go to bed at night and that is on your mind.

This is where it interests me, as a psychologist – you are thinking about these people. Do you think about them in a pretty neutral way, in almost a technical way, or do you think about them in an emotional way? Is there an emotional overtone to something like pace bowling?

I reckon that it's more technical, you're out there, you are watching a batter. They are probably in the batting net and you're probably at the other side of the nets and then you just have a glimpse. You can tell straight away and you say, 'I'll get this guy out that way,' or whatever, it is as simple as that. You probably know this guy and you think to yourself, 'Don't bowl such and such a way to him.'

So feelings don't enter into it, you don't have strong feelings for and against particular players?

Not at all. Feelings only come into it when I see a batsman going back to the pavilion as quickly as possible. I hate to see a batter out there accumulating runs.

Is it true that you were approached by the West Indies, that you could have played for them in the past?

Yes, indeed, in the early stages when I started playing for Derbyshire, I was told, 'Look, you have got a choice, you're qualified to play for England or you can make yourself available for the West Indies.' I said, 'Without a shadow of a doubt I will take my chances here.' If I was in the West Indies, I probably wouldn't be playing cricket. I have played most of my cricket here. I have played in the leagues, I have played for my school and this where I learned my cricket. I want to play for Derbyshire and if it so happens that I get good enough to play for England, it would be magnificent, it would be marvellous. As it happens, I did manage to make the grade.

Looking back, do you have any regrets about that?

No regrets at all, I had my chances here and I'm one hundred percent committed, despite all the horrible times I've had. If I had the choice again, I would make the same decision to play for England, I love it. Every ball I bowl for England I enjoy.

You must be very stunned by some infamous comments in *Wisden Cricket Monthly* about foreign players not having as much will to win as English players.

That was a load of rubbish. How can you say things like that, you have got to be crazy to write things like that or publish things like that. No reputable magazine should publish things like that.

Were you really shocked when you saw it written down?

When I saw that it was published in a reputable magazine I was very shocked indeed. *Wisden* is a magazine that I respect, it's a good magazine, but it was a bad misjudgement. I still read *Wisden*, it's still a good magazine, but it was misjudgement to put something like that in there. But all that is cleared up now.

What is it like touring the West Indies as a native West Indian?

The first tour I had back in 89–90 to the Caribbean was very hostile, without a shadow of a doubt, extremely hostile. The thing about Caribbean people is that they like quick bowling and after softening up Viv Richards – not softening up, I should say getting Viv Richards out a couple of times – they realized that I bowl quickly. After getting a lot of hassle in the first test match in Jamaica by the second or third day, I just couldn't get out because people wanted to chat and to know what is what. Especially when I had got Viv Richards out, because Viv was the king. That did help. I had a lot of flack, but once I got King Viv out they tended to tone things down a bit.

What sort of hostility?

They use terms. It's a little upsetting, things being said or things being shouted in the crowd, and you are there. The people in the middle don't hear, but I'm a bowler who fields fine leg, third man near to the boundary, it is very hurtful.

It must be doubly hurtful with these being your people.

Indeed. After a while it turned around and there was no problem after that.

Do you take stuff like that personally or do you reason that they are just trying to put you off, just trying to affect your performance?

As it turned around, you could see it was just a matter of trying to put me off, I could see that. At the end of the game they were all walking around chatting. I just saw it as a way of trying to put me off.

Could I change tack a little bit? Could you tell me a little about your childhood back in Jamaica?

Yes. Like most children brought up in the Caribbean, playing sport as a profession is out of the question. If I ever said to my grandmother, 'I want to be a footballer or a cricketer, or whatever,' she'd say, 'It's crazy, you have got to be a doctor or a teacher or a policeman.' Something that meant you had to do a job, not sport, that is something you did anyway. Any sport that is going, you must participate in at school. If it is cricket season, you play cricket; if it's football season, you play football. At school, whatever sports season it is, you participate in that. I must admit that I was a good sprinter. I used to love athletics and love football very much. When I got to England I didn't play cricket at all.

Could I ask you what your image of England was before you came? Did you have a clear image of the place?

No, not at all. The thing about the Caribbean is that cricket is being instilled and preached to you as a child. As a five-year-old my reading book was about cricket, 'Calypso Comes to Lord's'. That was my favourite story. I remember, as kids you have got to keep up with your reading book. I just got stuck on this 'Calypso Comes to Lord's'. When all the other kids were however many stories ahead, I was still on 'Calypso Comes to Lord's'. I was trying to create this Lord's cricket ground in my mind. I was building up this picture of Lord's. I could have recited the whole story right through. I probably knew a lot more about Lord's than a lot of kids who live in England, just from this one story. I believed Lord's is the home of cricket, cricket was born in England, discovered in England, Lord's was its home. It was all a dream. I never ever thought that I would ever play cricket at Lord's. The way cricket is portrayed in the Caribbean is, I would say, the one thing that bonds the whole of the Caribbean together.

When you came to England at fifteen, was your father already in England at that time?

Yes, my father had been living here for yonks really, before I came to live here, a long, long time before.

And he was in Sheffield, wasn't he?

Yes, he lived in Sheffield. I came over and joined him there.

Did your father write to you and give you any hint of what life in England was really going to be like before you came?

No, not at all. What he did do was gave me the choice. He said, 'Look, I believe you can make your own mind up now.' He was given the choice when he came here, he was pretty young at the time. So he said to me, 'OK, I will let you have the choice, now what do you think?' and I said, 'Oh yeah.' So, I came over and I went to school and college.

What was your first sight of Sheffield like?

I was very excited, it was quite a long flight. I got in the car and we drove from Heathrow to Sheffield. It was early spring actually, so there was a little bit of snow on the side, but I was so tired I fell asleep. Once I got to Sheffield, the style of housing was very different to what I was used to. You don't see houses in the Caribbean with chimneys, the houses looked like bakeries. This place was full of bakeries, what's happening here? After a while you get into things, but my first impression of England was that although it was spring it was cold. It was about eight degrees outside when I arrived here, and it felt really really cold to me. But after a while I began to love it.

Which bit of Sheffield were you living in?

I lived in Wincobank in Sheffield.

Quite close to where Brendan Ingle's gym is?

I was just across the road from Brendan Ingle. I remember, as a youngster in Sheffield, at times I popped across to Brendan's gym to watch the guys spar and box.

Were you ever tempted to have a go?

I must admit that I was tempted. But after I popped in to watch those guys box, I thought, 'That's not for me, I don't believe in somebody hitting me like that.' I normally would just pop across and watch those guys spar and stuff like that. I must admit that I love watching boxing on TV and getting out and watching a bit of boxing. I've sparred once with Herol Bomber Graham, and he was hard, it was very difficult to lay a hand on him. He was very fast.

Those were the famous days when Herol would put his hands behind his back.

Yes, I remember sparring against him for a bit of fun. We opened an indoor cricket school in Sheffield and we were just trying to raise a bit of money for Brendan Ingle, to give him a collection for his gym. Bomber would have his hands behind his back and he'd be putting his hands in my face and I'm swinging at him and turning around and he says, 'Hey over here, what's the matter Jimmy? What's up?' He was just incredibly quick. That was the closest I ever got to boxing.

If you were surprised by the housing in Sheffield and the fact that the houses looked like bakeries, were you also surprised by the English themselves? Were they how you expected them to be?

After I started high school, I won a scholarship and there were a lot of different races. The vice principal was Chinese, there were Indians, my chemistry teacher was Indian and there were white students around. The other kids on my street in Wincobank were very friendly. They realized that although my dad was living on the street for years and years, two of his offspring were now joining him. They came knocking on the door, bringing presents, wanting to talk. The accent was just a little bit funny at first. You have got to listen quite a bit to pick it up, although it was plain English. After a while I just picked it up.

Was there ever any racial tension in Wincobank? The reason I ask is that I always notice that on the wall by Brendan's gym, someone has written something about the National Front? I suspect that Brendan leaves it up there, people have said this to me over the years, that Brendan deliberately does not clean this off.

Brendan has got a psychological theory about things like this. As a matter of fact, I popped over to the gym the other day during his training and he said that there are certain things that he has got to teach his boxers. These guys are fighting machines, they are killers, there are certain things that you have got to instil in them because if somebody called them a name and they reacted straight away, without thinking about it, they could easily kill somebody. So, there are certain things that he can use to gradually try to get at these guys. So he probably uses things like that writing, even though he doesn't condone it, he says, 'Guys, look, there are people like that in the world, they are doing things like that because they are jealous, because they don't like peace, they don't like to see people getting together.' Even in the gym, if somebody makes a racial remark, instead of punching their lights out, you count to ten and then think about it. He's also saying, 'You who put the graffiti there, what have you achieved? There it is, have you achieved what you wanted to achieve? What are you trying to achieve?' I reckon Brendan is very clever. He is a great man manager. He knows how to get the best from someone, and he knows how to get the fighting instinct out because it's very important.

Could I ask you whether you think some managers of cricket could learn a bit from Brendan on motivational techniques?

Indeed. They could learn a lot of motivational techniques from him. There is a certain thing called natural talent. In the manual, it probably says that you can't play a shot a certain way but, in the end, it comes down to who can hit the ball for six off the bat first and things like that.

Presumably, there are parts of your own play that are slightly unorthodox but you are coming up against text-book descriptions of what a fast bowler should be like. The analogy there is that Brendan would never have gone to Herol Graham late in his career and said, 'Hang on, you're a good boxer but here is something you are doing wrong.' Or to Naseem Hamed, 'Here is something you are doing wrong, try to change the style of it.' That thing seems to happen in cricket. There was an instance, of course, in the last tour against South Africa.

Yes. Probably the lowest time in my entire career was last winter in South Africa. The last time I played against South Africa I took nine for fifty-seven and I did very well, I won the game. I went to South Africa with plenty of hope. I was all fired up and I said to myself, 'Yes, I am still going to be a major part of this tour.' I was very enthusiastic, my confidence was sky high. I just wanted to get out there and have a go at the South Africans again, and I could see that I had this psychological advantage over these guys. I could see from their body language that there was still a bit of nervousness there, they had not forgotten what had happened at the Oval. I knew that at the Oval they were totally shocked and I could see a bit of that, but I have learned that you have got to spend sixty per cent of your time worrying about your management and how they are going to see it, rather than worrying about the opposition, which is very sad. I found this to be true in South Africa. All I needed was the backing from the management, for them to say, 'Go get 'em, let's do 'em again.' But that wasn't the case. How could I operate when management turned around and said, 'This guy is no good, this guy is out'? I said, 'What have I done here, what is going on?' It was so embarrassing for me, but at the end of the day, all these things had been going around and talked about in the press and things like that.

As I said, it was the lowest time in my life in cricket, it was very very hard, it was so difficult just to pick myself up. It was kind of hard to describe. I was walking tall, but to be honest I didn't see myself as any higher than the soles of my feet, I felt as if I was looking down on myself all the while, and it was very difficult, very hard to lift myself. It didn't matter what I tried to do, it didn't matter that the other guys were saying, 'Come on, let's do it.' It was so difficult, I was isolated in a way, away from my family in South Africa. I must admit, going to South Africa as a first tour since, since the last English tour was cancelled, I was really worried anyway. I said, 'Look, the last tour was cancelled because of this colour thing. You only need one idiot in the crowd who wants to make an example of me.' In South Africa people carry guns around. A lot of the times I stayed in my room after the game because you only need one idiot, who wants the system to continue the way it is, just to come and say, 'Bang, there you are.' All they had to do was just blow me away, so all these things were in the back of my mind. There was just nobody to talk to. It was very scary to have left here and gone on the tour and tried to do a bit of work to build up for the three weeks prior to going on tour. Even after the tour, getting back here, I thought to myself, 'I've got a couple of months to get over it and get on with my cricket.' Until this day, at times I'm still having nightmares about it. I didn't realize that it had stuck in my mind so much. I now reckon that it will take a long, long time to clear up, it affected me terribly. Let me tell you how much it affected me. I hadn't played against a university side for a long while so I decided, 'OK, I'd better have a game against a university side just to see how I do.' And it was like playing a test match – I was actually scared to go out there and play. I was petrified, my first game after I got back from South Africa. I promise I was petrified to play against the university boys, and that is what South Africa did to me.

Did you think that there was anything in what the management was saying about trying to change your style?

The same action or coaching technique that was given to me was given to Darren Gough. Darren Gough tried this action and said, 'This isn't working for me, I can't do it. I need to bowl the way I bowl if you want me to bowl quick,' and in two minutes they said, 'You can bowl the way you do.' Yet for some reason I was told I had to do that. It's my willingness to learn and to go with what the management said that has caused me this problem. All this shouldn't have been known, it was something that was between me and the management. 'OK, give it a go, if it doesn't work no one will know and you can get back on to your own thing.' What complicated things even more was that I had a serious injury – I had an operation on my right knee. The problem was that I reckon the coach didn't have much idea because I got up from an anaesthetic on Wednesday and that afternoon I got a call from the coach. He didn't ask how I was. He said, 'When are we going to do this new bowling action? When are we going to bowl?' I said, 'Look, I can't move my leg, I'm still in bed, I've only just woken up from the anaesthetic. I've just had my first drink of water.' It wasn't, 'How are you?' it was, 'When are we going to try this new action?' But I said, 'OK, I'll try and do that.' I said to the coach, 'Look, have you ever had an injury?' He said, 'No.' He had probably forgotten, that is how long he'd been out of the game. He had never had an injury. He said, 'Have you had an operation?' and I said, 'Look, my knee is OK, but it could be something psychological. Look I have got to learn to do what I did before, that is, to bowl the way I used to bowl and after that I can practise this.'

Just before all this happened, when you met Nelson Mandela in South Africa, what did Mandela say to you?

Looking back, the real problem started the day after this. All those guys were there playing cricket, and no one knew the President was going to turn up, because of security reasons. There I was, running in to bowl, and all of a sudden the umpire put his hand up, we all started looking round. People were going 'woo' – you know the noise they make – and the President was there. We handed the ball to the umpire and we lined up. President Mandela met everybody and came to me and said, 'Nice to meet you, I know you're here to destroy us, you demolished us last time.' That was in Soweto, and as a matter of fact I shouldn't have played at that stage because I was still doing rehab. I was scheduled to play the game after that. But because of the importance of the game, the first ever first class game played in Soweto, in the township, the South African management asked my own management, 'Look, we would like Devon to play.' So I had to speed up my rehab just to be ready for that game. I wasn't ready, I must admit that, but I said, 'OK, I'll have to grit my teeth and go through whatever discomfort I'm feeling to play through this game.' Because it was a special request from both managements. It's my willingness to please and my belief in helping, but the real problem started the day after I met the President. We went to a press conference and met the President. He said a few words, and I said, 'Yes, it's obviously a great cause here and we will try to help the United Cricket Board as much as we can, but we are to beat South Africa in the test match series – that is what we have come here for.' That went around, and it was said that I was coy and that is probably what got up their nose. Contrary to what they were saying, I wasn't trying to be an ambassador for anyone. I was there as a professional cricketer because I like playing cricket, and if I can influence or help any kids or anybody in the townships, Black or white, I don't mind. As I said, you talk about cricket and that is probably the easiest way of teaching a young guy to read and count.

Do you have any theory for why management should be offended by that?

I don't know, but it was the following day when the real problem started. I was dropped from the game and sent an hour and a half away. It took quite a long while there, then I was batting and bowling for two hours and driving back and finishing bowling again. The physio was monitoring my leg, because I'd come back to playing early, and it was the first hard work I'd done on it and he had to put a bit of ice on it. Pulling out of the game too prematurely in both tours, I came back, and all of a sudden my knee got into real problems because I shouldn't have done that. It should have been monitored – ice and all that business – and my knee really started to play up.

You were talking about this sense of isolation in South Africa. Did you feel that was not just between you and the management but did you feel some isolation from the other players? Did you feel they supported you?

They supported me to a large extent, but they could only support me behind closed doors because of the way the management was. I was told that I was a nonentity and things like that. What can you do? The management made me actually feel embarrassed to be with my own team mates. I was totally isolated. I feel totally isolated from management and from my fellow team mates. As much as we have a beer and a chat together, deep in my heart, I was there but I said, 'Bloody hell fire, what's happening here? I'm here but I'm really not here.' It was very difficult at that stage to motivate myself. You are there in body, but boy, it is very difficult.

When you were so low you came out with a graphic image of how your ego had descended to the floor. How did you pick yourself back up again?

It was very difficult, it wasn't easy at all. Just talking to people helped, and I realized that all that energy I was using feeling bad, I had to try and turn around because if I had continued that way I would have sunk really deep.

Was there anyone who helped you? What about your wife?

Yes, my wife is a tower of strength. How would I have got through this without her? It was probably more difficult for her. She knows that wasn't me at all, it was very difficult for her, very difficult indeed. As I said, she was a tower of strength and for her to come through that – at least she was there when I was going through that. I could try and cope as much as possible but when she was away from it, having the kids to worry about ... as you can imagine it was extremely difficult. But eventually I pulled myself through it.

December 1996

KELLY HOLMES

There is one image from the 1996 Olympic Games in Atlanta that will stay with people for a very long time to come. And that is of Kelly Holmes, running in the final of the 1500 metres, when most people thought she was reckless to even attempt it. She was obviously struggling with an injury, but went ahead regardless. She trailed home in eleventh place. But why? What drives an athlete to push themselves in this way? What psychological forces compel athletes to push themselves beyond the limit? We met in her home town of Tunbridge in Kent, to talk about the disappointments of the summer and the psychological factors that drove her on against all the odds, in that fateful 1500-metre final. She described what it had been like for her.

I had a course of injections in my leg, over the whole of the Olympics. Coming into the final, I'd had my last injection and it actually hit a nerve in the lower part of my leg. It was like when you go to the dentist and you feel that numbness, that is how my foot was. So I think within that half hour of having the injection and me going out to the stadium, I changed my whole race pattern because I knew I couldn't sprint off my leg. The whole of the 1500-metre final was a nightmare, not just the last 200 metres. But obviously in the last 200 metres I just didn't have anything left. I think I'd had, maybe, one race too many. It's not just the physical side of it, it's the mental side of it too – you know, having knocks all the time and even that late in time, just having something else go wrong. It's just like, 'Oh God, here we go.' So it's one to forget really.

So, you literally had very little feeling from your leg.

Yes. There was just numbness, just like having a plate of steak slapping on the ground. That's just how it felt, I just really couldn't feel my foot at all. I obviously didn't feel any pain from it.

So, did it feel very strange even walking out with a leg like that?

Yes. I was hoping that it was going to ease off a bit, because I hadn't really felt like that before. It was the first time, after the injections, that I had felt that and it had actually hit a nerve. It was a risk that I was taking, it was no one else's fault. It was just a risk and it happened to be before the final, when I thought I could get a medal.

You obviously had quite a few injections, over those few days.

About four.

The British team doctor has said about you, 'I've never known a braver girl.' Did you feel brave at the time?

Not brave, it was just something I wanted to do. I had trained for it for four years since I've been back into athletics. I've wanted it since I was fourteen, for twelve years. I wasn't going to turn round and say, 'Well that's it, I'm injured, I'll give it up.' I still believed that I could get a medal.

When you came back from the Olympics, did you think, 'Goodness me, that was a bit reckless'? How did you feel about it afterwards? Did you feel that you were taking a lot of risks?

My spikes were in the bin, I wasn't going to do it any more! No, I'm glad I did what I did, and I would have done it again. At the end of the day, I felt that I was capable of getting a medal. I wasn't going to throw away that opportunity. I missed the bronze by a tenth of a second, I could have been on the other side of that tenth of a second and everybody would have been saying, 'Oh brilliant, you've done well to carry on.' But now, some people might be saying, 'You're stupid for carrying on.' But that's up to them. I did what I felt was best, and at the end of the day, I've got to two Olympic finals. Not a lot of people can say that.

Did you ever have doubts beforehand?

The only time that I had doubts about carrying on, was in the semi-final of the 1500 metres. My leg was pretty sore, and I had an injection which didn't really ease the pain. I was in tears after the injection. I was trying to prepare for the race and I was breaking down in tears, saying, 'Oh God, I can't carry on, my leg,' and all this sort of stuff. But everyone was really supportive, and then I just thought, 'Well I've got this far, I've got to carry on.' So, I wiped away the tears and got on the bus, and then I won the semi-final. So, it was like, 'If I can do that after I was so low …' It's more emotional than anything, because I was thinking, 'God, all that training I've done,' and I was at my fittest I've ever been. Suddenly, to have this blow, it wasn't just the blow. I'd had a lot of problems throughout the whole of the year, and I'd fought them off. I'd been ill and I'd been in hospital. I'd always come back and I actually got to the Olympics. However, maybe in January or February this year I thought I wasn't even going to get there, because I'd had so many problems.

I was surprised when I read all this stuff about you. You'd had a whole host of problems in the winter before the Olympics.

Yes, I had a lot of problems. I had my tonsils out in December, I had another operation for a cyst on the ovary. So, I was in and out of hospital, and then you have the rehab and you're completely unfit because you've been off for a couple of months. I'd been off for about two and a half months in total, after last season.

Did the determination build up during that period because you thought, 'My goodness me, I'm not going to make it to the Olympics anyway'? Did you have to fight your way through that?

It's the hardest year I've ever had for motivation and determination. I've always been a really determined and positive person, but I was very, very negative because I kept thinking everything was going wrong. So, I was trying to cope with all my negative thoughts, trying to make them positive but getting knocked down at the same time. It was very hard.

As a psychologist, I have to say, I am interested in how you actually coped with your negative thoughts. Do you have any special strategies that you use?

Not really. I think it's just the fact that I want to do well. I always think that it's the championships at such and such a time. It's like, say in December, when I was thinking I've got so many more months, and then it'll be OK. Then it came to January and I still had so many months. Then it got to February, then June and I was thinking, 'Oh my God, I've got two more months and I'm not ready for it.' To be honest, about three times this year, I've thought, 'That's it, I can't do it anymore,' because I was just going through so much, so many emotional setbacks. I was just getting on top of myself, and then another thing got bad, then getting on top of myself again and getting knocked down again. I think that it was because it was Olympic year, it's something that I have always dreamed of, and I'd finally got there and everything was going wrong. Trying to cope with all that and thinking, 'God, I'm not even going to get to the Olympics and I've worked for it for so long.' That was hard to overcome, but I think that it was just the fact that I believed I was good enough to get a medal, after last year. I wanted to get to the Olympics, so I just kept going.

Could I go back to your childhood. Have you always been this determined as an individual?

Yes, I think so. My mother says I have been anyway. My mother keeps telling me to slow down, she can't cope with me. Yes, I've always been determined to do well in everything that I've gone for. I've always set myself realistic targets, and I go out there to try to achieve them.

Have you succeeded in other domains, as well as athletics?

Yes, the army. At fourteen years old I wanted two things in life – one was to join the army and the other was to get to the Olympics. I was so determined to get into the army that at fifteen I went there. They said, 'You're too young. Come back again when you're seventeen and three-quarters. I went back at sixteen, and they said 'No, it's seventeen.' And then I actually went back and I got in the army. I got in just before my eighteenth birthday.

Could I ask you what it was about the army that attracted you?

It's just a completely different way of life, something that I could do for myself. I was determined that I would fulfil that part of my dream. I thought it was a challenge, meeting different people, doing different things, things that people would never dream of doing. The situations you come across in the army, it was just all a challenge to me. I love different things, I love attempting to do things and getting things out of myself that I thought that I could never do.

Did you have any family background in the army?

No, no member of my family is in the army, no one is involved with sport. I must be the milkman's daughter! But I've always wanted to be my own person, I've always wanted to achieve things. Like I say, I set myself dreams.

It wasn't that you were all part of a girl gang who said let's all join the army today?

No. I was a Girl Guide and I was a Brownie. Shame! I was into all that sort of thing, I just loved the outdoors, I did my Duke of Edinburgh award at school. I just missed my gold medal because I left school, I didn't carry on. I just like the outdoors, and I love outdoor pursuits.

It was the physical challenge of the army that appealed to you?

Yes. I mean, I wanted to be a physical training instructor, that was my main objective. It was the assault courses that excited me. I just wanted to see what I could get out of myself, and I became a physical training instructor two years after joining the army.

Was it as tough as you expected?

I quite enjoyed the basic training actually. Basic training for us then was just the Women's Royal Army Corps. So it was all female, whereas now it's amalgamated, men and women. I think that the situation was that everybody was in exactly the same boat. You were there to help people and you obviously weren't good at everything. I wasn't any good at buffing shoes or ironing, but I was good at running. So, I would take them out training and they used to do my shoes and my shirts! No one knows that by the way. It was a good laugh. It is tough, because I wanted to be the best and they're not just going to take anybody off the street. At the end of the day, they're training you for a role, they're training you for fighting. I fight on the track, they obviously train you for a role and it's very disciplined. I really enjoyed it, it is hard, but it's as hard as you make it.

I've also read somewhere that in terms of the army you like competing against men.

Yes. As a physical training instructor, I was in charge of a gymnasium at Beaconsfield, it was an officer recruiting place. They were all ex-soldiers who wanted to become officers, and there were maybe thirty or thirty-five guys in a platoon. I was in charge of them, and I always used to set them targets. In fact, the first time I took the first group of guys, there was me, a five foot four corporal, with all these guys there. You can imagine what that was like, me shouting at them and they took no notice whatsoever. So this one time I'd just had enough. So I said, 'There is this cross-country course that we are going to go on, it's four miles long and it's very, very hilly, very muddy, in and out of woods, everything.' And I said to them, 'OK tomorrow morning at half past six, we will go out for this run and anybody who comes in behind me comes back to the gym at half past five tonight and so on every day. Half past six in the morning for the run, half past five at the gym if I beat you back.' And they were saying, 'Oh yeah, yeah, yeah.' I said to them 'Anybody who beats me in doesn't have to come to PT for a week.' So I thought, 'Oh, God.' So everybody set off on this cross-country race. I beat every single one of these guys and from that day on they just respected everything that I said because I used to set them things to do, but I also used to demonstrate them beforehand. I never used to set them anything that I couldn't do myself, and I always made sure that it was of a high standard. After that day, they just respected everything that I did and didn't treat me like a woman that was just gobbing off because I had stripes and crossed swords on me. It was the fact that I could do what I was trained to do, and what I was passing down to them I was passing it to them for a reason.

So was it a fairly tough race with these guys or were they all pretty poor?

Oh no, they had to be good because they were going for officer cadets. So at the end of the day they have got to be at a fair fitness level to get in. I was quite chuffed. It happened for the next three courses, I think, and I wasn't even back in training properly, so I was quite chuffed.

Was this one of your strong motivations to get back into athletics?

I think so. I was just about on a turn around then because it was just before the World Championships in 1993. I had just started training at the end of 1992, so I was obviously back in and motivated. I used it as part of my training as well.

Can I ask you about women's middle-distance running? You said that it's like fighting. Can I ask you which is the more aggressive race, the 800 or the 1500 metres?

I think that they are completely different races. The 1500 is very tactical, and championship races tend to be quite slow because everybody is watching each other. No one wants to make the break because it might be too early, so it's very tactical and I think that is what takes the energy out of you. The fact that you're thinking all the time, and you're trying to dodge people and stay up on your own two feet, as well as place yourself and run at that speed. The 800 is just like a sprint, it's just flat out sprinting. I like the 800 because I feel you have got to be very strong, you have got to be fast, you have got to have endurance. You've got to have every aspect of racing within that event, and that is why I like it. It's another challenge really to beat all those girls. To think that the top eight in the world are most probably within a second of each other. This is just a click of the fingers, isn't it?

Is the 1500 metres more psychological then?

In a way, because the race is more tactical, but all races are very psychological anyway. Eighty per cent of your performance is how your head says you are going to do, it's not just the physical aspect. Obviously you've got to be one hundred per cent physically fit, but psychologically you have got to have belief in yourself. I think that it's very important in every event, not just the 1500 or 800 metres.

Presumably in the 1500 metres, when you say competitors are watching each other, they are looking for signs from each other. You're trying to look for signs of how strong they feel on the day and looking for signs of when they are going to go and so on.

That's right. You get to know about your competitors anyway, and I watch a lot of videos of my competitors to see how they are running and to see what their tactics are. Every race is different, so you have got to have completely different formats in your head. I'll go with a semi-race plan depending on the event, but most of the time it's just how the race goes. You're watching people all the time and just trying to stay on your own two feet. It's that part of the racing that I do like, getting in there and just having one up on the other competitors.

I suppose that the thing again that really intrigues me, as a psychologist, is that when you are in a middle of a race with all the adrenalin flowing, are these people all like blurs or something or do you actually see their faces? Are you reading their faces, do you get any information from their faces?

They're blurs until they elbow you! I race pretty much focused on how I want to run my race. These people are obstacles as far as I am concerned, but you've got to be aware of how good that obstacle really is. So you don't really see their faces as such and think, 'Oh they're tired, let's go.' You can tell, but at a world-class level, you have got to expect that everyone is capable of winning, so it is how you are going to be one up on those people.

Presumably, if you're watching stride pattern or something, are there any of the set of world-class competitors that are prone to be more misleading than others? What is Svetlana Masterkova like, for example?

No comment! Do I have to answer that one?

I'm just really intrigued about the similarities and differences between some of these great runners.

Masterkova hasn't really been out on the scene. It is the first time that I have come across her this year, so as a racer I am not really sure what she is like.

Was she a big shock in the Olympics then?

Yes – this whole year, really. She is strong, she is very strong, and she has got a very good finish on her. I feel she was very strong throughout the whole of the race anyway. I couldn't really pick out a point that she was noticeably strongest at, she's just a pretty strong person all round. That's it really.

Could I ask you what you think about Hassiba Boulmerka?

Boulmerka, she's obviously very talented. She has been around for a long time in the 1500 metres. She does look at her competitors, and she does see how they feel. I don't like the way she races, she is a messy racer and she likes catching people out. She is the kind of person who, when she overtakes you, doesn't overtake you to go, she overtakes you to slow you down, to cut you up and things like that. That is how she races, and that is just her tactics, you can't really fault the way she races because she does very well. She is the kind of person who does try psychologically to undermine your effort and your performance on the day. She is a person to watch out for because you never know what she is going to do, and I would say, most probably out of everybody, she is one of the people you don't really know how she is going to race. Maria Mutola is a person I respect very much. She is very, very strong all round, and at the end of the day, if we are to beat her, then we have to be so much stronger than her. I don't think that she is so outstanding that she can't be beaten. She is a very, very strong competitor, and she tends to push on the pace on the last 200 metres of an 800-metre race. A lot of people slow down in that phase, so that is where her strengths are, and that's a case of us trying to adapt our race pattern to be like hers, if we are going to beat her. She is a person that I really respect.

Is there any kind of psychological psyching out that goes on before the race starts? What runs through your mind before you line up?

You're pretty nervous actually before your race, so you are trying to focus on what you're doing, like your warm-up and your main preparation. You're trying to go through the routine that you have set – you always have a routine. You're stretching and getting to the track and everything, but you're always running past someone that you're going to be racing against. You're thinking, 'Just keep focusing,' but it always goes slightly off and I think, 'I wonder how they are going to run?' You are always looking around, because somebody on that day could just be a lot better than the other, or the person that you thought was favourite could have a bad day. You're always thinking, 'They are going to win' or 'I've got to beat that one person.' And then suddenly, in the race, they are at the back and your whole focus changes. Preparation is pretty nerve-racking. Actually, until you get on to that track and that gun goes, it's a horrible feeling. You get adrenalin and nerves mixed in together. It's not a nice feeling.

As someone who just enjoys watching middle-distance running, the thing that always strikes me is how the actual race often deviates from the script. You must have to go into a race with many different scripts in mind because you keep thinking, 'There are so many things that can happen.'

Yes. In a race you've got an idea of how a race is going to go because of the competitors that are in that race. You go into the race with a few options yourself. Like I feel I'm going to go at the bell, and once you set that target you have to go for it. If the race completely changes, where there is a lot of barging and pushing and something happens that you don't really expect, then obviously you have got to change your plans from there.

Could I ask you about your childhood again. Did you have any really big athletics heroes when you were growing up?

Mary Decker-Slaney, I was her biggest fan.

Was there anything in particular about her?

It was just the way she ran, she was very positive in the way she ran. She used to win everything and I thought that I wanted to be like that. Then there was Zola Budd and the confrontation between the two in the 1984 Olympics. That was the one that really stuck in my mind because of what happened there. The way that I thought Mary

Decker-Slaney was going to win and obviously Zola Budd was there as well, and I thought that it was going to be a big, big race and it just all went to pot. I suppose that was when she started going down hill, but up until then she was my greatest hero because of the way she performed. She always had something better than the others. She was very positive in the way that she was.

If I can remember correctly, she had quite an emotional reaction to the trip. Was she still your hero when she broke down like that afterwards, because my image is of this woman, who was very strong, and then suddenly she didn't look very strong any longer?

Oh yes, obviously. After that you change your attitude to different people, and a different person becomes your hero. I was obviously into Seb Coe. He was an outstanding runner. He was a great 800- and 1500-metre runner, and he was someone I have looked up to and I wish that I could be as talented as he was, and achieve what he has achieved. It was just amazing.

Was there anything about Coe's psychological profile that appealed to you rather than Ovett or Cram or anybody else? Was there anything about Coe, apart from the fact that he did win a lot of races?

I think that he was just a completely different athlete to Ovett and Cram. He was very positive, and he knew his race plan all the time. He was very good at tactics. He was very strong, very fast, and he could adjust to any situation within a race. I think him just having that confidence and his way of racing just stuck out in my mind. He was very good.

Ann Packer has commented on your mental toughness. Do you see yourself as mentally tough?

I believe that I'm a positive person and I think that is the way to be in athletics. I always run for medals – I run to win. I believe I am very strong-minded, or so a lot of people tell me, but I think that it's just the fact that I enjoy success. And I want those medals, and the money's good and records are there to be broken. But you've got medals for the rest of your life, and that is what I perform for and what I train for.

What is so special about medals?

They are there, they are an achievement. It means that I have done it, and nobody can ever take that away from me.

It is interesting, because in one sense the images of you at the Olympics will stand in the mind longer than if you had won the bronze and didn't have to fight through that adversity. That is why I was asking the question about what really are medals, because if you are interested in long-term effects, you could argue, in some sense, that you have already done that. You have shown something about the human character that the easy winning of the medal might not have shown.

That's right. Since I have come back from the Olympics I have had so much more recognition than I would have had for coming back with two medals. Like you say, this has stuck in people's minds and I suppose, in a way, that is really great. It has shown to me that the people have supported me in my athletics, regardless of whether I get medals, just because of the person that I am. That inspires me, and really that is why I want to come back next year. I have always wanted to do things for myself, which I think is ultimately the first priority anyway, because that is how you are going to succeed. Well, that is what I want to do, but now I've thought of all those people who have supported me through the athletics, all those letters I have got since I have come back, fan letters, people just saying how much I have inspired them to move on to something else or coax them into training or just get them to do something else in their life. I suppose I want to repay those thanks and come back next year and definitely get a medal and say, 'Look, I told you I could do it and thank you.'

Does it become a big responsibility, then? You know, if you feel people are looking up to you because you're pushing through this pain barrier?

You certainly can't take anything easy – that is, I suppose, one downside. No, it's nice, because I suppose that is what in the back of your mind keeps you going. I want to succeed anyway, like I said, I want to get medals. That is my motivation, that is my drive. But to strengthen that, is the fact that there are so many people out there watching me. When I set foot on that track I have to perform well just to bring back that pleasure to those people who are supporting me.

Do you see yourself as a role model and if so, for whom?

I like to think that I am a role model for kids. To say that I have achieved at both a career and had success in athletics and not because I am any bit more special than anyone else, but just that I have worked hard for what I have got. Yes, I've got a certain degree of natural ability, but natural ability only lasts so long and then you have got to start building on that. So, I hope that I pass on my knowledge from both my army career and the athletics and guide kids in the right direction. Also for women, I hope that they see me as somebody who goes out there and tries against adversity and never wants to be defeated. I hope that I can be a role model for both sets of people.

Is it difficult trying to balance two careers in the army and athletics? Do you think one is a safeguard for the other one because an athletics career can't go on for ever?

In a way. I wanted a career out of the army, and that is why I gave up athletics when I first joined the army. The army has been very supportive of me for the last couple of years, since I've been back into sport. It is very hard for anybody who wants to get to the top of sport to cope with two careers and become successful at both. When I first came back into athletics I was trying to be successful at both, I wanted to put one hundred per cent into my job and then I wanted to come back and be the world's best at athletics. There is only so much that you can do, and I suppose over the past couple of years the army have seen my potential as an athlete and they have given me the flexibility to be able to train. Like I say, since the age of seventeen there has been an income going into my bank and I suppose, in a way, that has enabled me to relax. A lot of athletes don't get money, they haven't got jobs, they don't get a lot through racing sponsorship and it's stressful. If you can't cope with your own personal life plus you have got to pay out for stuff to do with athletics, then it is a very stressful time for any sports person. In a way that has been good for me because I haven't had that worry and I have been able to carry on with my athletics and just get on with what I am doing. As for the army, I think in a way it has been good for me to have both those careers because the army has kept me very disciplined in myself and it's enabled me to get the best out of my life. It has taught me a lot. The army has made me grow up; it's given me confidence; it's given me respect for other people; and I think that is what you need for athletics. They both complement each other and I think both these careers are very valuable to me.

I've been reading this story about you doing some white water rafting. Was this some training programme for the army?

I went canoeing in Nottingham. They have got the white water rafting and a big set-up down there where they have the world championships, and I was part of the army youth team at the time. We had to be instructors in canoeing, abseiling, rock climbing and everything. Part of our team training was to go up and do this canoeing, so I said, 'I'll go canoeing', thinking it was going to be still water. It started off in the morning as still water, and I was quite OK with that, and then they said, 'Right, we have to go down the white water.' I thought, 'I can't do that.' But I didn't want them to know that because I was with a team of seven guys at the time. There was myself and seven other guys and, like I say, I always want to be the best and think that I am not going to be defeated. We got into these canoes and they are facing this white water rafting course, this slalom course with the poles hanging down. Three of the guys bottled out and I thought, 'Why are they going?' And they are saying, 'We'll do it later.' All these other guys go, and there is this one guy behind me and I said, 'Just stay with me.' I got down to the first stopper, which is the white water that you see churning, and I got over the first stopper, I was quite chuffed with myself. I was so chuffed with myself that I forgot what I was doing next and my canoe turned side on and I capsized. I don't like water anyway, I hate water, I only started swimming when I joined the army. So, I capsized, and I had to get out off the canoe. The thing that they told you to do was to hold on to the canoe and hold on to the paddles, well forget the canoe and the paddles – that was gone. I wasn't worried about that, I was being ducked under and spat out 20 metres down this river and I thought I was going to drown, literally drown. They have these poles hanging down and I was holding on to these poles with my legs dangling down the river and no one could help me. I was getting taken by the river and completely spat out. It was a horrible feeling, the worst feeling I've ever had, I really thought I was going to drown! One of my nightmares is drowning and I really thought that I was going to drown then. I had the major championships coming up, I think that was 1994, and I had the European Championship and the Commonwealth Games coming up that year. It was lucky that my coach didn't know this, all I could think was, 'My legs are going to be broken and everything.' I could imagine myself just coming out at the end a complete wreck, but I've never ever done it again. It was the worst moment of my life in water. But I still won the gold at the Commonwealth and the silver at the Europeans.

That is an extraordinary story because I've always had this image of athletes being very cautious people about their bodies and the risks they take. There are all kinds of things they simply won't do because of the possibility of injury.

I suppose that it happened because it was my first proper year back into athletics and I was still sort of army barmy, green and wanting to have another challenge and to do different things. The thing is, because I was with that team of guys and I was getting time off to go to my races, they were doing training, which was essential to my job. I wasn't going to miss that because I would get stick, 'Oh, all you're interested in is your athletics,' and I didn't want that sort of name on me – you know, that I was only interested in athletics and that I only turned up when they really needed me. I thought, 'Right, I'll prove to you that I can do whatever you do.' It was actually a week up at Nottingham, so I went there and this day it was canoeing, and I thought, 'Oh God.' I didn't want to do it, believe me I didn't want to do it, but I thought I've got to do it! I was quite chuffed at the end because these three guys, who bottled out at the top, never ever went down in the end. So I was really chuffed.

They never did it?

No, so they got some stick! In fact, I met up with one of them a couple of weeks ago and I still give him stick because he never did it. So yes, I was proud of myself more than anything that I did it. I mean, I'd never do it again. It was just horrible, really awful. I was proud that I did it. It's something else that I can say, 'Yes, I did it' and 'Done that.'

Is it fairly lonely being an athlete?

It can be, yes, especially this year because I've had so many things to overcome. It is a lonely time and it is only you who can achieve those things. You get support from your friends, your family, your coaches – there is everyone there to support you and to guide you in the right direction – but at the end of the day, it's me that has got to get on that track and it's me that has got to perform and win those races. It is lonely in the respect that you go out in the cold and the wet and the wind and everything, and all those horrible things about training, but in my mind I think, 'Well, I've got to do it, if I want to get those medals.' I don't really have a social life as such. All the mates that you used to go out with go to the bar all night and go to night-clubs, and, yes, you could do that, but I am pretty determined to do well in athletics and I'm pretty focused. I'm happy with what I do and I've got a close family. It can be lonely sometimes. I take my dog out for a run with me. No one else likes coming for a run with me, it might be all right if I had someone to chat to! It's a lonely life, but it has its ups, its bonuses and performing at the world's best level and, like I say, getting those medals.

When you say you have no social life, do you have to go to bed at a certain time each night? I'm just trying to work out how severe this actually is.

In the summer, when you are competing, you do have to think about your rest and your nutrition and things like that. You have got to be disciplined in what you do, and I'm bad in that respect in that I don't get enough sleep and I eat the wrong food and all this sort of stuff. I've sorted out my life now. I've seen a nutritionist. I've sorted out fitness training. I've sorted out a masseur. I've sorted out a lot of different things that I think are going to make me go on to a higher level next year. I feel that I have got to be one of the world's best. My aim is to be the best runner in the world and I am nowhere near that at the moment. I feel that if I stay how I am at the moment I am going to plateau in my sport, and I don't want to do that because I want to go on to be better next year and come back with another medal. So I have had a lot of things that have been changed in my life. People don't realize that even at the top level, the standard I'm at now, there are still things that I have got to change in my life to improve even more. They are, like I say, the rest and the nutritional advice, and I have taken that all on board and next year I'm going to come back storming.

Could you just give me a feeling for what goes through your mind on a wet night in Tunbridge, when the rain is pelting down? You are about to go for a run, you've got the dog, you've just put the lead on, the two of you are about to go through that door? Tell me what's in your head, just as you go out of the door into the wind and rain.

'Here we go again, I don't want to do this.' Everything goes into your head but, like I say, at the end of it there is always the plus and the satisfaction that you have achieved something. It's not what you do a week or a month before those medals, it's what you do all that time, a year before, two years before. All that build-up and all those things you learn about yourself and all the different types of training that you do – that is what makes you a successful person. So you just think, 'I'll just go out for this one and maybe in thirty minutes' time I'll be in the bath, in the warm.' So you just go out and do it. It does de-motivate you sometimes, and there are times when you think, 'I really don't want to do this.' But you have to think of the future and why you're doing it. I'm pretty lucky in terms of the fact that I have got medals and I am capable of getting medals and I have got the ability to get medals. There are a lot of people there in all sports who put in exactly the same work as me, they have the dedication, the motivation and the discipline and they are unfortunate in not getting medals. You think of them, some should be even more respected than I am. I'm capable of getting medals, I've got that ability to get medals, and I work on that ability, but there are people who put in as much as me and I respect them for that. They have got a lot of drive and obviously they never get recognized, but they must be very disciplined as well.

If you've just won a medal, who would be the first person you'd ring to tell them the good news?

My mum. I would ring my mum first, obviously, because she would kill me if I didn't. My coach is normally with me so that is OK, but yes, I phone my mum. In fact, when I won my silver medal at the European Championships they let me sit on the staging outside on one of the BBC phones, phoning my mother. She's screaming down the phone. So I always phone my mum because she's really proud of me and she was the first person who took me into athletics. Everybody else gets a phone call later on.

I read that your mum first took you to an athletics track when you were twelve. Is that right?

Yes, that's right. I had my first race at my local school in

Tunbridge, I did a cross-country race. I came second. One of my PE teachers said, 'I think you should get down to one of the athletics tracks,' and my mum took me down to Tunbridge AC. I met my coach, Dave Arnold, who is my coach now, and started training from there. I started training when I was twelve and I got to English Schools in my first year as a thirteen-year-old and I won it.

Was your mum quite keen on helping you develop an athletics career?

Yes, she was. I would have tried anything, and I think that's really important for youngsters these days, to try everything. It's something that I was good at and that I enjoyed and that's why I carried on. She gave me the support, but she never ever pushed me and I think that's very important – that parents don't push an athlete. I think that is why I carried on, because I enjoyed it and I wanted to go down training and I was self-motivated to train. I think that is why I have been successful. She wanted me to do my best, and she thought that I could get rid of some of my energy doing it.

You had too much energy as a child?

Yes.

You haven't mentioned your father.

I don't live with my father, I haven't done since I was, I don't know how old. My father, as far as I'm concerned, is my step-dad, my brother's dad. He's very supportive. In fact, my whole family always come up and watch me in, like Birmingham. I've an entourage of about twenty people who come and see me running in the UK, so that is really good.

How many brothers and sisters do you have?

I have got two sisters and three brothers.

Are they younger or older?

I've got a sister who is twenty-four; I've got a brother who is nine-teen, one who is sixteen and one who's eleven and a sister who is seven.

Are any of them interested in a career in athletics?

No, not at all. My two brothers are into football, like boys are. I don't know where I've got it from. The youngest sister, Penny, is very athletic. I think that she is going to be a dancer, she's pretty good in that respect. There is just something about her and I think that if she is coached in the right way that she could be successful at something. The others, I don't know, they're just boys and girls really. They like going out to pubs and that's it.

Are you running for your mum and the rest of your family, or are you running for yourself?

I'm running for myself firstly, to achieve those things but then, obviously, I want to please my family. Whatever I do in my life they are all very proud of me anyway. So I run for myself first, but just because they want me to win I always ring them and they are just as happy. If I've set myself up to win the gold and I come back with the silver, they know how down I'm going to be and they dread phoning because they know what I'm going to be like on the phone. It's like the World Championships last year. I was so determined to get the gold medal. I really thought that I was capable of getting the gold medal and I still believe that I was. I think that it was just lack of race experience and nerves and everything that lost me the chance of getting the gold medal. I came back with the silver medal and I was in tears on the phone to my mum, and she was saying, 'You have just won a World Championship silver, what are you on about?' She just knew as soon as I phoned that I would be in a state, so she was prepared for it and was trying to get me back on my own two feet. Everybody loves what I do because they know I go out there to win and they are all there thinking, 'She's going to win' and as soon as something goes wrong they are like, 'Oh God, she's going to phone us and she's going to go mad.'

She's going to be bad tempered?

They know what to expect.

Does it take you a few days to lift yourself after something like that?

Like I said, I came back with the World Championship silver medal and I was absolutely devastated. Everyone was saying, 'You're mad.' I suppose that was one of the hardest time I've had for coping with my emotions, as I was going from what I felt was a personal disappointment to the next day, getting back up and racing again to start off another set of races. That was really really hard and I could have blown it then because I was just not focused and not motivated. I was a bit negative. I got in as fastest loser in the 800 metres – I nearly blew it for myself. That just shows you that you have got to be so strong mentally in what you do and always believe in what you do. Otherwise you just falter. I mean I felt really tired. I'd done two minutes one, I think. I'd got fastest loser, I was really tired in that race and I couldn't believe that I had done so badly in that race and I think it was just because I was so disappointed from the day before. I picked myself up and I think what picked me up was that I saw a lot of fans in the crowd and they were all saying, 'Come on, Kel, you have done really, really well yesterday, you have got another race to go for.' The following day I won my semi-final and came back with a bronze medal. I was so happy to get a bronze medal, it was weird. I was so disappointed to get the silver medal in the 1500 and that is because I set my target. I just believe that once you set your aim and set your target and you believe you can do it, if you don't achieve it you feel that you should be disappointed because you've got nothing to go for next time. I was very, very disappointed. But for the 800 metres I just believed that I wanted to get a medal and to come back with the bronze medal I was like, 'Yes, it's a bronze medal.' It was completely different.

Would you describe yourself as an emotional person?

When it is to do with athletics and my performances then, yes. If
something goes wrong, if I've set a plan and I feel it should go along
with the plan and if something goes wrong, then, yes, I get very down
in myself. I'm emotional with my performances because I believe
that I should always do my best. But with respect to everything else, I
like to feel that I am quite sort of positive and energetic and I go for
what I want.

And in control?

Yes, in control of my life. I feel like I'm in control of what I do, as
long as you have got a good team of people to support you, then you
can do whatever you want.

January 1997

HEROL GRAHAM

In September 1992, on a cold night in Leeds, Herol 'Bomber' Graham lost his British title to Frank Grant, and soon after that he announced his retirement. Graham was the 'nearly' man of British boxing – he almost took the world title on two separate occasions, but he just missed out. But at the time of the interview, four years later, at the age of thirty-seven and after a lengthy struggle with the British Boxing Board of Control to regain his licence, he'd returned to the ring. Many critics in the fight game said this was folly of the highest order. Even his trainer said he should retire. So why was he fighting on? We met in his house in Sheffield. I asked him to reflect on his career and what he had learned from his years in the ring, and I probed him about the psychological forces that were driving him on in the face of so much opposition. I began by asking him about the fight against Frank Grant and how confident he had felt.

I wasn't confident at all, to tell you the truth. I mean, without getting into the nitty gritty of it all, something happened drastically in my family, to do with my sister. I can't tell you what because it's nothing to do with me, it concerns my sister and it's just awful. I was in the ring and I just did not want to be there. I had to look confident, I always look confident in the ring, but it was a case of 'What am I doing here?' I should be home with my sister, looking after her. That's how I felt then. Winning or losing didn't matter to me. I was just thinking about my sister.

Up to that point you'd only lost against the best in the world. How big a shock was it to lose?

It was a shock all right. It was a big shock, I must admit that. I was winning the fight anyway and it's like you're coasting along and then all of a sudden you come to a hiccup and something hits you on the back of the head, and it literally says, 'What am I doing here?' I froze in a corner, and I was thinking that I was cold and I started shivering. It wasn't a fright, but I was sort of shivering and thinking, 'I don't want to be here, I want to get out, I'm cold, I want to go home.'

Could the people in your corner sense it?

No, no way. I don't show it. I look great and I look good.

After the Frank Grant fight you announced your retirement. What was going through your mind at that time?

Going back to my sister again, for what she'd been through and what I'd been through on that night, I thought, 'I don't want it to happen again, I don't want to feel that way.' I could have won the fight but I didn't win the fight because of something that happened, something I couldn't control, and it was like controlling my inner self, it was controlling my own mind. I've always had trouble with other people's troubles.

Did you have any plans as to what you were going to do with your retirement at that point in 1992?

I wanted to be a teacher. I knew how hard it was going to be, but I still wanted to do it. I had to pass my maths and my English, and I'm bad on maths. Now I have maths lessons and I've taken English already at the Northern College.

Are these GCSEs you're taking?

Yes, yes. I'm taking them now. You know that old cliché, 'Herol, don't forget you need your O-levels and your spirit levels and all A-levels,' and I thought, 'I don't need them, I'm going to be a millionaire,' and what happens is you're not a millionaire and you need your O-levels and A-levels. So you're back to college again.

Is it tough to go back to school to try to pick it up?

It isn't tough, no, I quite like it actually. I'm like a big kid at the best of times anyway. It's fun because the teachers do help you on the access courses.

And what about your social circle when you announced your retirement? You were a big star – I mean you were one of the top boxers in the world.

It diminished, it went. You know you get your backslappers, you get your, 'I'm your best mate, I'm your friend,' and this and that and the other, but your true friends you could count them on one hand. I mean literally. There's my friend Glyn Rhodes and there's Johnny Nelson, they were still there, the rest just went.

And were these people who were associated with boxing anyway?

Yes, they were associated with boxing as well, and there's Brian – I can't forget Brian Anderson. They were still there and you know they helped me along. There were some people out of boxing as well who were still there for me, you know. There was a lot of, 'You're going to be OK. Don't worry about it. Think positive about everything you want to do,' and they gave me some good advice. I wish I had it about ten years earlier though.

But before you announced your retirement presumably you had a much wider circle of friends?

Oh yes, a much wider circle of friends, because you meet them day in and day out. When you say friends, they were acquaintances really, just people you meet now and again.

But did you think those acquaintances would be making you offers during your retirement? Did you think that because you had met a lot of people through boxing that you were going to be OK?

You think that sometimes, but it's not necessarily the case. Everybody likes a winner, and it is true what they say, that everybody needs a winner because you're always up there and you pull them along as well.

When you announced your retirement were you in a good financial state?

I was OK, I mean I wasn't brilliant, but I was OK. I was happy and that was the main thing but, of course, you need some extra pence now and again but so what, who doesn't?

Did you look after your money when you were in boxing?

That's a stupid question to ask me. *No I didn't.* No, I didn't look after it properly at all. I lent it to my friends. There are businesses I was in and I knew nothing about them, and you pretend that you do know something about them, but you don't and it's bad business and people just take you for a ride. It happens, and I was the foolish one and I was taken for a ride.

What kind of money were you making from boxing? Can I ask you what your biggest purse was?

The biggest purse was about 90,000, but I shouldn't tell you. That's all I'm going to tell you about my money situation, OK? Or else we're going to start fighting!

OK. Going back to before the Grant fight, how good a boxer were you?

I was as good as I was on my last fight, and that was against Jackson.

Could you talk about the Julian Jackson fight in 1990.

Do you really want me to talk about it?

Yes please, yes.

It was a brilliant learning fight for me, because I thought, 'I'm going to win this fight, the referee's going to stop it the next round. Great, I'm going to be the world champion.' I was counting my chickens before they had even hatched. Literally, as in 'I'm going to be champion,' then all of a sudden I stuck my chin out then *Bang*. I was out before I even touched the floor.

You were way ahead on points. Did you think that the fight was going to be stopped? Did you think that a stoppage was imminent?

Yes, because I heard the referee was going to stop it the following round, so I was, literally, just about to become the champion.

So you were that close to being world champion, and then what, just a momentary loss of concentration?

Yes, a lack of concentration for a split second, because that's all it took him. I saw him wind the shot up, and I thought, 'No surely not, you can't throw that'. Then bang, he did throw it and it came back so fast, and it just hit me on the jaw.

Psychologically how does that feel? Your whole future depending upon one second of your life.

That's why it's not that bad at all, my whole future, what's that? Future of being what? Wealthy? I'm still living and if it was a life or death situation then it would be totally different, but I'm still here and I've suffered the consequences. I wasn't world champion at that time, but there's still a chance now. There's still a chance now.

Of all the fights that you have fought which is the one you think about most?

The Grant fight really. I do think about the Grant fight. I mean, OK I do go back to the Jackson fight, I could have been world champion, but I can't dwell on anything. 'Oh dear, if only I did this, if only I did that.' You can't go 'if only, if only, if only.' 'If' is i-f, one of the smallest words and it means such a big thing. I can't keep saying 'if' all the time. I may as well go and put a noose around my neck.

But it's the Grant fight you tend to think about?

I think about that a lot, yes, because of what happened around it. Not just me losing the fight, but what happened afterwards.

All the bad things associated with it. OK. In terms of your own feelings about yourself as a boxer, how do you feel you compare to people like Nigel Benn and Chris Eubank?

Before I answer that, Eubank came down to the gym to spar with me, and that's one of the reasons we never fought, because they knew how good I was. The Benn situation – he never sparred with me but he knew how good I was and it was a case of the puncher and the boxer. It's like saying, 'Shall I do it?' 'No I'd better not. I'll keep what I've got and get some more.' Not easier fights, but fights that are easier for him, where he can have a war and he can win. I was definitely kept away from them. If I'd boxed them I think that I'd have beaten them either by stoppage or on points.

What was it like to have sparred with Eubank?

Well, the first time I sparred with Eubank I got chinned! He hit me on the chin, buff, I went down for three seconds, shot back up and I thought, 'Right that's the last time he's going to punch me or even touch me.' And that was the last time he did touch me. After that he hated being there. He literally hated it, because we sparred and I was tormenting him. At the time, I was training for the 1989 McCallum fight.

How long was this before the McCallum fight?

It was only about a week before the fight.

You came close to beating McCallum?

Yes, if I hadn't spun him round I would have got the extra point, so they say!

So you were that close again to winning a world title, you were that close.

Yes, because they took a point away from me.

And some people point out that McCallum delivered a low blow but wasn't ...

Oh no, he wasn't penalized at all for it, no.

So if he'd been penalized for that, it would have balanced out the two fouls.

Yes.

Again, can I take you back perhaps a little bit earlier in your career and your association with Brendan Ingle. Now there is Naseem Hamed, but can you just tell me a little bit about your relationship with Brendan. What was so special about him?

Well, you must remember that people tell me that I was the first boxer to do what I did up in the gym, so Brendan saw what I was doing, and he taught what I did to others because I didn't know what I was doing. I just did it.

Are you saying, Herol, that this was something that you brought naturally to Brendan's gym, this defensive boxing? Would you describe it as defensive boxing?

It's more defensive, yes, because I hate being hit.

You didn't like being hit. So was it a kind of natural skill that you'd got?

When you say natural, there is nothing natural, because you have to learn your job. So what's natural about it? I saw something and I took upon myself to teach myself how to do it.

Do you think that Naseem Hamed has got a similar style of boxing?

Naz says to me, 'Herol, of course, I got things from you. I got things from you and I turned them round to use for myself.' I said to him, 'Naz, no problem, I did that with Ali.' I saw what Ali did and I enjoyed it, and I liked looking at him because he didn't get hit. I took his style and adopted it for myself and I used it for me.

So to move now back on to your retirement, you were retired for how long before you decided that you really wanted to box again?

About a year, I think. Then I applied for my licence back.

So what prompted you to think about boxing again?

It was a case of thinking that I had something left. I said, 'Right, I've still got something left, I want to get it out.' I don't want to be coming back at the age of fifty-five saying, 'Oh, I could have done that, I should have done that, why didn't I do that?' I want to do it now. I want to get it out of my system and then if it's not there at least I will know that I've tried.

Was your pride important to you? Was it important for you to demonstrate what you could still do?

Pride, pride has got nothing to do with it really, because pride can kill you! You go out to do something that you can't really do, next thing, buff, you've gone. So it wasn't to do with pride at all. It was just something that I thought was still there.

So you were keen to box again. You applied for your licence. What happened next?

They said to me, 'Are you sure?' So I said, 'Yes of course I'm sure.' So they said, 'Well you'll have to have a medical.' So I said, 'No problem, I'll go to my doctors.' So they said, 'No, you have to go to the doctors in London.' So I went to London and had a test, a balance test, and I failed it. I failed my balance test!

What did that consist of?

It consisted of putting your hands out in front, closing your eyes and marching on the spot, and lifting your knees up quite high like a march, higher than a march really. He said that I swivelled round forty-five degrees when I was doing it. I said, 'Who else has taken these tests?' They said, 'You've taken this test because we've noticed something.' I said, 'What did you notice?' I don't know what I did, but they noticed something. I said, 'You're mad.'

Right, so there was a balance test, were there any other bits to the test as well?

There were all sorts. I've been through all sorts of tests. The psycho-metric testing is the hardest one. You'd fail it, I'm not being nasty neither, I'm just telling you, you'd fail it. You know Jonathan Rendall, *The Times* journalist, he failed it. You would definitely fail it.

What does it consist of?

It's like taking your eleven plus. They go 'two' and then they give you another number, like 'five', 'two' and 'five' is 'seven', right take away the last number they gave you, which was the 'five', so you take the 'five' away and add it to another number. They might say 'two' again, which is 'seven' again so you take the 'two' away this time and add it to another number, and you go like that all the way through.

And they actually read out all these numbers to you?

Yes, they go 'two, three, six', and then the second phase of it is a bit faster 'two, six, eight'. I'm going, 'Look I don't want to be a professor, right, all I want to do is box.' They said, 'This is what you've got to go through.' So I said, 'Why? Does everybody else do this?' They said, 'No.' So I said, 'Why just me?' They said, 'Well there's another person as well.' So I said, 'The actual same test? I bet it's not.'

Was there any reason why they were focusing on you for this test?

Well, I think that it was just a singling-out process. They wanted to single me out. That was the way it seemed to me. For what reason? OK, for a medical reason, but what is all this to do with the boxing? I can get lots of boxers, right, and say, 'OK take this test,' and they'd fail it. You can get some boxers who probably haven't been to school, so they'd fail it.

Presumably the psychometric test was trying to measure mental processes, but the point you're making is that they didn't have a baseline to compare it with. They were trying to say that your performance was significantly poorer because of your experiences in the ring, but they didn't know how good you'd be at these tests to begin with.

Yes, that's right.

How did you feel when you heard that you'd failed? Did you expect to fail?

Yes, I expected to fail because Jonathan Rendall failed.

Why did he take the test? Was it just to see how easy or difficult it was?

Yes, to see what I had to go through. He said, 'I failed it,' and I said, 'Oh, thanks for telling me.' But sometimes you have to go in with a positive attitude as well. It probably depends on what you eat on the day. Your mental ability depends on how confident you are. You have to think, 'No problem, just go for it.' And I did the second time around, I just went for it, and for some reason, not that I passed or failed, but I seemed to get through.

Did you do better the second time?

I think so, yeah, I must have done a bit better.

Because you got your licence back?

Because I got my licence back.

So you're saying it would be useful to have some psychometric measures, but what we need is a baseline for each boxer, to know whether they are getting significantly worse or not?

Yes, because everybody is an individual, everybody is different from everybody else. And they can't go from one point of view and say it's that level – what level? I might be a total idiot, and I might come in at that level.

Is there any other way of advising boxers? If you were trying to decide whether you are fit and capable of fighting, do you just look to yourself to answer that question, or do you go to some close friends, or do you go to your trainer? How does a boxer decide?

Running wise, training wise, I know my body from the time I have been boxing. Like I've got my records of my running, so I test myself on the running and if I dip or if I peak on it, I measure it from that. And then in the ring I know how I feel in the ring when I spar, who I spar with, and I know their reactions so I can tell by reactions again. So I'm looking at different angles all the time. For this fight I've just had, it was a case of I hadn't sparred with anybody significant.

And this was the Terry Ford fight. So you hadn't really done any serious fighting before that. How did you find that night?

It was hard, because of the timing. It is a timing situation, and you could be an inch and a half out. An inch and a half might not sound very much, but it's an awful lot if you're trying to knock someone out. You can't do it. It's like the commentator on the fight saying that my timing was gone. I started laughing to myself and I said to myself, 'Four years I haven't been boxing, my timing was one and a half inches out. Thank you very much.'

I think it's an interesting point you're making actually, which is that it's just small, small changes in skill that will make a boxer look very different. And what you are saying is that it is the boxer himself who knows how to get that skill exactly right, whereas the casual observer might think, 'He's just not the same guy any more.' But you might just think, 'Well hang on, it really is just an inch out, and if I'd just got that inch back I'd look like a different fighter.'

Yes, definitely.

So you won the Terry Ford fight, and you won on points. How do you feel about the win?

I felt great about the win, before I even got into the ring I knew my timing was going to be out. That was no surprise.

Were you shocked the day after the fight when your trainer Glyn Rhodes said that he thought you should retire?

In a sense yes, but the reason he said it was because he doesn't understand me. In the changing room I'm so placid. It's like if you come in to visit me, it's 'yes,' 'no,' 'I'm not sure,' 'OK are you leaving now?' And that's it. That's me normally. Glyn thought something was wrong with me. He thought that I didn't want the fight. He literally thought I didn't want the fight. If you ask him he'd say, 'I thought he didn't want the fight, he was so quiet.' He's never seen me like that before. So he made the comment, and I said, 'Glyn whatever you do, please don't make any comments without seeing me, right, because there's nothing wrong with me at all.' I wanted to fight, I was ready for the fight, I couldn't wait for the fight, but I was controlling the pressure around me. I knew I had to do well and it was pressure, which I had to contain and use in certain ways. You have to let the energies out in different ways.

Do you have any explanation as to why Brendan, your ex-trainer, thinks you should retire?

It's like someone owning the best team in the land and they want the best players, and if the best players are not there they are going to get them somehow. But if they're not going to come to you then they shouldn't be playing! Brendan said, 'He shouldn't be boxing, he wasn't like that when I had him.' Of course not – I hadn't boxed for four years. When I was near the top, he wasn't saying that then. And I can remember when Brendan said, 'No you don't retire. You can go on until you are forty, you can go on until you're forty-five. You can do this and you can do that, you keep training and you'll be all right.' Of course, while you're with him, fine; if you're not you can't do it. It's impossible. It's as if to say, 'I'm the only person who can keep you going until you're forty-five or fifty.' Look at Larry Holmes and those guys in America, they're doing it. Anybody can do it if they look after themselves.

Can I ask you how long you can go on as a boxer? You're thirty-seven now.

Thirty-seven going on twenty-eight, you know.

I mean the point about you, Herol, was that you were famous because no one could lay a hand on you, and obviously some people might say that as you get older it's going to be the speed of your reflexes, the speed of your defensive actions, which are going to go first. Does that mean that you are going to have to change your boxing style to accommodate those changes?

Sometimes yes, of course. Reflexes go, all reflexes go, but it's like saying, 'When do they go?' Do you know when they go? I can say, 'Right, OK, you train for a fight, you're quite fit anyway, come down the gym, right, put the gloves on and now hit me. Oh sorry, now try to hit me.' And like, 'Oh your reflexes haven't gone!' It was like one lad came down from London and he said, 'I thought your reflexes had gone.' I said, 'My reflexes are still there.' I was training with the kids and some adults in the gym, and I've still got my hands down, but they still weren't able to hit me.

This is something you always did, which is you stand in a ring, with your hands behind your back, or your hands down and you ask people to lay a punch on you. They can't do it. This is something you've done all your career, and this is something you still do.

Yes. Harry Mullan was watching me and he says, 'They still can't do it. And there was all this talk that your reflexes had gone, where did this come about?' It's just vindictive talk. That's all it is.

There have been stories or rumours circulating about you being knocked out in training. Are they true?

I wasn't knocked out in training; I was downed in training. The best place to be downed is in the gym training instead of in the ring by people like Julian Jackson. It happens. I mean, I can tell you a lot of people who have been chinned. Tyson's been chinned in the gym, but there's hardly any talk about that. 'Oh Bomber Graham he's been chinned, oh he's finished.' These simple people, these simple people!

Do you get angry when you hear these stories?

When you hear the stories and they don't ask you what happened, yes, there's room for anger there. And I feel sorry for them, if that's what they're going to go to. If they're going to go as low as a snake's belly, then fine, they can do, because it's like saying, 'You got knocked out, didn't you Bomber?' 'Yes, but do you know why? Do you know what happened?' 'Oh no, but the thing is you got knocked out.' 'No, I got chinned and I went down.' 'Yes, but it's like getting knocked out, isn't it?' OK then, do you want to know what happened? I went in there, and I thought that everything was OK, it wasn't. I was training and I thought that I was fit and I wasn't fit and I got chinned, right. That's the end of the story.

That's a very good point, actually, because it's almost as if someone has written a script now, isn't it? All they look for now is confirmatory evidence to back up the script, and they're not interested in understanding the details of the event any longer. They just want stuff to fit in with the broad story.

It's just like all the nasty talk. I can't be dealing with it. I think I'm more adult than that.

What was the build-up like for the Terry Ford fight? Did you find that you could get motivated again?

Yes definitely. I was motivated about four years ago. Terry Ford is not a mug, but everyone said, 'Oh, bringing a mug over from America again.' He's boxed there for the Golden Gloves in America, I found out later on. Although he was lighter than me, he still had very good credentials. Anyway, I had to beat him, whether by knock out or by points. It didn't matter. The points would do, and it happened that way. But I felt really good.

Before you went in with Terry Ford, did you have any doubts at all about what the outcome would be?

Look, in life there are doubts about everything. You don't have a day when you're not thinking about what could happen to you or your next of kin. Yes, of course, there's a doubt, but there are doubts when I walk across the road. 'Is that bus going to hit me?' You doubt yourself before you even do the thing, but then you take the doubt away and you bring the positive out, and you say to yourself, 'Right, I don't care. I'm going to win. I'm going to make myself win. I'm going to do it for me and better myself.' That's how I am, but, yes, of course you have a doubt in your mind. You always do, I think.

Do you have butterflies before you go in the ring?

If I didn't have butterflies I wouldn't be human. It just means that I was focused on the situation, I was very focused. Yes, I did have butterflies.

Again I'm fascinated psychologically by what it must feel like to literally step into the ring after a four-year gap – suddenly you're there again. What does it feel like?

'Have these people come to see me? Have they come to see me getting beaten or winning? I think most of them have come to see me win, but there might be a few who have come to see me lose. But I'm not going to lose.' And that's the way it goes.

Were you pleased with the turn-out?

Oh yes, very pleased. It was just a hundred less than a sell-out. But people were still very sceptical about it. 'I could see this happening, I could see that happening. No I don't know, it might, oh dear, I'll wait until he's had this fight and then I'll go and support him next time. If it's a good fight then I'll hear about it.'

So were you pleased that people hadn't forgotten about you?

I was very pleased. I mean, although I keep saying that I've done it for myself, I like to share it with everybody around me. But in the past it's, 'I'll do it for you, I'll do it for you, I'll do it for you,' and you're doing it for the wrong person. You've got to do it for yourself first, and then you share it with whoever wants to share it with you. But it's got to be primarily for yourself. You've got to do it for yourself. It's like maths exams at school, you've got to do them for yourself, not your mum and dad. It's you who's going to benefit from it. So I was very pleased with the turn-out, and I think that even more will come next time round.

So what's happened with you and your trainer Glyn Rhodes now?

Well I've been down the gym since then. I've been training since then.

So you still train in Glyn Rhodes's gym?

Yeah, yeah, yeah. And he's been training me. It's as if nothing's happened. We go on like nothing has happened. We're quite similar in our own ways.

So has he publicly said now that he thinks you should continue?

He hasn't publicly said anything.

So what does the future hold for you now?

The future. Let me see. Who shall we have now? We'll have another warm-up fight, first. Two more warm-up fights, I think. But whether I box abroad this time, I don't know. I will probably aim for a British championship.

And over what kind of time-frame are we talking about here?

If I can do it all in three years, then great stuff. But I don't want to go on till I'm forty-six, you know!

And after you finally retire, finally, finally retire. What kind of career might you be thinking about then?

After boxing I'd love to work in the TV world. I mean, I know that it's cut-throat, but I'd love TV presenting. I could work in Meadowhall, the big shopping centre just outside Sheffield, as they've offered me a job there. There's a TV station inside the Meadowhall complex. They go out and they film and they show it while you're having meals. It's very good, so I might do it there just to brush up on things.

So what kind of TV slot would suit you?

I think something stupid. Kiddies' programmes, because I'm stupid. Right. Because it's like this thing I have with kids, you know. They see me and they say, 'Oh, he looks funny,' and I say, 'What do you mean I look funny?' 'Oh you look funny.' I say, 'The word's fanny. I mean, oops, sorry. London accent! Sorry.' No wonder we say funny up here! Anyway, TV programmes, kids' programmes, something hilarious. It's like I went to a drama studio, and I played in this two-man busker band. And it was absolutely brilliant; we wanted to film it. I think that someone got it on one of those stupid videos, sort of thing, but it didn't come out right. I love drama. I absolutely love it, and they want me to do this production with them again as a bumble bee, but I don't want to be a bee. They had a bigger part for me, but with the boxing I couldn't concentrate on my script. But I love things like that. I love it, love it, love it, love it.

Do you ever see a long-term career in boxing training? A career in training other boxers?

Well, I help Glyn anyway, down at the gym. If he goes somewhere, then he says, 'Herol can you do this for me please?' I say, 'All right then, fine.' It's good fun watching them do something and improving. They've got to be improving, or if they don't improve they say, 'How boring.' With some children it takes a little bit of time, because the training side of it is quite easy for them but the coordination side is quite hard for children to cope with. Some children get it in a click of your fingers, with others it's a long time waiting, but it's fun watching them.

Are you a good motivator of people?

Yes. I like shouting at them. But shouting the right things to them. And the expressions on your face, they know when it's right. It's like they do something, and you shout 'yesss', and they like to hear that 'yesss' sort of thing. With the little kids in the gym, it's brilliant, you can see the smile on their face. It's like I made some skipping ropes for them out of wire and a plastic sheet. Some of them will treasure it.

When you said that you were coming back to boxing and you announced that you were going to fight Terry Ford, did your family give you any advice about whether you should or should not go ahead with it?

Yes, they gave me some advice. They said, 'Just look after yourself.' All of the family said, 'If you want to do it then do it, but look after yourself.' And they all said a prayer for me and said, 'God willing, God will be on your side.'

Could you sense any anxiety on their part?

No anxiety at all. My mum would say 'Are you sure?' and I'd say 'Yes mum' so she would say 'OK then, fine.' And when I talked to my dad I said, 'Dad, I'm going to start boxing again.' 'I told you, you was, you know.' He always thought that I was going to go back to fighting.

And if they ever said to you that they thought that you shouldn't, would you listen to them or would you go ahead anyway?

I don't know. If my mum says, 'Don't box,' I'll think, 'Why? Why are you saying that?' And if she can't explain why, then I'd probably carry on. It's something that I want to do, and I don't want to let it go past me. The future is in front of me, so either I box now and earn some money, or I don't box and I just think about earning money. Or do another job. So I think to myself, 'Oh no, I'll box instead.'

Your whole family are religious. What about yourself, are you religious in any way?

Yes I am. I read the Bible. I read from the Psalms actually, they're short passages. When I question myself, what I do sometimes is that I open the Bible, and the first page it hits at in the Psalms I'll read. And if it's to do with what I'm doing and it's saying, 'Yes carry on', then that's great stuff. Something happened to me a long time ago, I can't tell you exactly what, but I opened the Bible and I read from it. Ever since that day I always open the Bible at any page and read it. And I do read it quite regularly. I find comfort in it, believe it or not, and I've got this thing and if I have any worries, it's like, 'Why worry, when you can pray?' It doesn't give the answer to you but it relieves pressure within you. The problem doesn't disappear, you haven't solved it, but it's not a problem any more. You think, 'Well when it happens, it happens,' sort of thing. You can't do anything about it.

So are you pleased you've got this kind of bedrock of Christianity to fall back on?

Yeah. When I have trouble I look at the Bible. I just open it out. It's like a comforter to me.

I get the impression that not all of your troubles have come from boxing.

It's all around the boxing. If I didn't box, it's like saying 'OK, would I have the girlfriend I had?' It's a case of, 'Is she only around me because of the adulation you get and the media situation or would she be here because she wants to support me?' You don't know. I think that in the early years it was a case of people being there because, 'Oh he's going to be in the papers. Oh it's the high life sort of thing, the sports life sort of thing.' And now it's like you find a person who's not bothered about that at all.

Can we talk about the pressure of fame? It's a bit of a cliché, but you're really saying that it brings its own very special problems

with it. Because there are all sorts of people who just want to know you because you're in the public eye and it must be very hard trying to work out exactly what you mean to them. I mean it must be impossible, because you are that famous sports person.

Yeah, it's like the same thing when you go back the other way and they say, 'Who wants to know a nobody?'

It must be difficult to cope with the transition from one state to another, from one day being world famous to next minute being just a retired boxer.

That wasn't too bad actually, I could cope with that. It was a case of finding something else to take the place of it, and the thing that was taking the place at the time was college, going to college and taking different modules and writing down certain things, that's quite easy. The toughest thing is doing the maths and the English. That is tough.

And this is absolutely essential for you if you want a career as a teacher, you have to have maths and English. So have your psychometric tests put you off maths?

No. I know what you are saying, 'If I can't do the psychometric tests, how can I do the maths?' But I know I'll do the maths, and with English it's the same difference.

Deep inside, did those psychometric tests rock your confidence?

Yes. They do rob you of confidence, definitely. I was never good under pressure anyway, in the sense of taking examinations at school. I did brilliantly in the mock exams, but come the actual exam I was so nervous I couldn't do well. Some people love it and they go through it quite easily, others just can't accept it. And I'm one of those who are frightened by it.

Are you frightened by the prospect of GCSEs looming?

Well, I don't know. I think because I'm a mature student, I'll be able to accept it more this time. Not that I wasn't mature, but I couldn't accept the fact that if I failed, 'What do I do?' You don't want that side of it, you want to pass.

And is that kind of fear of failure pretty reminiscent of emotions in the past? With your fear of failing as a boxer, does it remind you of emotions you've felt?

No, I haven't failed in boxing. You can't fail in boxing. Even if you lose in boxing, you don't fail. It's still an achievement, and it's your own aspirations in life, you haven't failed in life at all, because you've achieved something that other people cannot do.

Is that why the psychometric test was different, because that was like saying you have failed? That was a judgement on you – it wasn't a judgement on a piece of work, it was a judgement on you.

Yes. It was a judgement on me and my boxing, because it was to do with my boxing. That's when I said, 'How can I fail? You don't know anything about me and yet you have failed me.'

Did you feel you were up against the system then?

Yes, definitely so.

A system kind of conspiring against you?

Yes. I felt it was, 'We don't want you. We're going to get you out some way, we're going to get you out.' And I fought the system and I got through the system. Whether by luck, it doesn't matter, but I got through.

So you feel you've beaten the system to get back? Just to get your licence back?

I don't want to get my own back on the British Boxing Board of Control, but it's like saying, 'I've beaten something, I've won something, I've won something.'

So anything else is a bonus now?

Yes, from now on definitely. I'm glad that they passed me and said that I could box on, because there is totally nothing wrong with me. I was doing all sorts of things, I was standing on one leg and leaning over at an angle and I said, 'Look, does this count?' They said, 'No. You've failed the balance test already.' I failed that and then I went back again and passed it, and I said, 'Once your balance has gone hasn't it gone forever?' And he couldn't answer my question. He couldn't give me an answer to that.

December 1996

GARY McALLISTER

In years to come, Euro '96, will probably be remembered most for its penalty miss – that is Gareth Southgate's fateful miss against Germany in the semi-final of the competition – but people have already started forgetting about Gary McAllister's miss against England, a miss disastrous for the Scotland squad, because England scored almost immediately after it. But how does a miss like that affect someone psychologically? Someone with such a reputation among his fellow players – the captain of Leeds, the captain of Scotland and then the captain of Coventry City. When we met in an office at the Coventry City training ground, I wanted to know how would someone who aspires to perfection on the pitch cope with such a fall from standards, such an embarrassment?

I've always been very confident taking penalties even from a young age, right through primary school, through secondary school and into boys club level. I have always been the guy who has stepped forward to take penalties. It has just been a natural progression up into professional ranks and then to go and play for my country. When I'm asked, 'Who wants to take penalties?' I have always put my hand up. That responsibility is always something that I've wanted. When we were awarded the penalty in Euro '96 at Wembley against England, I had no hesitation in grabbing the ball, putting it on the spot and taking the penalty. My decision-making that day was off. I've scored a lot more penalties than I have missed, and when a penalty is given to my team in the future I will always step forward and want to take it.

Do you have a plan of where you are going to place a kick? Is that all worked out beforehand or is it very spontaneous?

It's very much to do with the goalkeeper. You have got to know the goalkeeper. The fact that a lot of football is on the television means that you get to see a lot of penalties, and you get to see the different techniques of the goalkeepers. Dave Seaman is probably one of the best penalty-kick savers in the country, and he is always difficult to beat because of the fact that he watches a lot of penalty-kick takers himself. My thinking was that he would know where my favourite side was, so I decided to go down the middle. The only problem was that it wasn't as high as I wanted it to be. If it had have been high down the middle, or on the line that I hit the penalty, it would have been a goal.

Is the goalkeeper trying to look you in the eye to get some information from you?

Players have got different techniques. Very few players look into the goalkeeper's eyes and try to psych him out. I would say that the majority of penalty-kick takers make their decision before they hit the penalty and stick by it. The worst thing that you can do when you are hitting a penalty is to change your mind on the run-up. There are a few players who watch the goalkeeper on the run-up, but this is a very tough technique.

If you miss a penalty, how easy is it to get over it?

It was made even worse that day by the fact that England went right up the park and scored a second goal. On that day, it seemed like hours, but I imagine it was only a couple of minutes, it was difficult to get it out of my mind. I thought we had responded well as a team to the penalty miss. Even after the game, when you are reflecting back, it is always difficult, but there have been penalties missed in the past and there will be penalties missed in the future, and that is just one of those things that happens in football.

Could I ask you about this sense of responsibility because you have been captain of Leeds and captain of your country as well. Where do you think this concept of responsibility that you have inside comes from?

There are different types of captains, I think. There are captains who lead by example; there are captains who try to pass on information on the pitch with their voices and their actions; and there are captains who try to get other players to follow suit by showing natural enthusiasm. I don't know what type of captain I am, but I would like to think that I am a little bit of all the things that I have just mentioned.

Have you always thought of yourself as a natural leader?

To be perfectly honest, that is not something that I have ever sat down and thought about deeply. What I can say is that when I'm playing football, if I can help a colleague by one of my actions or through my voice or through the experience that I have gained over the years, then that is something that I will always do, even if I am not captain.

Do you find it fairly easy to motivate people?

Well, I think when you are at the level we are talking about, when you are playing in the Premiership, I don't think players should really need much motivation. There are some big prizes in football. Playing at a club like Leeds United, which is still a massive club, the players should have ambitions to go and play for Barcelona or Real Madrid. It is the same here at Coventry, you should never settle for what you have got. That is something that you have got to look at.

I get the feeling that you are always aspiring to something greater. Do you think that is true of all players in the Premiership?

Well definitely. I don't necessarily think that all players have that aspiration, but they should always aspire to be better. There are players in the Premiership now that people might think are the finished article – guys like Alan Shearer, Peter Beardsley and John Barnes, they have played loads and loads of football. But I'm sure if you asked them if they were still learning and still watching football from other parts of the world, they would say that they were still on a learning curve. They would still want to improve and get better, even though they've played so many times for their countries and been stars for years.

Do you still aspire to some other clubs?

I'm still waiting for Barcelona! The ambitions I have now are to try and lead Scotland to France for the next World Cup and at this precise time with Coventry I'm trying to get them away from the bottom of the league along with nineteen other guys.

I suppose the thing that fascinates me, and I suspect it fascinates a fair number of other people as well, are the financial rewards that footballers get and the idolization they get from fans. They get this regardless of whether they are performing at their peak on a week-to-week basis or not, and it must be hard to keep the specific motivations up on a week-to-week basis.

I think that sort of ideal has been pushed on to players a little bit – the fact that the game has overtaken everything and everyday life. I think that football is the game of the people, and everything you see now is mainly football – all other sports come second. The fact that Sky has put so much financial backing into the game means that players have become the stars of their country, or of their part of the world. It is something that they have got to look at and they have got to try and show that the so-called earnings that they get, they do actually earn them.

Do you think that it is very hard for footballers to keep their feet on the ground?

Yes, definitely. I would say that I have been quite lucky in the fact that I have come up from Motherwell to Leicester; I went to Leeds and now I am at Coventry, which has been a gradual progression. I haven't been pushed like some of these young guys that come from one of the lower divisions right through to Manchester United. They have come from earning, say, £200 a week to £2000 a week. It must be very difficult for them, and that is where the clubs have got to give some help. I've been lucky that I have had a natural progression through to the bigger club, but it must be so hard for seventeen- or eighteen-year-olds to be pushed straight into the limelight the way they are these days.

There are obviously a fair number of temptations for players in terms of drink and so forth.

That's right, they do have a lot of spare time. The fact that we play so many games, it means that the management at most clubs have got to give the players a lot of rest time because we are playing Saturdays and Wednesdays right through the season. The players get days off and they get afternoons off. There is not that much temptation abroad, because they play Saturday to Saturday and most players abroad train morning and afternoon. By the time they get home they just want to rest, so they don't really have that much temptation.

People have made the point that in Italy footballers consider themselves primarily as athletes, they look after their bodies in the way that an athlete would. You get the impression, I don't know if it is just a media impression, that footballers drink a bit too much after a game and so on. Do you think that this is just part of the winding-down process? Do you think that it is necessary?

I've got to disagree with you entirely here. I think that these days that this is a myth. I think on occasions these things get publicized, but in general players are now as fit and as dedicated as any foreigner. I think that this has been proved in international matches when England did well in Euro '96, and I think they will continue to do well, and Scotland has been getting some great results over the past three or four years. So, I don't really think that comes into it. I think players are focusing right on their jobs these days.

So, you think that it is just one or two cases that the media are focusing on and giving far too much attention to?

Yes.

Is it hard to come down from a game of football?

Yes, it can be. It definitely can be.

Do you come off on a kind of high?

Yes, you're still flying. You don't sleep. I don't think any player sleeps the night of a match. You are on pure adrenalin until the next day, and it's even greater when you have had a good result.

So, you are lying in bed and you can't sleep, what do you do? Are you going over things you did well in the game or things you did badly?

You actually go right through all the game and you watch some strange programmes at strange hours in the morning, especially on the Sky channels. You are watching re-runs of all these talk shows and stuff like that. Every player will know every one of them.

Do you think that is why some players, a small proportion, go and drink to excess because they're desperately trying to come down?

I don't necessarily want to talk about players doing this sort of thing. Players have different ways of coping. I don't think that there is any harm in a player going and having a drink after a game. There is a time and a place for that sort of thing, and it is just a matter of a player picking the right moment. I wouldn't want to touch on it too much – I don't necessarily associate footballers with the image that some people have got of them.

I was just trying to make sense of it, that's all. OK, changing tack, you were growing up in Motherwell, but your big ambition when you were a school boy was not to play for Celtic or Rangers, it was to play for Manchester United. Was there any reason for that?

There was a big reason for that. I was born in Motherwell and grew up near Motherwell in Bellshill, Bellshill being the village where Sir Matt Busby is from. We are very, very close to the Busby family. Every second weekend there were quite a few of us who went down to Manchester to watch the famous side of the Sixties and early Seventies. I was always getting memorabilia, programmes and stuff from Old Trafford, so I grew up being a Manchester United fan. I was at Manchester United for trials quite early, through Sir Matt really. I continued to go to United for four years, I was going from when I was twelve to sixteen every holiday. I thought things were going quite well until they said they didn't want me.

How did that feel?

I was in bits really. I can remember going up and ripping all the Manchester United posters off the bedroom wall. I was about fifteen and a half then. I immediately signed for my local club, Motherwell. Of the guys I was growing up with from twelve to sixteen at United, a lot of them managed to create brilliant careers. There was Norman Whiteside, Mark Hughes, Clayton Blackmore. United is one club where they do give youth a chance, but if I'd signed there I might never have got my chance, for every one success there is maybe twenty or thirty failures. Who is to say that I wouldn't have been one of the failures that maybe drifted out of the game? I've been quite fortunate in the way that I have come up from Motherwell to Leicester to Leeds to Coventry.

Could you tell me about your reasons for leaving Leeds and moving to Coventry?

I think it is well known that I wasn't happy at the end of last season with the way things were happening at Leeds United. I felt that we were under-achieving and we were short in many ways and I felt that I needed assurances that the club was going to progress, that we were going to get the right sort of players in and make the sort of push that they made three or four years previously when we won the League. I didn't feel that was going to happen, and Leeds United accepted an offer from Coventry for three million for me. It wasn't actually the first offer that Leeds United had accepted for me – I don't think a lot of people know that, but they had previously accepted two offers from two other clubs, which I turned down. The moves then would have made me better off financially but I refused them and stayed loyal to the club. At the time, when Coventry came in and their offer was accepted, I thought that maybe I wasn't wanted as much as I thought. So, I decided to go for the move.

Presumably, the fact that Gordon Strachan was at Coventry was important?

There was also the fact that Gordon was here and I had been at Leeds United for six years and had worked under Howard Wilkinson for six years. You do get used to certain things and maybe you get too used to each other, hearing the same things from each other's mouth, maybe a change was a good thing.

I'm interested in the psychology of that; it seems that you have spent quite a time at each of the clubs that you have played for. It must be interesting and different for you, because every year new players come in and are hearing the manager and his psychological techniques for the first time but you have heard it all before.

I don't think it is a problem if you have been successful, you are on a roll all the time and you can see success, even if it is not the ultimate success of winning the League or a cup, if you can see that things are improving and you are going in the right direction. For two or three years I felt that we were just drifting along a bit at Leeds.

Presumably, yet another season starts and you hear the same things being said to motivate you and you think, 'It didn't work last year, so why would it work this year?'

Yes, possibly. But players shouldn't necessarily rely on what the manager has got to say. I think that they have got to get out there and be their own men. I find it strange when managers come in for all the stick for the team performance. There has got to be a stage where it is up to the players. They shouldn't rely on what the manager has got to tell them, where they have to run and where they have got to go. They have got to show a bit of initiative and be their own person.

Is loyalty something that is extremely important to you? I get the impression that it is very important to you. I'm just trying to work out psychologically where that might come from?

The thing about loyalty is, when I was at Motherwell for four or five years, from maybe two years into my career at Motherwell, I wanted to leave and go on to do better things. I wanted to play for a better and bigger club. When I went to Leicester, I was there for five years, and after a couple of seasons there, when you sign for a club you have got to commit yourself, you've got to get to know the area and know the people, but you have got to be ambitious and go and do better. When I was at Leicester I wanted to go on to a bigger club and when I got to Leeds, to be honest, I thought I would finish my first-class career there, but it wasn't to be. But it's not as if I have set out to be greatly loyal to every club I have played for. That is just the way it has been. I'm not the type of person who, after six months of not doing well, starts asking for transfers, I don't think I've ever asked for a transfer.

When Coventry play Leeds, what does it feel like to go back to Elland Road?

I've not been back yet, but we played Leeds at Highfield Road and we managed to get a result but it was strange playing against my old club. I had got to know a lot of the fans just by seeing them on the terraces. They started throwing stuff at me and it was disappointing. I don't think it will change when I go up to Elland Road, so I'm ready for it.

Do you get comments from previous team mates when you are on the pitch?

No, there wasn't a lot said. Of the guys that I was really close to at Elland Road, there aren't a lot of them left there and the ones I got on well with weren't playing that day.

I would imagine it would be quite intimidating playing against your friends.

As soon as you are on a football field that all goes.

Could I ask you about your relations with managers? And about footballers' relations with managers in general.

I was at Motherwell first, and I was there for five years and I had five different managers because they changed manager every year. I got to know that all managers are different and they have all got certain things that they are good at, but also things that they are not so good at. I would say that of all the managers that I have played under, they have all given me something.

Are there any particular styles of management that suit you?

I suppose that when I was at Leicester, I was about twenty-one or twenty-two, and David Pleat got the job. I can remember him influencing me greatly, I think simply because he had come from Tottenham and had been working with the likes of Glenn Hoddle, Chris Waddle and Ossie Ardiles. These were the kind of players that I admired. When he was doing team talks and trying to give us ideas he would talk about these players that he had previously worked with, so he instantly got my ear. He passed on a lot of stuff and I was at that age when I wanted to learn and become better, so I would say that David was probably one of the most influential managers that I've worked under.

At one point in your career there was a possibility of your moving to Nottingham Forest.

Yes, the deal had been done with Brian Hill, who was the assistant manager to Brian Clough. The deal was done, and then I met Brian Clough. After the meeting with Brian Clough I had a tremendous gut feeling that it wasn't right and I just walked away from it. I decided to go and speak with Leeds United, and I got the feeling there that this was the place that I wanted to go.

Was it something about Nottingham Forest Football Club or something about Brian Clough's personality that made you feel that it wouldn't work?

I think it was something to do with Cloughy's personality. I just had visions of it being very difficult to work there. It's something that I might regret when I've finished playing – the fact that I have never worked with Brian Clough – because he achieved an unbelievable amount at Nottingham Forest. He managed to win League Championships and European cups with a club that is not as glamorous as the big boys in our League now. So, I might regret that later on, but I think that I made a good decision joining Leeds United.

When you met Howard Wilkinson for the first time, what was so different about him?

I suppose it is like any other person going in for an interview or going in for a new job application; I think sometimes it is wise just to follow your gut feeling and that is purely what went on here. I wouldn't want to put Howard Wilkinson above Brian Clough as a better guy or as a nicer person or say that he made a nicer cup of tea! It was just the fact that after sitting and listening to Brian Clough and then going up to Howard Wilkinson's house and meeting him and the coach, I just felt more at ease and more comfortable. I knew that I could go to Leeds United and work with Howard Wilkinson better.

Was there any particular moment in your interview with Clough when you thought, 'No, this is not for me'?

Yes, there was. Yes. And I've always just left it at that, to be quite honest.

Presumably, you have some management ambitions?

Yes, it's way down the line. I still think that I have got three or four years playing in the Premiership. Then, I would maybe start looking at that side of the game.

Is it tougher as you get older as a footballer? I'm intrigued by this.

As far as fitness and stuff goes?

Yes. Could you talk about fitness first? Do you feel as strong now as you did when you were younger?

Yes, it was good that I signed for Leeds and Howard Wilkinson, who has got a reputation for having fit sides and concentrating on the fitness side of the game. That has definitely improved me and that will stand me in good stead. I think that the fact that I got to Leeds United and Howard Wilkinson at twenty-five or twenty-six will lengthen my career when I get to thirty-three or thirty-four because I do think that I have got a good, solid foundation of fitness, and it is just a matter of topping it up when the season has ended. Now that players are better advised on hydration and their diet, that can only help as well.

Do you get some stick from the younger players at the club?

Yes – where's your zimmer frame? That sort of thing. I'm not at that stage yet, but there are a few players at the club who are a wee bit older than me and they are bailing me out at the moment. I'm not quite the eldest statesman.

Do you feel that you have got things to prove as you get older as a footballer?

I think that you have just got to look at guys like Wilkins, Gordon Strachan, Bryan Robson and Peter Beardsley, who are still playing at the highest level. I don't necessarily think that they have got anything to prove. You just want to play until you are no longer picked.

Have you any idea what that is going to feel like when you get to that point?

That is probably the most difficult thing about being a professional footballer – when you come to that time when you can no longer affect the game the way you want to affect a game. When you play football at the level that I'm playing in the Premiership in England, the day that I can't affect the way a game is going, I can't score a goal or make a goal, or help create something good, it's going to be difficult to accept that. Speaking to players in the game, that is the hardest thing I'm going to have to deal with.

Is that something you talk to players about? Is this the big dark cloud over the horizon?

Hopefully, you will have some friends about you, fellow pros. If I'm working here with Gordon in three or four years' time and he says to me, 'Look I don't think you are producing what you could before,' I would trust his wisdom. Most definitely.

Is it something, when you have got a group together socially, that is discussed? Is it something that there are jokes about, when your playing days are over, is it something that is dealt with, with humour?

I think so, because you are still in a good position. If you are a player who has played years of top-level football and international football, then you can always stay in the game in some capacity. There are always radio stations looking for guys to go along and watch games or some club wants a scouting mission somewhere. If you want to stay in the game there is always that reassurance that there is something, some bit of work to coincide with the game, and that makes it a wee bit easier.

I saw a quote from Craig Brown, the Scotland manager, about you in which he said, 'He likes to be one of the boys and yet he is not one of the boys.' Have you any idea what he meant by that?

I don't honestly know what that meant. I think that a dressing room spirit is a must for any team that is going to do well. I don't think that you can distance yourself from that. You have got to be in among the crack and the banter that flies around a changing room, and when we get together for Scotland, that is something that Craig has worked hard on, trying to get the same sort of feel between international players that you get at club level. Maybe he is touching at that, the fact that everyone gets on so well.

Is he suggesting that there is a little bit of a psychological distance between you and the rest of the players? Is that part of being a captain? Does there have to be something, a slight gap there, you can't just be one of the boys?

I don't necessarily try to drift away at any stage, but there are times when I have got to go and do the duties of a captain. Dealing with the press immediately after games, they always ask for the captain, so I suppose that is when I am drifting the other way.

As captain, there are obviously special responsibilities on the field as well. The responsibility of knowing what's going on, picking out individuals who are weak links and having a word with them.

At international level we don't necessarily have weak links. When Scotland play, Craig Brown has picked the best eleven players that

Scotland has got on that day. If there was anybody better, they would be in the team. Before games, the manager will sit with me and he will brief me on what sort of shape and what sort of system we are going to play before he speaks to the rest of the guys so that no one is struggling.

Are there any psychological techniques that you use just before a game to psych yourself up?

Just one that Brian Hamilton used quite a bit when I played under him for Leicester. He simply said, 'No regrets, don't have any regrets after the game.' Also, other bits of information that I have taken in quite well, just go out and lose yourself in the game and enjoy it, lose yourself in the hard work of the game and just get lost in the game of football.

Could I ask you who your role models were as a child?

My first answer is always Glenn Hoddle. He is the player that I tried to copy as a young player, basically trying to copy everything that he did. His movements, his style and just the way he kicked the ball. He was a guy that I liked to watch.

Were you disillusioned when you met him as a person?

I've never actually met Glenn Hoddle socially, but I've played against him a couple of times at Leicester, just before he went off to play with Monaco. I've not been disappointed with him, and he has now gone on to be a successful manager and he has tried to impress his style on the players that he has worked with. You can see it in Swindon, Chelsea and now England. They are going to play with a certain amount of flair.

I suppose what I was getting at was, is it possible to have a role model whose football you liked but you didn't admire the more personal side of the player?

Well, yes, I think you can still have a role model even if you might disagree with some of the things that they might do off the pitch. Maradona is a perfect example. He is the only player who has managed to win a World Cup on his own, I don't know if many people can name the other players in that Argentinian side that won the World Cup. But you can't agree with some of the things that he has done off the field. As far as having someone to look at and learn from, I think that you just have to look at his movement on the football field, and if you don't learn something from Maradona then there is something wrong with you.

If you weren't a footballer, is there any other career that you would have been particularly interested in pursuing?

On a sporting level, I would have liked to have become a professional golfer. I've managed to meet some of the guys over the years and I know it is a tough lifestyle, but it is something I would have liked to have done. In the real world, at school I was most interested in technical drawing. I would have looked towards maybe becoming a draftsman.

Definitely not a psychologist?

No.

Shame. Any comments on the changes in football over the past few years with all the foreign players?

I think it is pretty obvious that the players that are now coming into our League are going to enhance the game. Even though there are a few journalists who say that the players are just coming in for the money, I think that these players are world-class players and they will make our League better. I would say three, four or maybe five years ago when there was an influx of players from Scandinavia, that I don't think were good for our game, and I don't think they were any better than the players that we had here already. I think that if we continue to bring in the world stars that we are bringing in at the moment, our young players will benefit from it, just by watching them.

Will it benefit them just in terms of technical skills or also because they are bringing in different kinds of psychological characteristics?

That's a point, they have got different mentalities from us. On the downside, they struggle to cope with the fact that we play two games a week, every week. On the other hand, even though they don't always play with the same amount of passion as us, it doesn't mean that they are not trying. They have got different methods and a different outlook on the game. They don't understand why we play at one hundred miles an hour all the time. Italians are quite fiery people really, but on the football field they are quite calm. Sometimes you just see them walking around, like Zola, Di Matteo and Vialli, but they are just waiting for the right moment and then they will explode. I think that is something that we have got to recognize and try to learn from.

I was interested to learn that your mother died at a very early age, when you were eight years old. Has that had any effect on your psychological development?

Until I sit in front of somebody who can analyse that, I don't really know. I don't really know a mother, that's a sad thing now when I look back. I've grown up and I don't really know her. I don't know if that was a good thing or a bad thing. My brother, who is three years younger than me, has even fewer memories of my mum. The only thing that I can say is that my dad has done a great job. I think that there was always plenty of help and love near by, and I was never left wanting for anything. I'm not talking about materialistic things, but things like company and love and friends and family, they were always there.

Do you think that if you lose a family member early in life it causes you to mature more quickly? Do you think that there is pressure to mature?

I don't necessarily think that there was pressure, but I definitely think that does make you grow up a little bit quicker. There were times when my dad was out working and we were at an age to be left alone. I was the senior guy of the two lads in the family, and I had to look after my younger brother. I suppose you shared the household chores a bit quicker than if there were two parents about the house. I think the fact that we had to do that makes you become older and wiser a bit quicker.

Interestingly, there is a lot of psychological research to suggest that if you lose a parent early on in life it has a big psychological effect on you. There is a huge proportion of very successful people who have lost a parent early. I'm just wondering if you have any explanation for that? Is it that you are trying to achieve something for the parent that you no longer know?

I must admit that, at times, when I have had a little bit of success at Motherwell when we won the League or at Leicester, I have sat and wondered if she was up there watching me. I was hoping that she was and that she might be a little bit proud to see some of what I've achieved over the years.

January 1997

VA'AIGA TUIGAMALA

Va'aiga Tuigamala, more commonly known as Inga Tuigamala, is a formidable winger from the southern hemisphere. Originally from the Polynesian island of Western Samoa, he was brought up in Auckland, New Zealand. At the time of the interview he was playing rugby league for Wigan, and rugby union for Wasps. At international level, he has represented the All Blacks and his native Western Samoa. Tuigamala is an awesome figure of a man, built like a boxer, but more Mike Tyson than Naseem Hamed. But how awesome is he psychologically? When I met him at the Wasps club-house in north-west London, I wanted to know how this warrior from the Polynesian Islands, prepares for the imminent battle on the rugby field.

Well, I prepare myself in a lot of different ways. I suppose as a sportsman you mature and become wise about yourself and, through time, you get to know what patterns suit you best prior to you performing on the field. I've been one of the few who's been fortunate to go through rugby clinics when I was young, and there we learned about sport psychology and how to prepare ourselves, both physically and mentally.

So what kind of psychological strategies do you actually use? Do you think specifically about your opponents, the ones you're going to be coming face to face with on the pitch?

I think it's important to dwell on your opposite number. Part of this is that you've got to respect his ability to play the game. Therefore, I would do my homework and make sure that I look up video-tapes to see how he's been performing in his last three or four weeks leading up to us clashing. But most of the time I try and dwell on the points of my own game which could benefit my team. About two or three days before a game I get really nervous and a bit itchy and twitchy and ready to go. I have a lot of quiet times to myself then, in which I can dwell on the things that I'm looking forward to trying to develop in the game or trying to achieve in the game.

When you start to get twitchy before the game does that make you difficult to get on with?

No, it doesn't. There's a fine balance there where my Christian faith comes in. I draw a lot from my personal relationship with God. I need to be absolutely focused, and to concentrate on what I need to achieve on the field for the team. I need quiet times. So, when I'm being twitchy I keep myself away from everyone else.

And everyone respects that, do they?

Yes, yes. So no one gets interrupted or gets disturbed or feels uncomfortable with me. I'm not a very emotional person. I keep all my emotions inside and therefore I find a space, or a little place in the changing room, whether it's in the toilets or in a corner, where I just meditate on what I need to do. But a lot of my strength is drawn from within me and certainly from my Christianity. You know, the Bible has a lot of scriptures and sayings that really calm me prior to a game, and it is important for me to be relaxed going into a big competition.

So would you bring a Bible with you to the changing rooms before a game?

I do, I usually carry the Bible with me. I don't open it in front of the guys and read it out loud, because I think I've got to respect the ways that they prepare and what they believe in. But I will have my quiet time, and I might take my Bible to the toilet and sit there and read the scriptures from the Book of Psalms or the Book of Proverbs, which gives me the inner strength to say, 'Right, OK, I'm relaxed and I'm focused, and I actually know what I want to achieve.' But I'm not an emotional person, so I don't get hyped up, or what you psychologists call 'over-aroused'.

Are you a little under-aroused then?

Well, I don't try to be under-aroused, I mean I try to be in the middle. So I know that I'm not losing energy, by sucking myself out physically. That's the danger if you get too aroused. You just get sucked out physically and mentally.

I'm sure that the dynamics of the group must be fascinating at this point before a big game, because you can imagine the captain of your team trying to get you more hyped up.

Everyone has his own individual way of motivating himself, and it's funny because, like I said, I'm not the kind of person who will fill up with emotion and just explode with emotion. And it's quite fascinating when you are able to sit in the corner and just watch the guys around you and how they prepare, especially in rugby union as opposed to rugby league.

Is it more extreme in rugby union?

Yes, I don't know why really. I can't really put my finger on it, but I see a lot more emotion erupt out of rugby union players compared with league players.

Do you have any explanation as to why this might be the case?

I think a lot of it is that rugby union becomes a mental battle, especially for the forwards. When you sit down and watch the way the guys develop themselves before the game, it's absolutely hilarious. I mean, you can see guys spewing and guys pulling funny faces, and you just sit there and you just get so fascinated with it all. And it actually motivates you in some way, not to a huge extent, but it does motivate you to say to yourself, 'Well, if that guy is so psyched up to want to play and to give it his all, then I have to give it my all.' Like I said, I get inspired by what I see, but I don't get influenced by the way they prepare. I don't try to copy them, everyone is different.

It must be fairly draining for some of them actually.

Like I said, when you see a guy losing himself you know he's ready to play and ready to explode, and all that he needs is not a soft talk. He just needs to be put on the field and let loose. There are other guys who would just sit there and just glare at the wall, imagining that they're doing a great run and scoring a great try. I'm a realist, I know that in the real world I'm not going to run 100 metres and score a try every time I get the ball. It is an important part of my preparation before kick off to sit down and, in my mind, go through the things that I need to do, which are usually the basics and if I believe that I can do the basics right then everything else will follow. Anything else on top of that is a big bonus.

And are you visualizing your opponent at that stage? You use this term respect, but obviously you can give someone too much respect. I mean, that's a very fine balance, just getting the right level of respect, you don't want to be shocked by what they're doing on the pitch.

Oh definitely. I mean you've got to be confident in your own ability and when you don't feel confident in your ability then it's game over, and you might as well pack your bags and go back inside and have a shower. But like you said, there are different levels of respect. But the important point is that you try to justify in your own mind that you're just as good as the opponent that you'll be coming across on the field. So therefore the confidence within you is being projected in your own mind, knowing that you have enough faith and trust in your ability to get one over on the opponent you're marking. And he might be the greatest player that's played the game, but if you have this self-belief within you, then you know that you are to able to go out and compete with this guy.

Can I just ask you about the psychological battle right at the start of the match and the famous *haka*. Can I ask you what the *haka* actually means to you first of all?

A lot of people look at the *haka* and interpret it in their own way, and a lot of people who are not from New Zealand, or not from a Polynesian background, wouldn't understand what it really means. Now the *haka* to me represents my country. It represents the identity of the people who live in my country or come from that area. It's like the American Indians, before they went out to do war against the cowboys, they would chant prior to doing battle. And that chanting gave them psychological bravery and boldness and courage to be able to go out there and do the battle and represent their village, their group or their tribe. And that's no different to the Maori people. The *haka* is a representation of their identity, of who they are and what they stand for. And that's the same for me. I'm a Polynesian, but the Maori people are exactly the same as me. You know we come from the same basic group. We also come from the same group as the American Indians. And in the old days, that's what they used to do, they used to chant, when tribe came out to meet tribe. They would chant, for bravery and encouragement and boldness, to go out and fight. And it was seen in the old days as a blood-thirsty thing, but they've used it over the years, down the line, as a way of making peace, as a way of showing respect for the opposition, and we've carried that through into our sport. The *haka* is a sign of respect, and it's laying a challenge to the opposition, but in a certain way. It's saying basically, 'We appreciate you coming. Now it's time to do battle.'

So it's actually a war dance?

It is a war dance. I've always said the *haka* is a war dance, and I feel really proud, more proud than most people who do the *haka*, because to me, it's me, it's my people, and it's my identity, and it's something that everyone should be proud of.

So it makes you feel proud. I mean, does that get you from under-arousal, or moderate arousal to high arousal?

Oh yes, usually.

What does it do to you psychologically when you are actually doing it? What does it feel like?

It's hard to explain unless you're doing it. It does psych you up, and the All Blacks use it as a way to get themselves so aroused; and this is one of the few seen advantages of the *haka*. Also, much of the opposition who come across the *haka* feel intimidated.

I have to say that, as a psychologist, it has always been fascinating watching the opposition's reaction to it, because there are some people who just leak fear when they see it. But obviously, these days you see people trying to cover their fear with a mask, this kind of blank facial mask with a fixed expression or a slight smile, but again you can read through that. When you're doing it, can you really notice what emotions the opposition are displaying?

Oh yes, you can tell what they're feeling. I mean the whole idea is to look at your opponent and say, 'Yes, you're my man today, and I'll be hunting you.' And to a player who's not prepared for the *haka*, it's a big psychological blow to have to face it. So he has to prepare himself, and the best way he can answer the challenge is by looking at me straight in the face and saying, 'Yes, I'm here. I'm ready for you.' That's the best way to respect me, it's to stand up and look at me face to face and say, 'Yeah, I'll accept the challenge. I'll take you on.' But I've come across loads of different people who have had to face it, but in all that time there has only been one person who has ever looked back at me when I've done the *haka* in such a way that he almost put me off. That was a big psychological blow for me.

Could I ask you who that person was?

David Campese. He just stood there poking his tongue out at me and laughing at me. But he knew what the *haka* was all about, and he knew that if he stood up to me, then he wasn't going to get intimidated. He knew that a lot of the time people do get intimidated, but he wasn't going to crumble.

And was your reaction to Campese anything to do with Campese's reputation as a rugby player, or was it specifically to do with what he did when you were doing the *haka*?

I think a lot of it came down to the mutual respect that we had for each other. I mean, he is one of the greatest players who's ever worn a rugby union jersey and will continue to be so. And for me it was such an inspiration to be able to stand before him and do the *haka* with pride and just see a guy that I really admire stand up to it. I, on the other hand, could easily have folded. I could easily have gone, 'Right that's it.'

How did you stop yourself folding on that occasion?

Well, I've just to be absolutely focused deep within myself, and to know that 'OK, this is just a game.' But it's more than a game, it's a test match, it's my representation of my country. And I knew that if my knees were to buckle in front of him, then I would have lost the battle, because, people might not say it, but sixty per cent of the time in rugby it's essentially a mental battle between you and your opposition. Well probably more than sixty per cent, you know. So I respect people who are able to stand up to it and take it on.

Have you ever destroyed the opposition just with the *haka*? Have you watched someone just completely crumble in front of you, and thought to yourself, 'He's gone'?

Yes, I mean I've been really fortunate physically, in that I'm a lot bigger than most of the opponents that I've come across. And I've seen players, and I could see from their eyes or from their body language that there was a real fear there. There's a difference between fear and respect, you know, and you can see real fear in some players, knowing that they're coming up against me. And that's always going to be to my advantage, because it means that I've got that part done. The next bit is to go on and to play well. But yes, I've come across guys who have crumbled in front of me simply because I've done the *haka* to the extent that they feel really intimidated and thought to themselves, 'I don't really want to be part of this!'

Is there any particular body language cues you would use for reading fear, because the psychological literature suggests that the emotion 'fear' is often confused with 'surprise'. I could imagine the *haka* taking people by surprise, shocking people, and given that the behavioural cues for fear and surprise are very similar, how can you really tell if someone is really fearful?

Yes, you're right there, but players already know what to expect. They know that we're going to do the *haka*. They shouldn't be that surprised. Then he knows that he either stands up to me, or he turns his back on me. That's a personal decision he has to make. But I can still read him.

If he turns his back on you, is that a good strategy?

That's a good strategy. If someone stands up to me and faces me I say, 'Oh, I've got a battle on my hands,' but that doesn't intimidate me, because I know that they're going to have to work hard to beat me. But I've known guys who wouldn't look at me, and you usually can tell because they're always nervous – they can never stand still, they're always twitching – and you know straight away what they're feeling inside. When I get that ball I make it a priority to run straight at them, I don't try and side step them, I just go straight into them and see what they do. And you can really find out by that very first reaction whether they've got it or not. So not only is the *haka* a great way of psyching them out, but it's also a great way of knowing whether they'll actually stand up to you, and whether they're up for the game or whether they're not.

So the game's all over in the first few minutes really, or at least important psychological parts of it are?

True, but it's not just fear. I've known guys who have been really surprised by the *haka*, they just stand there with their eyes wide open, and the *haka* has finished, and they're still standing there with their eyes wide open. You know they've been that surprised by the actual event. And then there's been guys who have literally just looked at me and just glared but you know deep inside that they've been shocked by the whole thing.

What has been your greatest moment on a rugby pitch?

My greatest moment? I've been really fortunate in that I've had a lot of great moments in my career. But I would say, if I had to choose, that it would be the 1992 test against the Springboks in Johannesburg in Atlas Park. As a youngster, growing up, the pinnacle in rugby was to meet the South Africans but to actually beat them. So that was probably the greatest moment I've ever encountered as a rugby player.

What about your own performance that day?

I was marking a guy who was very strong. He was very, very good, and he was very competitive. I had a very decent game. I didn't get on the try list, but it was still very good. I came off the field feeling that I had contributed to history in the making, being one of the few All Black teams undefeated in 1992. So that was a great moment for me, to finish the tour on a high note against the Springboks. I think that there are a lot of reasons for making it the highlight of my career. The atmosphere was absolutely tremendous, it was in front of 104,000 people, shouting at the tops of their voices. It was such an occasion to savour. Not only that, we were also the first official sporting team to be allowed into South Africa for about fifteen to twenty years.

Did you get a big reception from the crowd?

Yes. I remember very clearly when we turned up at the airport and there were about 5000 people to meet us there, which was a remarkable reception, and it typifies South Africa's passion for rugby. So that, in itself, was a great occasion. But to be able to play against South Africa at Atlas Park was the pinnacle. The ultimate challenge.

Can I just change angle then and ask you about your transition from rugby union to rugby league. Was that a difficult move?

It's like anything, you know. If you go to a new job you're going to find it difficult in the first few stages; once you get used to it and you understand it, then you can adjust yourself and you're away, aren't you? And the same thing went for me when I first came from rugby union to rugby league. I found it hard because there's a different type of fitness involved, there's a different technique and different game plan. And I had to work twice as hard, or maybe even three times as hard, to try to adjust myself and condition myself to a point where I could be as competitive as the league boys. That took a little bit of time. It took about three or four, maybe even five months, to get myself used to the aerobic capacity that was required in league, the physical intensity that was needed and the mental toughness that was needed to compete. It was very difficult. It wasn't easy coming in midwinter into this country, it was really hard, it was really difficult. But I had to dig deep and believe in my ability, and rely a lot on my Christian faith to get me through.

Could I ask what prompted the move? What made you interested in moving over to rugby league?

There was a time when rugby union in New Zealand was going through a hard period. It wasn't really solid and players themselves were unsure about their places. I remember that one of my greatest heroes got dropped for no apparent reason. And I thought to myself, if it can happen to him without a reason given, it can also happen to me. During that time I was also finding it really hard to get employment, because I was away as an All Black. I travelled and toured and I was away a lot of the time. So no employer was going to employ someone who was going to be away all the time, regardless of reputation, and not only that, I had to give something back to my family. I wanted to give them some sort of security. I wanted to offer them some of the fruits of my success, and the only way that I was going to be able to do that was to make a clean break and to look at the opportunities elsewhere. The first time Wigan offered me a position, I refused, because I didn't want to leave. I wanted it, but I didn't want to leave the family and the country and my friends. But eventually, after six months, I decided to take the challenge up and I knew that deep within me I always wanted to try league to see what it was like and to put that urge within me to rest straight away. So, I've been here three years now, and I've been really thankful that I've been given such an opportunity, not only to give something to my family, but also to fulfil the passion that has been within me, to be able to play rugby league. I've been very fortunate.

It must have been a huge culture shock to suddenly end up in Wigan.

Not really. Like I said, the All Blacks provided a lot of opportunities to travel. I saw a lot of the world through the All Blacks and what it has to offer. It was more of a shock to my family, to my wife and my two boys, because it was something that they've never done before. I, on the other hand, was quite used to travelling and experiencing different cultures. But, you know, it was good. I've always said to people that the best education that you can give your children is travel, because they see so much more, they experience so much more, and they remember so much more. And that's what I'm hoping to try and do – continue to provide that for the children.

Was the fitness a big struggle to begin with?

The fitness was a big struggle, simply because I had a good Christmas! I had a really good Christmas and I had put on a lot of weight. When I came to Wigan I was a bit overweight, but that was soon dealt with. The physios and the doctors and the coaches brought me through a real hard programme, which was absolutely mind-blowing. I had to get up at six in the morning and train at seven, in the snow, up in the mountains, on the rugby field, in the weights room, in the swimming pool. And that was constant for three or four months – now you understand why it took me about six months to get used to it. Not only was the game difficult to learn at first, but getting myself physically in shape and mentally prepared was another big issue.

And did you lose a lot of weight in the process?

Not really, I didn't lose a lot of weight. What they did was pump me up to the weight that I could handle comfortably, and then they made me run fast, and then they made me a lot stronger and then they made me a lot fitter. In that order.

In your opinion, is rugby league a much tougher sport than rugby union?

I think that it is, because it's not only a test of physical toughness, it's also a test of mental toughness. In a game of rugby union, the ball is in play for an average of about twenty-two minutes; in rugby league, it's in play for sixty-five minutes, so you've got to concentrate more for a much longer time. That is a big, big difference. So you've got to get yourself aerobically fit, physically fit to cope with this. It's a long time for the ball to be in play. And during this time you're taking knocks, you're getting battered, and you're chasing, you're tackling, you're doing all these things within that sixty-five minutes, which takes its toll. Rugby union, on the other hand, is more tactical, more of a mental thing. It's all about putting your opposition down psychologically, and a lot of it requires kicking for position and positional play. Union players realize how difficult the game is at times, when you're sat out on the wing and the ball hasn't come to you for seventy-nine minutes of the game and the last minute you get it, and then it's a psychological thing. Rugby union is a lot harder to learn and it's a lot harder to understand than rugby league. League is a simpler game, but it's a harder game.

Is there any difference in the level of aggression of the players in the two codes? As a psychologist, I'm fascinated by the control mechanisms for aggression in the sport.

Well, you've certainly got to be in control.

What about rugby league and rugby union, are there any differences between these in terms of levels of aggression?

Not really. But I think there is more emphasis on controlled aggression in rugby league as opposed to union. Because in union you can hide, you can punch someone and you can hide. In league you can't, because there's only one line of defence, so it's more obvious if you're going to punch someone. It's going to be pretty obvious who punched who. Unless it's a brawl, which is something you don't really want to get involved with. In league it's a much more demanding game physically, because the emphasis is on defence. Everyone knows that the team can score tries and there's only one line of defence. If you've missed that tackle everyone knows about it. In union, if you miss that tackle, you've got so many lines of defence that you can get away with it.

So there's much more focus on the individual in rugby league really, on individual strength?

Yes. So therefore one mistake or one lapse of concentration from someone can cost you the game. I've always said it's harder to score tries in union as opposed to league. League has a one-line defence; if you break it, you've got a fifty-fifty chance of scoring. In union, on the other hand, if you break the first line of defence, then you've got one, two, three, four or five lines of defence to break down still. In union everyone is vying for the ball, and if you've got the ball everyone targets you. In league, because the emphasis is on defence, it's a one-on-one defence and a one-on-one attack.

So it's much more like boxing really?

It is like boxing.

One-on-one. There's no hiding place.

That's right, there is no hiding place. I mean, even though there is a big emphasis on team work, it can become a very one-on-one battle, both physically and psychologically.

I was going to ask you about other sports that you enjoy or other sportsmen you respect. Would boxers be a set of people you would look up to, or admire?

Well yes. Definitely boxers. I mean boxing has got to be right up there in my calendar, because I come from a boxing family. My family were all boxers, my great grandfather, my father, my brothers – all were boxers. And then I go and decide to take up rugby for some reason! And I can see the respect that boxers get, because it's so tough. It's a lonely sport to be involved in, because you can't put the blame on anyone else. When you're feeling tired, you can't excuse yourself for not performing. It's only you and your opponent. And that's why I respect individual sportsmen and women, more than I would those involved in team sports, because it's a real leveller. It comes down to you alone, and what you produce is what you get. And to me, individual sport can cause more of a psychological blow. I mean I could play real bad, but I could hide it, couldn't I? In team sport I could always put the blame on someone else. When we lose they can't say, 'You lost it for us.' It's a team game. You can get away with it. In individual games, like tennis and golf and boxing, it's very hard to point the finger at someone else, because it's just up to you. You're the only person who can do it. So I have a huge respect for individual sportsmen, who are able to go out there and achieve what they want to achieve.

If you weren't a rugby player what sport would you like to have excelled in?

Boxing. Definitely boxing. I've got a cousin who's a professional boxer in the States and he rang me up three nights ago and they'd just got the new rankings. He's fighting in the heavyweight division over there, in the Holyfield's camp. He's got good prospects.

Is he built similarly to you?

He's bigger than me. He's shorter, but he's a lot stockier. He's had about twenty-seven professional fights and no defeats. He's had twenty-five knock-outs and two have gone the distance.

Can I ask you how old you were when you moved from Western Samoa to New Zealand? At what age did you and your family move?

I was four years old when Mum and Dad decided to pack their bags and get on that canoe and row to New Zealand! Only joking! It was 1974, I was four years old. I come from a small family of fourteen, and Mum and Dad decided that New Zealand was the land of opportunities, and, therefore, we were going to go. But there were twelve of us children at that time, so Mum and Dad, by law, had to give up the other eight kids for adoption, because the law in New Zealand was that you were only allowed four children to come with you from the Islands. So Mum and Dad decided to give the rest up for adoption, and they were so grateful that their granddad adopted them. So we came over to New Zealand, and over the years we had to work hard and finally we managed to earn enough money to bring the rest of the family over.

That must have been psychologically very tough for your parents.

Yes, it was for my parents, because we had nothing when we came to New Zealand. We were a very poor family when we came over. We had nothing and we've worked hard over the years to be able to sustain a good living. And my dad passed away about sixteen years ago now, and it was a really trying time within my family and especially for my mum. My mum had to be a father-figure as well as a mother to all of us. And it was difficult, because dad worked himself to the grave and we hardly saw him, he was away somewhere six days out of the seven. So I only saw him one day a week, and that was a Sunday evening before we went to sleep, because he'd work right through. And when he passed away mum decided to sell all our furniture to buy sewing-machines and she got a little job as an out-worker sewing pillowcases and that's what we did for about eight years. I can remember in our house and our garage we had four sewing-machines, and we would be sewing these pillowcases all the time.

And were the kids involved as well?

All fourteen of us were involved. This was from 1981 to 1989. And we would sew these pillowcases to make a living to put us through school and put food on the table. It wasn't a lot really, because one pillowcase was worth two cents, which wasn't even a penny in this country. And we sewed thousands and thousands and thousands of these, there'd be four on the machine, there'd be four folding, there'd be four tying up and marking and then delivering. And that's what we would be doing all the time. So it was a hard time. We struggled a lot of the time. I suppose the good thing that came out of it was that we put a lot of effort into it together, and there was a real closeness in the family to be able to mix and work together. But what my mum did, she was very bold and she had a lot of courage and a lot of care and love for us that she persevered through those trying years and now I'm able to reap the benefits of all the hard work.

It must have been very tough for her playing the role of a mother and a father.

Yes, but she had to. She had to discipline us, physically as well. And at the same time, she had to make sure that she could give that time over to us, to be able to grow and to be independent, which is very hard for a mother to do when you're by yourself and you've got all this responsibility. So one of the things that my mum did, which was very moving, was that she taught my older brothers how to be fathers to the younger ones. This took a lot of effort and time and patience. I could see that all this was having an effect psychologically on my mum, because it wasn't easy to be a father and discipline us as a father would discipline his children, and to care for us as a mother would care for her children. So she had two roles in one person. And, yes, it had side-effects on my mum, because she was under stress all the time and then she had to provide for the family. It wasn't easy. But I saw a lot of courage in my mum and a lot of peace as well, while she was doing it. She knew that she had to do it, in order for us to survive. So it was a trying time, but you know I've got to give it to my mother. I know I've been better for it.

So what kind of role models did you have at that time? Did you have a clear image of what you wanted to be as a man?

Not really. While I was growing up sport was a big part of my life and this has continued to this very day. As a youngster I didn't really know what I wanted in life. All I wanted to do was be with my friends, I suppose that was my ultimate goal as a youngster – just to be with my friends. I thought that my friends would get me through life. I thought my friends would get me out of trouble. I thought my friends were going to be the cornerstone in my life. But I grew up and the world that we live in just doesn't work like that. It would be nice if we had friends we could rely on, but that's not the case. When my dad died, I questioned my mum, I said, 'Mum I don't know what death is.' I was only ten years old. I heard about it, I saw it on television, but I didn't really know what it was like to lose someone forever. And I said to my mum, 'Where's dad, why isn't he coming back?' And she explained it to me and she said something very, very clear to me about life. And I didn't understand it at first, but over the years I look back now and I can see what she meant. She said, 'Son, the only thing that I can give you right now is this advice – where there's a will there's a way.' I didn't understand this as a ten year old. But looking back on my own personal life and what I've achieved and what I've strived for and what I stand for today, I really understand now what she meant. 'Where there's a will, there's a way,' and I've held on to that.

Were you already a strong Christian when your father died?

I was very fortunate that the presence of God was instilled in me at such a young age. I was made to go to Sunday school. One of the reasons that I went to Sunday school was simply that mum and dad decided that the only way we were going to learn English was to put us in an English-speaking church, while they went to their own Polynesian church, where they spoke our language. So we had to go and sit, and I'll never forget, we went to a Baptist church, all of us walking down the road, bare foot, to sit there and we didn't understand what the preacher was talking about! But over the years we came to understand and appreciate and we learned our English that way. I'm still learning now.

What about your brothers and sisters, have any of them gone into sport?

I've got one younger brother who plays for Orrell, and he's here with me. The rest of my brothers were all boxers. But they've all retired because they're all older now, which is a good thing because otherwise I would have got beaten up by them all the time. But I was fortunate at a young age that, like I said, God's presence was instilled in me. But it didn't really hit home with me until my dad died, when I was ten. Then I started to see the reality of God coming into place, in our family and in our lives. I saw this through my mother, because I knew my mum had something that most women didn't have. To be able to persevere and be bold and to stand up and to survive with fourteen children on her own. I knew there was something more than her as a mother. And I can still remember my mother standing up in front of the congregation and she never cried, you know, when my dad died. She never cried right through the whole service, and she just stood there with all that emotion kept inside her. She just said to us, 'Don't worry.' OK, she had lost a husband and a father to her children, but she stood there with a lot of faith and a lot of

composure and said, 'Don't worry, it's part of life. We must all one
day address this issue.' Over the years I was able to see her faith in
God as the cornerstone, as the backbone to her as a mother. And
while I saw this, I was growing up at the time and there were a lot of
things that went unanswered in my own life, that needed to be
answered. Like I said, I thought my friends were the bees' knees. I
thought that my friends were going to carry me through, but it
wasn't to be. And I remember as a sixteen-year-old I was surrounded
with friends who were always mischievous, who were always getting
into trouble. Their ultimate goal was trouble. They went out and
searched for it. Honestly, we would go out on Wednesdays,
Thursdays, Fridays, Saturdays, and go out into town and we would
cause riots in town, with other school gangs. We used to meet in
town in downtown Auckland, and we used to have an all-out brawl.
I never got involved in any of the brawls. I used to be among these
friends of mine, and I used to thoroughly enjoy watching my friends
beating others up, but I never joined in.

Is there any particular reason why you yourself didn't get involved?

I think that it was the discipline that was brought through my family.
I mean, if I did anything wrong, not only would my mother beat me
up, but my brothers would beat me up, my father would beat me up,
even my older sisters would beat me up and my neighbours, when
they found out, they'd kick me around as well! So I knew that I
didn't want to get involved, because if I got caught, I knew that I was
going to get it all over again. And I had that kind of fear in me, not
scared of them, but I just had a real respect for my family, you know,
when it came to this kind of problem.

**Did this get you into trouble with your friends? Did they say, 'Why
aren't you joining in?'**

No, that's one thing. My friends took drugs, they drank, and I was
right in the midst of it and not once did I ever take it, you know. And
I'm so thankful to this day. I was never pressurized, that was the
funny thing about it. I had all these friends who were involved in

trying to be gangsters and taking drugs and alcohol, but I never once took them. And it was a big winner for me, because over the years, I mean even now, the players ask me, 'Why don't you drink? Have you ever drunk?' And I've said, 'No, I've never drunk in my life.' 'Have you ever smoked?' 'No.' And they can't understand it. They can't understand that I can be in the midst of all this, and yet they cannot understand why I can't be one of them. But I'm fortunate, like I said, with the principles that I was brought up with, with the morals that my parents taught me. They helped me all the way through. It wasn't until I was sixteen that we had a Christian fellow-ship going on, and in this Christian fellowship they were talking about the claims of Jesus Christ and God and what the Bible talks about, and life in general, and I said, 'Yeah, yeah.' And all of a sudden my friends stopped going out and partying and taking drugs and drinking. And I thought, 'I want my friends, I want those old friends of mine.' But the whole lot of them decided to go and sit and listen to this preacher speaking about Jesus. And I said, 'No, no, no.' And I waited and I said, 'Right it won't take long.' And when they came and told me I didn't want anything to do with it, because I thought that all I had to do was to go to church on a Sunday and I would be forgiven. But they had something more real than this, something that I didn't experience. And they were telling me about this man called Jesus, they were telling me about what he'd done, and I said, 'No, no, it's a lot of rubbish. What's happened to you guys?' I said to myself, 'Right, I'll give them two months.' Two months went by, then four months, then six months, and then eight months.

And they had all just changed?

They had all changed. And I said, 'No, no, no.' But what I saw in them was something that I'd never experienced before. And that was love, joy and peace. It's called the food of the spirit. Love, joy and peace. And I said, 'No, no, no.' And I started envying them. I started getting jealous, because they had something which I didn't have. I thought I had it, but I'd missed out on it. And I said, 'What can make these people, these friends of mine, these so-called drug addicts, alcoholics and gangsters, change so dramatically?' They told me about this personal relationship with Jesus, and what they'd accepted which was the salvation. The a, b, c – A, accept that you're a sinner; B, believe that Jesus is the son of God; C, confess that Jesus is going to be the lord of your life. And I thought, 'No, no, no, no, no, no.' And it wasn't until the teacher, who had brought all of these youngsters, all my friends to this fellowship, told me about it. And I said, 'Well, I thought I had to go to church to be a Christian.' She said, 'No.' She turned round and she said, 'No, you don't have to go to church to be a Christian. Going to church doesn't mean that you're a Christian, just like being in a garage doesn't make you a car.' And I started thinking, 'Oh, OK.' And I took a step of faith then, and I took God into my own life, and I said, 'God, if you are the God that you say you are and the God that my family worship, then show me through your divine power that you are who you say you are.' And that was the first time, when I was sixteen years old, that I became a Christian. And it hasn't been easy. It's been the hardest challenge of my life. It's harder than rugby league or rugby union, because I've got to stand by my principles. I've got to stand by what God says, and it's hard to walk away when all your friends are doing the opposite to what you've been brought up to believe in. It's very hard. But at the end of the day, you know, every time I go out there the guys are looking for an opportunity to pull me down. They're testing me all the time – 'Inga, have a beer with us' – and I've got to stand my ground.

But do you find that people would also try to needle you, perhaps on a football field as well?

I get that all the time. It's their way of trying to psych me out. I mean I had one guy punch me in the face, I turned around and said, 'Look, was it really as good for you as it was for me?'

How did he react to that?

He didn't know what to do. He was absolutely shocked. He stared at me and went, 'Oh my goodness. This guy is cuckoo in the head.' And another guy knocked me out. I got up and said, 'Did you know that Jesus loves you?' He just looked at me! I'm playing rugby because it's a God-given talent to be able to go and express myself and to be a role model and stand up for God, and I know it's corny but rugby is the vehicle that I use to do that. Christianity is the hardest thing that I've ever done. But it's the best decision I've ever made, to be able to have this personal relationship with Jesus, and with God. A lot of people misunderstand it, a lot of people criticize it, and blame things on God very quickly, because of their misunderstanding – or lack of understanding. But for me, I know that one day, my life is going to come to an end, you know, and my ultimate goal is to be right with God. And it's been a real blessing to be able to come over here and enhance that talent that he's given me. And it's been a real mind-blowing voyage in this country in rugby.

Do you feel you've been changed by your success?

I don't think so, not deep within me. The people who really know me, I know for a fact that they know, that I haven't changed. Success has made me a more confident person, but it hasn't changed me in terms of how I see life and my outlook on life. Like I said, I've been fortunate in that I'm known as a rugby player, but that has not changed me in terms of what I believe in, what I stand for and who I am. And I've experienced a lot of success at such a young age, but I'll be thankful that I've been blessed with brothers and sisters who would tell me if something was wrong. Just because I was an All Black it didn't mean that I could come home and get my breakfast served on the table. I had to get up and make my own breakfast and wash my own dishes and do my own washing. So I had no privileges, which is the best thing that ever happened to me. When I'd just become an All Black, and it was the pinnacle to play for the All Blacks in New Zealand, my mum said, 'You know my only advice to you my son, is this: I know you'll make friends and you will come across a lot of people and a lot of people will be your friend and I know right now you've got a lot of friends, but you've got to choose your friends wisely. In this world we live in you don't know who you can trust. But my advice to you is this – know that your real friends are the friends who would come up to you and confront you and tell you what's wrong with you.' And I said, 'Oh mum, give over. You don't know what you're talking about.' But do you know that no friend, except one, has ever been like that with me. I came here as an eighteen-year-old, when the All Blacks toured England, and I went back and I was on cloud nine. I thought I was it, to be honest. As a teenager you think like that. Of course, you have every right to think like that, but it took one friend of mine to come up and say it to my face, and it hurt me real bad because I thought he would support me. You know, friends should always be supportive, but this particular friend came up to me and said, 'Inga, you've got such a big head that you don't know what to do with it.' And it really hurt me. And to be quite honest, we've been friends for twenty-two years now and that friend has been the best friend that I've ever had. Today, he's still the best friend that I've ever had. And again my mother was spot on with what she said. You know not many friends would come and say that to you, but because this friend decided to do something about it, and because he cares so much about me, he was going to do something about it straight away, and he did it. It hurt me at first, but it was the best thing that ever happened to me, because I soon learned that I'm not the bees' knees. I soon learned that you can sink really quickly, if you don't have your head firmly on your shoulders and your feet firmly on the ground.

What was it like when you moved to England? What kind of perception did people have of you then?

I don't know. It was quite fascinating really, because they don't know what to expect. They don't know how to accept me because I'm not Black Black, and I'm not white white, I'm in the middle. But I suppose if they had to class me I'd be in the Black category, which is something that I'm really proud of. I'm proud of my identity, I'm proud of my colour. At the end of the day, I can't try and say I'm John Smith when I'm really Inga Tuigamala. I mean my skin says it, my colour says it, my language says it. I am who I am, and I am who God made me. And it's quite fascinating when you come to places where people don't see much of you and then they start calling you names and making racial comments. I quite like it really. I suppose that it hurts me deep down that they don't know any better, but it doesn't worry me. It makes me very proud of who I stand for and who I represent. I'm Black, that's how God made me. I'm not trying to be anyone, I'm not trying to impress anyone, if they've got a problem with that, that's their problem. Rugby, and sport generally, breaks down the barriers so many times, but it's fascinating to stand on the side line if you're a winger or a centre and listen to all these racial comments that are thrown at you. I mean the most hilarious one was when I went to Hull. I ran out and they were throwing banana skins on to the field for me. I just laughed and the more I laughed, the more violent they became. But like I said, if people have got that problem then it's sad because they're missing out on so much in life, whereas I'm enjoying life to its full. You know, whether I'm Black, brown, yellow, pink, red or whatever colour God made me. I'm proud to be who I am and I'll stand up for it. In Wigan there are not a lot of coloured people, but what I try to do is to mix as much as I possibly can with the English people. They need to know that there is another side to life that they're missing out on, and that with a little bit more effort they could come to appreciate that it's not all about whites and it's not all about Blacks, it's about being able to get along with each other. At the end of the day, if I cut my skin and the Englishman cuts his skin then we're the same underneath it.

I think that people say these racial comments simply because they've got nothing else to shout about. And it's unfortunate. I get a bit cheesed off now and again when I hear people say it, because it's not what you want to see in sport. Sport can do without it. To me sport is a way for people to be able to come and relax and appreciate us as human beings. Unfortunately, we live in a society where they don't see that side. You know people can't get along, people can't accept each other for who they are, not who they've become. And it's sad because I would say that in society today we live in this world where we wear a mask all the time. We live in a world where we can't see the real person and we won't allow each other to see the real person because of some stupid reason. And unfortunately, I see it more in this country than any other country that I've ever been to. More even than within South Africa. I don't like racism.

**Do you have any explanation as to why racism might be more
intense in this country than in certain other countries?**

Not really. But I think that it's growing more and more, especially in
football. It's sad. I don't know where it stems from. Through sport
people are given the opportunity to appreciate what we as human
beings really stand for. But in the world that we live in this is just not
the case. Sometimes I sit and think that we could all learn a lot from
the animal world, to learn something about the way that they get
along.

December 1996

JONATHAN EDWARDS

Jonathan Edwards is the vicar's son and physics graduate from Durham University who lives in Newcastle with his wife and two sons. At the World Championships in Sweden in 1995, he leapt into the record books with an unprecedented performance, breaking the world record twice in successive jumps. And yet he describes his triple jump achievements as 'jumping a long way into a sand pit'. He seems to downplay his achievements to a bizarre level. This makes it all sound like child's play, which clearly it is not. He is a committed Christian in a world that is, in his words, 'consumed by Satan'. Up until 1993, because of his Christian lifestyle, he felt unable to compete in any events taking place on a Sunday, missing out as a result on the 1991 World Championships and two European cups. When we met in Newcastle I wanted to find out who this Jonathan Edwards really was, this enigma who seems to find it difficult – psychologically speaking – to take in all his achievements. So what does he think about when he is waiting to jump that long way, into the sand pit?

I've been asked that question quite a lot, and I'm really sitting here now and thinking that I'm not really aware of anything in particular and I'm only vaguely aware of the crowd clapping. I'm just trying to focus, without actually having something definite to focus on, but all my concentration, everything is just on what I'm about to do, and then just going. And at that stage, I think it's automatic pilot, I would have to say. I'm certainly not aware of anything particular that I do. I know that Mike Powell, the long jumper, has this visualization sequence he goes through – for the first six strides he visualizes himself like a raging bull, and then he's like a gazelle and then he's like a leopard, but I've got nothing like that. I get on the runway, I put a hundred per cent into this and pheow, off I go.

You make it sound very easy. Does it just come naturally to you then?

Yes, I think it does, to a certain extent. I have worked on the whole mental side of things in training, in my weight training particularly. There's a lot going on in the gym, a lot of outside influences, people chatting away, wanting to take my attention from what I'm doing but I try to focus on that particular lift and cut everything else off. The guy I work with on my weight training says, 'Just talk with your mouth and not with your head, just forget about what everybody is saying to you and just get on and do what you're doing. This is the most important thing you've done, everything else is history, nothing else in the future matters, just do this.' And that's kind of been ingrained in me. I was good at responding under pressure anyway, but it's just become slightly more formalized, through my training. But it is a quite natural thing, I think.

I was going to say, does this kind of mental discipline come naturally to you?

Yes, I think to be an athlete you need to be reasonably well-disciplined in all aspects.

Were you focused like this as a boy?

I think that I'm very different now from how I was as a boy. I think the thing that's developed over the last two or three years in me is the capacity to be independent. Before, I was very worried all the time, I was very tied up with what people thought. What should I do? What would people think if I did this? What would they think if I didn't?

And I've become much more able to make a decision based on what I feel I should do, regardless of anyone else. I don't mean to their detriment, but just that I can go down a line that I believe is right and go for something without worrying what everybody else is thinking. There's a verse in the Bible, in Proverbs, which says the fear of man is a snare – if you are so worried about what everybody else is thinking about you, you just end up tying yourself in knots.

Were you very hesitant before making any decisions in the past?

Oh very much so. I was a bit of a girl's blouse, a bit woofy as a boy, if I can use that expression. My dad or mum will disagree with me, but I was very diffident, you know, I didn't like to do things on my own. I wouldn't even read a lesson in church in public, I'd be so nervous about what people would think.

So when did all this change?

I had a wonderful upbringing, but it was quite sheltered in many respects, I think. I think I've changed since I left home and moved up to Newcastle after university in 1987. I've probably just developed as a person, particularly in the last two or three years.

Right, so even at university you were still very concerned with other people's views of you?

Yes, definitely, and I didn't like to take on responsibility, probably for fear of failing, or not being able to do it, or pressure. Looking back I feel that I've missed out on a lot of good opportunities though, I don't really have any regrets, it's just the way it's gone.

So going back to the last world championship, you broke the world record, did you think you could do it in the next jump as well?

I've always got a very good idea of how I feel physically and whether or not I'm going to jump well. On the second jump I knew I was still focused, physically I was still up for it. So I knew I could still jump well on that second jump, but on the third jump, I knew that I might as well have not stood on the runway, I knew nothing was going to happen. It's like that in training, I get to the point in a training session, when I'm on the end of a run-up and I know, no matter what I do, it's just not going to happen.

Now 1995 was an absolutely remarkable year – I mean, was there any indication that it was going to be so remarkable for you?

No, not to the extent it was. The year before, I'd had a very bad year, following on from a good 1993, when I'd broken through into world class with a bronze medal at the world championships. I'd trained very hard and then got one of these viral problems, a glandular fever type thing, and so at the end of 1994, I had a long rest. I was quite down mentally as well and I started asking myself, 'Did I have any talent any more?' With a virus, it's not like you're injured and you've got an excuse, you can't touch it. You can't see it. A lot of people are very sceptical about viruses anyway and think maybe you are making it all up, that maybe you just had a bad year. So I went into my winter training for 1995, probably January time, very low key, with no great expectations and still not a hundred per cent sure in my mind that I was a hundred per cent physically fit. I was also not sleeping particularly well. I was obsessed with my pulse, because I thought that once my pulse went below sixty that I would be OK. And I went to America in February and things started to turn around a little bit then, particularly mentally, and then I started to train really quite well – my weights improved, my jumping was good in training. So I thought I was going to have a good season, but not to the level that I did have.

And was it easy to cope with it when you had it? I mean, how easy is it to suddenly be the world champion and the world record holder?

I think that my way of coping with it is that it's still somewhere away in the distance and I'm just getting on with what I normally do. I've not really taken it down and made it my own and said, 'That's me.' I look at it and I just shake my head and think that's incredible and I'm very thankful for what's happened. But it's almost as if, in one sense, I put it to one side and I'm just getting on, trying to do the same things, because I feel the same, I feel exactly the same person, I don't feel any different.

Not even slightly different? I mean you must feel ...

It's weird, it's still weird. I mean I've never really talked to anybody about this. Take the likes of Linford – he gives the impression that he was born to greatness and that it's no great surprise that he's doing what he is doing – yet for me it is, and it is even now. And I still think, 'Goodness can I do it again?' I mean I'm not unique in that, I'm sure.

So how do you feel, do you feel extremely lucky about the whole thing or do you feel blessed in some way?

Yes, I do feel blessed. I think it was Roger Black who said, after I'd jumped in the European Cup, to his coach, 'I've got to get God,' he said, 'It's obviously working.' But it's not because I'm a Christian that I'm having the success I'm having, I don't think. I mean, there are many, many people who are successful in all walks of life who don't believe and in fact, quite the opposite. But I believe God has blessed me and it's ultimately because of his plan and purpose that I am where I am and I've done what I've done, and I'm thankful in that respect. But I don't think that it's because I've been a good Christian and because I know God that what's happened has happened.

Do you pray for sporting success?

Yes I have, yes. I didn't used to, but I have done. I've asked God to make me successful. Not making it a priority, but as I go out, I do want to win and I'm honest about that, but at the same time, it's not everything.

Are there any pitfalls, do you think, in praying for success? I mean, for example, if you're not successful?

Oh there can be. I've no guarantee that my prayers are going to be answered. There are certain things the Bible makes clear that if you pray for them I think you can expect answers, but success isn't one of them. I would ask God for success, and I think that's a valid prayer because it's a want and a desire within me, but it's all subservient to what God wants in my life and the overall aim is, 'yes, grant me success God', but most of all, whatever happens, I can glorify God. My philosophy of life is to glorify God in what I do.

Could I ask where your strong religious views come from? Your father was a minister, so you were brought up in a Christian household?

That's right, in a strong Christian home. My personal faith is based on the fact that I'm a sinner, Jesus came and he died and rose again, to pay the penalties for my sins so that I could know God. So that's the basis of my faith, what Christ has done, and he gave his life for me, and in turn I want to give my life for him.

Right. What kind of age were you when you first found Christ?

I didn't have a dramatic conversion, like a Damascus road experience. I think that because of my upbringing, it was very much a gradual thing. When I was six, my mum said that I came to her and said that I'd asked Jesus into my life and I wanted to trust him, so I might look upon that as the time. Later on, probably my first really independent religious experience, if you like, was when I went to a boys' camp, you know, I remember that being a very emotional kind of experience, wanting to live for God.

Did the boys you grew up with also have strong Christian views?

Our main friendships came from within the church. I was very close friends with my brother. I was never one of the lads in any particular way. I went to a private school and although I was in with the 'in-group' it was because of my sport. That always gave me an open door into popularity and having friends. I was never actually part of the in-group, because a lot of the time I wouldn't feel comfortable with all the things they were into. This was nothing more than lads would normally do anyway, but as a Christian I wouldn't feel comfortable with them.

Did you get ribbed a lot about your Christianity?

Not really, no. Sport enabled me to be slightly separate and yet be part of it all because of my sporting ability. Had I not had sport, then I might have felt that I had to compromise to be accepted. My sport allowed me to be more independent, I would say.

Do you feel the kind of scrapes that lads get into as they grow up are kind of important for their psychological development? In some sense do you have to learn by your mistakes?

Yes, certainly, but whether all the things are positive I don't know. I think I've learned from my mistakes anyway.

Did you ever feel envious of your friends when you saw them getting up to the kinds of things that lads get up to, but you thought to yourself, 'I can't really get involved in that'?

No I didn't. I was quite happy with my belief and all that it entailed.

Did you ever have a period of teenage rebellion when you thought that you perhaps didn't want to live for God?

No, not at all.

You never had any doubts? Even when you went out into the world at large?

Never. Vicars' sons always seem to go that way, don't they? They get very rebellious. Sometimes with religion parents can be over-zealous in a desire for you to believe what they believe and they can force it down your throat, and it can become just a set of rules, something very dead and ritual. But in my home there was a lot of love and a reality of God's presence. There were the rights and the wrongs, but it was more than that, it was something that came from inside.

Do you feel the presence of God no matter where you go?

I know it. The Bible tells me. God said, 'He'd never leave me, he'd never forsake me.' So I know it. Sometimes I would feel it more than other times, but primarily my religion isn't based on feelings, it is based on fact, it is based on the Bible and what I know. If the feelings are there then that's great, but sometimes they're not there, but nevertheless that doesn't change the truth.

Do you feel the presence of the devil at work in society?

Yes, very much so. I mean, it's stated very clearly in the Bible, but I look around and see the type of world that we live in and yes, I do see it. I mean, in injustice particularly, and in poverty. I do work with the homeless in society and you know you see people living on the streets, and that's something I think success has made me think much more about, the different lots that people have in life. In some ways, it's quite a difficult thing to come to terms with.

Do you feel the devil tempts you?

Yes, I think there are a lot of temptations – money, success, thinking of myself more highly than I should, and that I'm somehow better than everybody else. I think in my success there are many more temptations, much more subtle than there have been in failure, because in failure it's like, you can say, 'I'm no good, there's nothing in me,' and you throw yourself totally on God. With what I've had there's quite a lot of power associated with it, and people want to listen to my opinions and you can think, 'Oh yes, actually I know quite a lot,' and all this sort of thing. I think that pride is a big area for temptation, thinking of myself more highly than I should.

Right, pride and vanity, which are very biblical concepts, of course.

Yes. Vanity, vanity, always vanity.

Yes, and in terms of your own success, do you feel that there are even more temptations out there waiting for you? Do you feel that it's going to be a difficult path to tread?

Yes, I think it is and it has been already. One of the things that I laid out from the beginning was the priority of my family, and it still is very much so, but I have been spending much more time away from home than I should really, I think. You know today, for example, I left home at nine o'clock this morning and I'll be back just for a short time at tea and then I'm out again and speaking at a dinner, and it's not on really. You know, we've got two young children and Alison is under a lot of pressure, so subtly I have been moved away from the stand that I made at the beginning.

Now of course you are fairly well known for your position on not competing on a Sunday and you missed the 1991 World Championships because of this. But in 1993, you changed your opinion on this. Could you talk a little bit about what made you change your mind?

Right. It's very much a question of conscience. I was brought up to keep Sundays different, but I think that the Sabbath of the Old Testament for the people of Israel and now the Christian Sunday, which has replaced it, are subtly different. Through my own Bible study I really understood that it wasn't necessary, if you like, to have this Sabbath, this Sunday, when I didn't do any sport, when I didn't do any work. I'm still very much in agreement with the rest principle on a Sunday, but as a Christian that wasn't something that was obligatory for me.

Is it not pretty clear in the Bible that you should keep the Sabbath free?

Well it isn't. We could get into theological issues here, there is great difference on this. The Sabbath formed part of something called the

Mosaic Law, which was given to the people of Israel, on Mount
Sinai through Moses. I think that has finished with the death of
Christ. There are many things that are still similar, for us to do now
as Christians, but there are some things that are different and I think
Sunday, or the Sabbath anyway, is one of those things.

**In that case, do you think that some other Christian principles are
also contextually bound? One can understand the principles of, for
example, not stealing for the children of Israel, but is that the same as
pinching from a hypermarket or supermarket today? I mean is everything not contextually bound?**

I think that's very important. Whenever you study the Bible you have
to look very much at its context, but also at the same time to try to
understand if there is a wider application. Certainly some things are,
as you say, very contextually bound, and they are very specific to a
specific time, to a specific person and to a specific place. To use the
example of stealing, it is quite clear in the New Testament, it is given
as a rule of life for the believer now, that stealing is wrong. But say,
for example, the eating of certain foods, which was not allowed for
Jewish people in the Old Testament, now is a question of conscience,
for us, since Jesus has ascended into heaven. Similarly, I believe this
is so with Sunday, but there are great differences of opinion on this.

**How did people react when you changed your mind about this?
Because, in some sense, you got an awful lot of respect for keeping
Sunday sacred, so what was the response from people generally
whenever you decided to compete on a Sunday?**

It was very positive, and really that became the deciding factor. I had
no problem with competing on a Sunday, but what would people
think? I'd made such a stand and I didn't want to dishonour God and
to compromise my faith, but this is perhaps where the idea of being
independent comes in and I thought well, 'I believe it's right, I think
it's going to be positive for my witness as a Christian, as an athlete,
I'm going to go ahead and do it.' And people can make their own
decisions, based on what they see of me as a person.

Right, so do you think it was important for your own psychological development in a way, because you've talked a little bit about your kind of boyhood and so on, but do you think that was an important stepping-stone in your development?

I think it probably was. For example, my parents were not for the decision and, given the strong influence they have been, it was quite a big thing for me to go ahead and do it regardless. I obviously asked their opinion and they didn't agree, but I said, 'Well, I believe it's right, I'm going to go ahead and do it.' So yes, I think it was probably very important.

Right, and was it strange to fly in the face of their opinion this time?

Yes, it was. It was a new experience on something that is so big. I mean not that we hadn't ever disagreed before, but this was something which was quite a big issue and also had ramifications, not just in the circle of my family but nationally. It certainly made me think and if nothing else it made me really know and think through the implications of it.

Was it strange the first time you competed on a Sunday? What was it like competing for money on the Sabbath?

Well actually it was the European Cup, so it wasn't strictly for money. I didn't actually get paid, so that complicating factor was removed. The funny thing is that on my first jump I had a massive foul and they gave it to me, my foot must have been two inches over the board and they gave it to me, so draw your own conclusions on that.

In terms of your relationship with God, did you feel that he was advising you?

I think in the Bible this is quite clear, it was up to me. It was a question of my conscience. The Bible talks about that, one person keeps one day above all others, another considers all days the same, each should be convinced and do it unto God. And I kept Sunday different to God, and I jump now to God. For me, it's no different, and it's never been a problem. It's not an issue. It's a question that a lot of people ask and I don't mind you asking, obviously, but it was a long time ago and it's not an issue now.

You've made some interesting comments about the triple jump as jumping into a sand pit. Are these just funny remarks you make about it to amuse, or sometimes do you step back from triple jumping and think, 'How significant really is this?'

Oh yes, I do, and in the grand scheme of things, it isn't that significant is it really? I mean sometimes, I look at the whole sports world and think about how much attention, money, time and effort is put into sport and what does it achieve? I mean people enjoy themselves and I know this sounds very corny, but you look at all the various problems that there are in the world, you know, in the whole former Yugoslavia and yet on the other side of the world, people are enjoying themselves on a beautiful golf course in Barbados earning a million dollars. I think that there's something not quite right here.

And do you ever step back and ask yourself if it's all about false idols? Obviously you look at the whole sporting edifice from the Bible's perspective.

Yes, there's a lot of idolatry and, you know, people worship. There's no greater example than here at Newcastle with the football team. It's nothing short of a religion – they talk of Keegan being the Messiah coming to take Newcastle to its new glory, and it's remarkable.

How does that make you feel? Are you offended by that?

When they talk about the Messiah and they call footballers God, that does offend me. I mean I am realistic, I think that I can say that people are lucky to be fulfilled in all sorts of different ways, and sport fills a void. I would say that man was created to be in a relationship with God and man should find his fulfilment, his direction, his purpose in that, but people look in different areas to be fulfilled, because they reject God.

In religious terms, do you think they get anything out of it? Do they get anything spiritual from that experience?

I would say probably not. I mean they could. God could speak through it, but in and of itself, no I wouldn't think so. I mean, when you go into Saint James's Park, there's a tremendous atmosphere and a sense of unity that's all about communion together, but I wouldn't call it a religious thing. People might liken it to a religious experience, but no, it's not the real thing.

Which people do you draw support from?

I think I first look to my wife, Alison, and my family. My children, Sam and Nathan, are young, but they are an inspiration. I still look to my parents very much. A close circle of friends in the church, and I've got three main coaches who are all very influential, I have different training partners, the whole group associated with Gateshead stadium are very much behind me and, in a sense, the whole region is actually. I'm the only athlete in the northeast really doing anything at the moment, and I very much feel the support of the whole region. There is a very tight-knit community here. Sometimes you can feel a bit cut off from the rest of the country here, but I think that probably increases the sense of belonging.

Do you see yourself as a role model for coming generations of northeastern kids?

It's not that I see myself as a role model, but I realize that I'm in that position and I have that responsibility. I think that is one thing that weighs quite heavily on me. As a society we are quite into our rights and what we should have, and not quite so much on the flip side of the coin of the responsibility that comes with being part of society. As an athlete, I'm given a great position and a great status in society, and I think there is a lot of responsibility with that. I do take it seriously.

And is it important for you to demonstrate that you can have strong religious beliefs and that's perfectly compatible with having a successful sporting career?

Yeah, absolutely. Primarily I think I'm an ambassador for Christ in what I do and, whether it's as an athlete or whatever I'm doing, I want to speak about Christ and what he's done. I want to speak about the gospel. Man can be reconciled to God because of Jesus Christ – if I can do that through my sport and be a normal guy, then I'll be happy.

That's the interesting thing really, because one strand of you is this very normal guy and what's happening to you is surprising, and you have these strongly held religious beliefs and then you have these sporting accomplishments, which are out of this world. It's amazing how these strands all exist together in a single person!

Are you saying I've got multiple personality disorder?

It must be very interesting for you just keeping it all together! Do you almost have to act normal, because in some sense you are so extraordinary and your beliefs are so strong? Or does it just come naturally?

I'm a Christian first and foremost, and everything comes out of that. I have a relationship with God and I try and glorify him, and everything I do tries to come out of that basic desire.

Do you ever wake up in the morning and think, 'I'm an absolute superstar,' and you have to try and talk yourself into being normal for the day?

No, no. I'll be training and I'll think, 'Goodness, I'm the world record holder and the world champion.' It's such a funny feeling, it really is strange. I was thinking about this the other night, and the level of success that I've had has made me more grateful and in a sense perhaps more humble, because I don't think I deserve it more than anybody else. I've been given a gift and an ability, but at the same time more than that I've actually been able to express it to its full extent. Or perhaps, there's more to come. A lot of athletes have got a lot of ability, more ability than me, but they have never quite made it either because of injury or because it's not gone right on the day. Because of the level of my success I think I can only be thankful. I can't say that it's happened because I'm wonderful. That is probably rooted in my belief in God and my understanding of perhaps how the world works, I don't know.

Is jumping a kind of religious type of experience for you? I mean when you're sailing through the air?

No.

No?

No. I mean God's very much part of it, but no, it's not a religious experience. Generally my feelings out on the track are very similar to most other athletes, you know, a mixture of fear, of excitement, of wanting to do well.

But if you feel that you've been blessed and you're expressing God through your jumping, surely you must feel in some sense that this is what you've been born to do and therefore feel ...

Yes, but I mean, I've had lots and lots of down times. This has been an incredible year but in a sense I was equally blessed, God was as much with me, when things weren't going well and that's what has given me the broader perspective. So I don't get carried away with what's happened this year.

So the virus was pretty important to you really, I mean that whole period of the virus?

The down times that I've had – in particular not qualifying for the Olympics in 1992 and the virus in 1994 – have been the most incredible times of personal character development, particularly of spiritual growth, and I can never say absolutely for certain but I think I would look on those as preparing me for the success that I've had now.

In 1994 when you had the virus and you were resting from athletics, what did you spend your time doing?

A lot of Bible study actually.

Did you get a lot of inspiration from the Bible at that time?

Yes, I just love to study it and to know what it says and to try to apply it to me in my family life, particularly, and then in a broader way, with other people and friends.

And you had no religious doubts, even though things just weren't going well for you?

No.

You just thought this was part of the plan?

Yes, I trusted God.

Right.

God is the object of my faith, and I believe he loves me and he cares for me and he'll look after me, and if I'd never jumped again, if I'd never jumped well again, I would hope that I would still have trusted God and moved on to whatever I thought was the best thing to do next.

But I think earlier you've said that psychologically you were a bit down during that period, so what do you mean by that?

Just not being able to compete at a level I felt I could, wondering if I'd lost it forever, you know the young family. I suppose concerns about what direction my life was going to take if I couldn't carry on as an athlete.

Did you come to any conclusions about that?

No. I felt I could probably carry on till after the Olympics in 1996 and then it might be decision time. I was fairly committed to go on until the Olympics in 1996, but it was a difficult time.

Did you ever get depressed, I mean really depressed?

I wouldn't say really depressed. Even in my sort of downside I'm generally quite optimistic in my outlook and thankful for what I have, so I never got really depressed.

What things sustain you as an athlete? Is it working for God?

I think that is a hope. The Bible says the heart is deceitful and wicked above all things. I think working for God is my main motivation, but maybe it is deep down wanting to be the best, I don't know. I mean I'm sure that is there, you know, a desire to be number one and to express my talent to its fullest. But certainly the idea of glorifying God is fundamental to it.

Is it true to say that you want to be number one because that will give you a much better platform for you to express your Christian views?

Certainly that is part of it. I strive to win in a sense because I'm an athlete and I want to do my hundred per cent best, and that's just part of being an athlete. I'd like to win in a sense for winning's sake because that's part and parcel of it, but it's not the be all and end all.

Do you have any role models out there that you use?

No, I'm often asked about heroes and things like that. If I looked at one person as far as preparation for competing, dedication, focus, I'd have to pick out Linford Christie, because I've been contemporary with him and have seen the way that he's dealt with pressure and the way that he comes through. Not always in the way that I would do it, but I do respect the way that he prepares and his professionalism.

Are there any other role models outside athletics that you would use?

There's one particular scholar who used to lecture at a theological seminary in America and I've read a lot of his works and I have a great respect for him as a person. He's a great scholar and a great theologian but he's also intensely practical as well. I think that is my desire, to know God's word, to be a theologian but for it to be in my everyday life and for it to be a reality. If I was looking at one thing that I wanted to be it would be that – to know God's word and to interact with it intelligently, for it to be very practical.

Right, I think that's interesting. Christianity as a practical activity, not something that is distinct from the world but something that can be used in the world, and I think through your life and through your athletics you're demonstrating that that's a perfectly practical approach. OK. I believe you studied physics at university. Could you find the scientific view of the world reconcilable with your Christian views?

I'm not really a physicist. I did physics, but I'm not a physicist. I went through my degree and I learnt my equations and bits and pieces and I got my degree without ever really interacting with it in a very meaningful way! That's not a very good advert for Durham University is it? I never really looked at the conflict between science and religion at all. It never entered my mind. My faith was very strong and I just thought this is true and there is going to be nothing that changes that. But recently I have looked a bit into evolution as evolution seems to be indisputably true, so I wondered, 'How does it reconcile?' As I said, I've looked into it recently and my feeling is that you need more faith to believe in evolution!

How do you argue against the apparent evidence for evolution? You know, fossil evidence and stuff.

Well, I'm not an expert, but some of the things I've read say that a lot of this fossil evidence could be accounted for by worldwide flood. And a lot of the arguments about age and fossil records are often quite circular arguments, one is argued from the other and the other is argued and so on, and it goes round in a circle. Actually, concerning the fossils there are a lot of more complex states underneath the more simple forms. I'm not saying there's not a lot of good science in evolutionary theory, but it's portrayed as being true and people accept it as true and yet there are a lot of problems with it.

What about physics theories concerning the creation of the world, such as 'the big bang theory'? Did you never get into any of those arguments?

No. I believe that God created the world in seven days.

After your degree, what kind of work did you do?

Well, I left university and my aim was to try and be an athlete. I moved up to Newcastle and applied for various jobs. Most were at a sort of clerical level as I thought that, 'I'm not going to get a graduate job if I want to concentrate on athletics.' But the only job that I applied for and got an interview for was to cover maternity leave at a genetics laboratory at a local hospital. It was a degree-level job and I applied for it – and this isn't a joke – I didn't know what a chromosome was. I knew nothing about genetics, I'd given up biology at O-level. The night before the interview I went around to see one of my friends who studied at Durham with me who had done zoology, and she gave me the basic a, b, c of genetics. Forty-six chromosomes, an X and a Y are male, two Xs are female, all this stuff. This is no exaggeration. I went in the next day as an obvious total dunce as far as anything genetic was concerned and I was given the job. I was very surprised and I think they were as well. So I'm not a genetic scientist by any stretch of the imagination. I wasn't much more than a glorified technician there, although I did become a post-probationary scientist. This was not a career thing; it was just to fill a gap. I believe, looking back, that God provided very miraculously for me. They gave me a lot of time to train, unpaid leave for the Olympics, they allowed me to go part-time when I got a bit more serious. So I was almost a bit of a fraud as a genetic scientist.

What about your plans for the future, what do you see yourself doing after all of this? Do you ever give retirement any thought or are you far too young to think about that yet?

Well I do, but not a lot. I hope that it's still a long way away. I think I could possibly carry on until the next Olympics in 2000. Being an athlete, you've always got to be flexible with your plans – an injury could come along and I could lose form or I could just think I've had enough, I'll do something else. I do feel that I'd like to be involved full time in sort of Christian work of some description or other. I don't know what that would entail but certainly that would be a general long-term plan. At the moment I'm just starting off doing a theology degree by distance learning. So when I do retire as an athlete I'll have some qualification there which then might lead on and open doors in other areas.

December 1995